on pilgrimage

on pilgrimage

A TIME TO SEEK

JENNIFER LASH

BLOOMSBURY

Published by Bloomsbury Publishing, New York and London.
Distributed to the trade by St. Martin's Press

A CIP catalogue record for this book
is available from the Library of Congress

ISBN 1-58234-090-0

First published in Great Britain by Sinclair-Stevenson Limited.
First published in the U.S. by Bloomsbury Publishing in 1999.

This paperback edition published 2000
10 9 8 7 6 5 4 3 2 1
Printed in the United States of America by
RR Donnelley & Sons Company, Harrisonburg, Virginia

For Margery Kempe
Her memory, her fervour
and human frailty,
above all — her inspiration

Acknowledgements

I WOULD like to thank all those kind people on my Journey who gave me hospitality, advice, general enthusiasm and a measure of their own experiences.

I would particularly like to thank Janet and Arthur Bell in Wales and John and Jill Horsman in Suffolk for their shelter, support and every kind of sustenance – the 'magistrate's dressing room' was an unforgettable workspace.

Many thanks also to those kind friends who read the MS: Nick Boulting for his wit, wisdom and endearing authority; Catherine Reihaug, Marie and Laura Hugo.

Finally I must thank Nic Barlow for a brilliant, intense printing session in his cellar/darkroom.

J.F.

Contents

Preface

The Stars are setting and the Caravan
Starts for the Dawn of Nothing –
Oh make haste!
E. FITZGERALD

POOR CANCER, the word is dark and terrible, full of fear to the medical profession as much as anyone else. I believe it is a constellation; you become simply one of thousands and thousands of stars within it. It is a common, everyday disease. A star may be sharp, and full of pain, but it may also be a guide, a useful companion on a dark night.

There is a hidden current within every individual. It seeks and stirs, hides and yearns. Sometimes it is bewildered, a mixture of anger and pain and certainty. It may recede, but it never escapes. In moments of crisis, it is often full of voice.

Make a Pilgrimage. Go to ancient places. Go wherever there are contemporary seekers. Go in whatever way it works out. Just go!

Raising a large family keeps you more or less pegged down in a fairly domestic space. To leave that space, and the roles of wife and mother, might be to discover those intangible threads that unite practical living to a purpose beyond the particulars of name and time and gender.

Margery Kempe, that emotional miller's wife of the fifteenth century, who dictated the 'Booke' of her life to a priest, has always been a great love and inspiration to me. Margery was an eager pilgrim, travelling with much weeping and adventure, from her native town of Kings Lynn in Norfolk, to Rome, Jerusalem and

xi

Compostela. Margery was variously loathed and loved, scolded and encouraged, by a variety of priests and fellow pilgrims, but above all, it is her struggle for complete honesty, which is so endearing. Her 'Booke' is a vivid and lively account of a woman on the road. She refers to herself as 'this creature'. This creature, without much means, or any foreign tongue, made these journeys on her own, in the company of diverse persons who frequently found her very difficult indeed. Her eccentricity and her honesty were my inspiration.

Suddenly there were just days before my departure. In Kensington Market I found a lovely, blue leather money belt. The stall holder was Saïd. I told him I was going on pilgrimage, ending up I hoped in Compostela. He asked me to pray for him there. I promised I would. He had a severe and painful skin disorder. He was a gentle man. As I watched him put the leather purse, in a small, crumpled, brown paper bag, I felt that there might be some kind of blessing in his soft hands.

Rucksacks, I discovered, are sold by the litre. I chose a strong blue one, thirty-five litres, with a mass of exciting, hidden pockets. The young men in the camping shop at Shepherd's Bush told me it was far too small for three months; it was simply a day sack. But I couldn't have handled anything bigger. Once strapped into it, I felt different; there was great freedom in the feel of it. I couldn't wait to be off, on the move. Different beds. Different places. Different people. Keeping only the company of strangers. But a nagging kind of panic did seize me every so often, not for the practical side of the journey, that would be a straight forward adventure. It was the idea itself. I sometimes wondered, rather fearfully, why I had thought of such a book.

I had ceased long ago to be a practising Catholic. I look back on eight years of convent boarding school education as a mixed blessing. The good things were many of the nuns themselves, extremely interesting, well-educated, sensitive human beings. Then there was the experience of silence, the singing, the Liturgical Year, and the really inspiring idea of a God, and Love, as an available, transforming force, enabling you to love your neighbour and your enemies. An exciting and rather radical thought. It certainly fired my imagination.

But there were uncomfortable memories; dark, nagging guilt bits left over. They were probably part of the turbulence of youth. It was all so long ago, but nevertheless, I was definitely planning a return to convent corridors and all that goes with them. I wanted to be simply an observer, open to anything, interested in what is going on in this particular groove of contemporary Europe.

Where are the seekers? What inspires them? What are they finding, maintaining, and creating?

Goodbyes are terrible, always somehow inconclusive and unsatisfactory. In the end you just long to be off.

Finally I was alone in the departure lounge of Brittany Ferries at Portsmouth, waiting for the 11.30 night crossing to Caen. I sat there surrounded by excited, boisterous school children and several families. Anxiously I kept checking and rechecking; passport, glasses, Visa card, penknife, pencils, camera. I had brought another bag, with even more zip pockets: it was for books, film, maps and things. I began to realise that all this double checking might become feverish and neurotic. I had once had a great friend, an Austrian psychoanalyst, who earlier in his life had had a nervous breakdown. He had told me, 'I used to check and recheck the letters I had written, opening them again and again, finally I even called out the Post Office to open up the post box; I knew then that anxiety was master of me.' I kept thinking of this. I realised that I must never let practical anxieties overwhelm me. Nothing mattered. No loss was irredeemable. Even death would not be a real disaster, as it was the one certain event in life. Why worry? It was only a book, a puff of thin air, less than a spider's web in a rusty bucket.

There was only one other obviously single traveller waiting with us; a tall, weathered man, probably in his thirties. He had a thumb stick as I did. His stick was far more robust, gnarled, and beaten about. His rucksack was greased and dark, marked with the patina of constant travel. He was Zen-calm, quite detached from the noise and clatter of the school children, although he did eye my stick every so often. He was probably about to walk to Compostela, if not round the world; maybe he was a mountain man. My stick kept slipping down on to the hard floor, snagging at people's legs, and tripping them up. Obviously staff control was the first thing I had to learn! The mountain man's staff never moved, it just seemed to rest beside him like a well-trained hound.

At last the right words came up on the flickering screens and we were off. There was a small bus waiting to take us to the boat. I purposely got on last, I was so fearful of bashing people with the baggage. Instantly, a rather bossy school teacher demanded of her students that I should be given a seat. I realised that I probably looked like a rather frantic bag lady, instead of a keen adventurer.

It was a fairly bumpy crossing. I was very surprised to find that I had a four-berth cabin completely to myself. It was a great temptation to spread things out over the empty bunks, but I was fearful of forgetting something, I hardly dared to unpack my toothbrush.

During the dark uneven hours of the night, I was grateful for the clear sounds of girlish 'ooh's and 'ah's and little screams from the cabin that backed on to mine. It was so odd to be alone. I remembered ferry journeys with all of the children, tired, sleepy and excited. We had crossed several times to and from Ireland with dogs and rabbits, the latter smuggled up into the cabin under anoraks to spend the night away from the heat and noise of the car deck. Travelling with children you see any voyage much more through their eyes than your own. Their excitements, their fears are the pace of things, you are simply the eyes of responsibility that must be a step ahead all the time. Being alone made me feel younger and older all at once – an odd sensation.

I

Alençon and Lisieux

Health is the state, about which medicine has nothing to say;
sanctity is the state about which theology has nothing to say!

W.H. AUDEN

IT WAS A very bright but bitterly cold morning when we docked.
Everyone was muffled up to the eyeballs; hats, long coats, gloves,
scarves. I had brought no coat, just a long black mac, that rolled
up into a plate-sized, sticky mass when sufficiently urged. I had put
on every layer of vest, shirt, jersey that I possessed and topped it
with the mac, which, although thin, was very efficient at keeping out
the wind.

Just as I had been told, French public transport is amazing,
efficient and most welcoming. There was little time to wait before
the arrival of the bus into Caen. The blossom was fully out on the
cherry trees, just as it had been in London, but the plane trees were
like dark, mutilated fists, without any sign of unfurled leaf. Caen in
the early morning looked handsome and prosperous. Devastated in
the war, it had been rebuilt with great coherence; fine civic buildings
in broad streets which lead off one another on either side of the wide
river. There was no sign of litter or detritus. There were few people.
Several young men were sweeping the pavements in front of small
bars and cafés. An elderly man gingerly crossed the street in front
of the bus, his hand clasping his hat against the wind, two long
loaves of bread sticking out under his arm and a small white dog on
a narrow lead, the dog pulled back against the bitter cold, it had to
be tugged. The silhouettes of these two in the gusty morning
reminded me of a wonderful drawing by Pissarro of the same subject.

The station building is modern, full of coloured curves, blue-

I

green and bright red, with tinted glass, reminiscent of a great deal of eighties London architecture; determined brightness from a play-school catalogue.

There was a train from Caen direct to Alençon. The windows of the train were extremely dirty, the bright sun made the rather dull, frosty landscape more or less invisible. I could just detect the two spires of Sées Cathedral.

The bus from the station dropped me off in the market square of Alençon, directly in front of the large church of Notre Dame, with its heavy flying buttress and domes, it seemed like a broody hen nursing the market place. My first thought was coffee, strong, black coffee and crusty bread. But finding a bar or café proved quite taxing. There were elegant provincial shops, opticians, chemists, florists, boutiques ... but no bars. Eventually, to my surprise, I came to a red telephone box in full operative working order. A present from Basingstoke, which is twinned with Alençon. Twinning seems such a random, vaguely surreal business. Do the city fathers simply call one another up, or does some authority pronounce on this urban intimacy as a 'fait accompli'? I wonder, are there derelict, sad, untwinnable towns?

Beside the telephone box there was a bar. The coffee was weak and not hot. The only edible item was a *croque monsieur*. It was quite disgusting. It could aptly have been called a 'croak monsieur', white fat, limp bread. I realised I should try and avoid eager anticipation of any kind.

The reason for making Alençon my first stop was to visit the birth place of Thérèse Martin, the youngest child of Louis and Zélie Martin. Thérèse, who was born in 1873, only just survived infancy. Her mother, who had given birth to eight other children, previous to Thérèse, was suffering with breast cancer: she was unable to feed her babies. In the space of three-and-a-half years she had lost three infants and a daughter, Hélène, when she was five-and-a-half. In order to save Thérèse's life, she was sent to be nursed by Rose Taille who lived in a small farmhouse eight kilometres out of Alençon. Thérèse returned to her mother a strong and happy child with a great love of the country. At only fifteen Thérèse followed her two sisters to become a nun in the Carmelite convent in Lisieux. She died at twenty-three in 1897 after appalling suffering with tuberculosis and gangrene of the intestines. After her death, her spiritual diaries, written under obedience from her Mother Superior, who was also her sister Pauline, were published. The impact of her writings, her 'Little Way' was immediate.

'Not to do extraordinary things, but to do ordinary things extra-ordinarily well', and all for Love. 'Love is my Vocation', she wrote. After her death, favours and cures ascribed to her intercession were numerous. Devotion to her spread like wildfire. By 1925 the process of canonisation was complete. She was proclaimed a saint. Later she was made Principal Patroness of the Universal Missions with Saint Francis Xavier. In 1944 she was proclaimed second patroness of France with Saint Joan who had not herself been canonised for long. Saint Joan was a saint Thérèse had fervently admired. The huge basilica built in Lisieux to honour Thérèse and the convent of Carmel both escaped the violent bombing of Lisieux. Today there is hardly a Catholic church in the world without a statue to her. There is certainly one in every church and chapel in France.

My first clear memory of any serious mention of Thérèse, was in an attic dormitory, having my hair brushed extremely hard. Someone had said that their mother was making a novena to the 'Little Flower'. 'Who's the Little Flower?' we asked. Then we were told about Thérèse, who sounded depressingly good: she ate the fat and gristle from other people's plates as an offering. (I can find no trace of this.) But the same nun, as she wielded the hair brush from one small head to the next, went on to say with great emphasis, 'but for me, the great Teresa, Teresa of Avila is the one'. This personal partiality to particular saints played an important part in many of the nuns' lives and devotions. They all seemed, as it were, to have their celestial best friends, Saint Antony for the careless and forget-ful, Saint Jude for the deeply depressed. Thérèse, we were told, was greatly loved by soldiers in both world wars: they frequently carried her picture to assist them in the protection of their lives.

Perhaps because of that first moment of prejudice, I have always felt more inclined to study the life and writings of that passionate, dynamic Spanish woman – Teresa of Avila. There is something so gutsy, so uncompromising about her. The fact the Church saw fit to make her a Doctor, albeit centuries later, also influences one: there are so few. Hans Urs Von Balthasar wrote, 'The theology of woman has never been taken seriously, nor has it been received by the corpus. After the message of Lisieux, at last it will have to be

taken into consideration in the present day reconstruction of dogmatic theology.'

Reading that made me think of what Simone de Beauvoir wrote,
in relation to the inherited confidence, or lack of it, in women. 'The
individuals who seem to us the most outstanding, who are honoured
by the name of genius, are those who enact the fate of all humanity
in their personal existences, and no woman has believed herself
authorised to do this.' Simone de Beauvoir attributes this lack of
confidence, this lack of authority, to the mediocrity of the status
women had been obliged to accept. Thérèse is remarkable because
she creatively chose an extraordinary level of self abnegation. She
chose systematically to drop self, and seek Love in everyone and
everything; sleeping and waking. She understood that to be truly
united with Christ, her Beloved, she must be utterly 'of Love' and
from that position she could work for all mankind.

Thérèse, with the fervour of an artist, was determined against all
the odds to become a great saint, and she was quite sure she would
achieve this goal. In the manner of going for the goal, saints and
artists seem to have something in common. Henry Moore said in
relation to the artist, 'If you believe you can do it, you will do it.' I
suppose artists, like the saints, know they are receivers, their job is
to summon every skill, every kind of attention and remain skinlessly
alert in order, as Picasso said, 'to find'.

From a tiny child Thérèse longed for heaven. Sanctity was her
clear ambition. She would, as she wrote, 'have happily gone for
martyrdom ... flagellation, plunging into boiling oil, her throat
offered to the sword.' She longed to be priest, apostle, missionary,
but all those jobs were not realistically available to a young woman
in nineteenth-century France. Undaunted, she found her way. Her
little 'lift' to heaven. Before entering Carmel, her father, her beloved
'King of Navarre' as she called him, took her and her sister Céline
on an extremely up-market pilgrimage to Rome, it included visiting
Venice and Switzerland. Staying in the various hotels, Thérèse was
most impressed by the new lifts. It made her think, might there not
be a quick way like this to heaven. (Interestingly Van Gogh decided
that the great diseases of tuberculosis and cancer were quick lifts to
heaven.) Thérèse discovered her master plan: to subjugate the
desires of the ego at all times; sit beside the most irritating nun;
choose to work in the hottest, most disagreeable part of the laundry
etc. But – and this was most important – every act must be an act of

Love, an act offered for others; sinners, priests, the suffering, the abandoned. The overwhelming desire must be that all souls should finally be able to love Jesus, her spouse, her most beloved.

Perhaps because, frequently, a woman's domain is small and domestic; teaching, nursing, the general minding of others: perhaps it was only natural that a young woman should be the one to express so powerfully, long before Schumacher, that 'small is beautiful'. Thérèse would seem to have much in common with Saint Francis of Assisi. To them both, no instant, no occasion, cannot be made huge for the glory of God.

After my salutary experience with the *croque monsieur*, I began to make my way through the careful, dignified, well-maintained, provincial town of Alençon. I was looking for the Rue de la Demi-Lune, where, at number seven, there is the Monastery of the Poor Clares, just as it had been when the Martins lived in Alençon. I had been corresponding with Sister Monique. I hoped they were expecting me. It was nearly midday. The smart deft shoppers, mostly women, with, so it seemed, a universal, very short hair cut, that went well with the clipped kissing and crisp pavement greetings, were now nearly all home with their full shopping baskets and narrow lengths of bread.

Although it was very cold, the bright sun was full on to the handsome buildings. Basingstoke might get a bit of a complex, there is nothing as handsome there. I came to the top of the street. I was just debating when and where to cross when a very tall nun, dressed unmistakably in the brown of a Poor Clare leapt like a deer across the street just ahead of me. I was looking forward to all the radical cloister changes that I should find, but I had assumed that the Poor Clares were still an enclosed order. I crossed the street and turned down into the Rue de la Demi-Lune; a narrow pavement, high stone walls and a bell tower. In the distance ahead of me, the tall brown figure vanished into a doorway. There are three doors from the monastery into the street. I rang the bell of the middle one. Sister Monique came to the door. She had received my letter. She was expecting me. The extraordinary thing about stepping off a pavement into a convent is how immediate the sense of silence is: you are enveloped at once by another world. Instinctively I lowered my voice.

5

The windows on to the street were high and small. There was a faded, grey quiet about everything; the stone flags; the simple chair; the small cabinet full of crocheted and knitted garments for sale, proceeds to assist the nuns. Looking at the spotless, acrylic matinée jackets and shawls, I imagined the Sisters in their recreation, making them with love and care for unknown, little bodies.

Sister Monique asked about the journey; were the bags heavy? She suggested we should go at once to my room, but before that she must explain the keys. There were a great many keys. Keys for the outer door, the inner door, the yard, the stairway and finally my room. I followed Sister Monique down a narrow corridor off which to the right there were various small rooms. Then we came to the kitchen. It looked most unused, everything was neatly put to bed behind little curtains. There was a huge, wooden cupboard, the shelves lined with red-checked paper. From the state of the kitchen I realised that guests were not frequent. To get to the bedrooms we crossed a stone-flagged yard, with high, wooden double doors on to the street, and a glass door on the other side on to a little garden. Sister Monique led the way. She indicated towards various closed doors and said in a whisper ... 'the priest's room; a young woman who lives with us; a very sick sister; a little chapel for the infirm sisters ... ' On every doorway there were postcards of Assisi or other Franciscan houses – Caceri, Narni. Sister Colette, a great reformer like Saint Teresa, was pinned on the dining room door. She wore a wide-brimmed pilgrim hat and held a staff', she was making her way alone up a stony mountain road.

My room was at the top of a very beautiful, curved oak stairway. The pale light from the street, and the pale, bleached, smoky oak, all added to the quiet and calm. My room, by contrast, was bright and cheerful. Sun poured in through lace curtains from a public garden; doves cooed, almost purred. I realised that I was to fend for myself, using the dining room and kitchen as I thought fit. I was most welcome to share in the Offices and to join the Sisters for mass etc. Beaming Sister Monique left me.

Silence is strange; it is really palpable. It seems to have different colours. The silence here seemed grey-blue to me. If you listen to it, it draws you in. Rather like water, it very soon takes up any emptiness that you might have thought was there. I unpacked. Already the pace of me felt different. I didn't feel any anxiety, or the need to check things. I knew that the little house in the Rue St

Blaise where Thérèse was born would be closed. I decided simply to mooch about Alençon, generally get my bearings.

On my way out after much locking and 'clacking' as directed, I made my way down the narrow street to the chapel. It was a simple, ordinary room, with a modern feel to it. Once again the windows on to the street were high and small so the chapel was a peering, stealthy, kind of brown darkness. The altar was a square table with a white cloth on it. Ordinary wooden chairs were arranged in a semicircle round the altar. There was absolutely no hint of sentimental, plaster statuary, with mournful eyes and streaming blood. A small repro-duction of the famous Cimabue Crucifix in Assisi hung on the far wall. To the right of it there was a group of objects: a large trunk of dead wood with twig-like branches; a wooden bowl; three candles at different heights; a brown pitcher; and a small reproduction of an icon of the Resurrection. Behind the dead tree, written in the form of a scroll were the words *Tous Responsables*. It was quite unlike the chapels of my childhood. The feeling was more reticent and yet more certain.

Out in the street it was snowing. Sister Monique remarked to me later that the snow was a blessing for me from Thérèse: she had loved snow. I made my way back to the market place, to the great church of Notre Dame where, daily, the Martin parents had attended the workers' mass at 5.30 in the morning. It was colder in the church than in the street outside. There is a side chapel dedicated to Thérèse. There is a huge oval font where the saint was baptised; it has a bronze lid with openings either end. It felt rather like a magnificent cooking pot, out of which one might be scooping piping-hot broth. I stared at the the saint's christening robe and, on the walls, all those white marble tablets of gratitude for favours received. But I couldn't think of Thérèse. I could only think of her parents; their extraordinary faith and unusual betrothal.

Before they met both Louis and Zélie had tried to be accepted as religious. Both had been refused. Louis was born in Bordeaux, his father was a soldier, he had grown up in military barracks. He chose to become a watchmaker. At twenty-two he asked to enter the great contemplative monastery of Saint Bernard. He was refused because he knew no Latin. He went away to study it. By 1850 he was settled in Alençon with his parents who had a jeweller's shop on the Rue du Pont Neuf. The shop is still there, and it is still a jeweller's. Louis

7

gave up Latin but he continued to live an intensely christian life; his only relaxation was fishing.

Zélie Guérin had not been a happy child. She too had wanted to be a saint. Having been firmly discouraged from entering a religious order she came to Alençon to master the art of lacemaking. By twenty-two she had set up her own business. It was Louis' mother who introduced Zélie to her son. Within three months they were married. But Louis proposed that they should live together as brother and sister. It was a father confessor who later encouraged them to break their monastic lifestyle. There were nine births from this union. Later, all five of their surviving daughters were to become nuns. Léonie even tried to enter with the Poor Clares in Rue de la Demi-Lune, but she didn't stay. Thérèse visited the monastery. She describes it with horror, she couldn't wait to get away.

I remember reading somewhere, it might have been Jung, I cannot be sure, that, so often, children live out and accomplish the dreams of their parents. This would seem to be the case in the Martin family.

Lace is a big part of Alençon's life and pride. There is a Museum of Lace and a Lacemaking School. *Point D'Alençon* is very famous. It is frequently finished with a jutting, uneven fringe, the *point* which looks rather like pointed teeth. Apparently the secret of the lace was this final stage when each *point* was ironed cold with a lobster's claw, this made it stand out. Each part of the process was kept secret even from the workers. A piece of lace, the size of a postage stamp, represents twenty-five working hours. Zélie Martin took the orders, organised the workers and assembled the final length of lace.

The Musée de la Dentelle is amazing, the rooms are kept in semi darkness. It has a very rarified atmosphere, like some cave, storing vintage wines. The variety is enormous; the names romantic. *Point de Venise. Point de Burano. Chantilly. Blonde de Caen* (very tiny) *Point de France*, a very textured open work, like rough ground, it could be a page to illustrate *Le Pré* of Francis Ponge.

The museum is on the third floor of the Musée des Beaux Arts, where there is a spectacular public library. The reference library is housed in what was a Jesuit chapel. The ceiling is made in very narrow tongue-and-grooved wood, painted white, that floats round the elegantly proportioned windows, which bend up and over the space, like billows of cloud. Although the library was marvellous, the young librarian from Brittany said she found the people of Alençon 'cold, very closed, without any warmth'.

Maybe too much attention to civic splendour and maintenance mitigates against a more open, human countenance.

Because of the bitter cold and a slight nervousness to pull back all those little curtains and sully the silent kitchen space with the noise of taps and cutlery I rather guiltily settled for a menu outside the monastery walls.

Earlier, after the 6.30 Office, I was introduced by Sister Monique to the Mother Abbess, Marie Thérèse and several of the Sisters.

Before the Office starts, the Sisters are all there in the dark. They seem like a still circle of rough, brown stones. There are no hands to be seen, they are folded into the deep wide arms of the habit, which is a generous, shapeless garment of grey-brown cloth reaching to the ground. Sometimes there is a glimpse of thick sock bulging out of the open leather sandals. The veil is darker in colour than the rest of the habit, now and then a crown of hair shows giving you some feel of the hidden woman; of course it is the expression in the eyes that tells you most of all.

The community was small, about fifteen nuns, many of them old and infirm. Sister Monique and Anne Chantal were the only younger ones. It was Anne Chantal who plugged in the electric zither and turned on the lights when the office was due to start. The high, very controlled voices chanted in French, one side after the other. They sang so quietly, even the note on the zither seemed hardly to be a real sound. At the back of the church there were several women. They eyed me with extreme curiosity.

After the office, as the community processed out of the chapel, at a sign from Sister Monique, a few Sisters, all smiles and laughter, crowded warmly round me. Their eyes bright with keen interest, why was one here? I asked about them, their vocation etc. Yes, we are contemplative, but not like the Benedictines, we are less formal, more of a family. The silence, yes, but within reason. Yes we are enclosed, we never leave the convent. Suddenly there were peals of laughter from the very tall Sister, Thérèse Francois, who I had seen leap across the street earlier in the day. 'I know, I know,' she said 'you saw me earlier. I was coming from the dentist.' More laughter.

*

The next morning, I overslept, although sunlight was pouring into the little room and the birds were making a tremendous racket. I found the Café Douet, where the coffee was excellent, a real *coup de noir* to rouse one. Suitably awake, I made my way up the Rue St Blaise, to the little house on the dark side of the street that was the Martin's home. It faces the extremely impressive building of the Préfecture. After the death of Thérèse, the house beside number fifty was bought to be a memorial chapel. A double sweep of stone steps leads up to the chapel which opens out into the actual bedroom where Thérèse was born. The bed is still there under its red canopy, beside it a prie-dieu, chairs, tables, photographs and flowers. It must have been a very taxing bed from the midwife's point of view as top and bottom are high, solid, wooden-scrolled ends.

In the chapel there are white marble tablets from floor to ceiling and high above them, the saint's life depicted in various paintings designed by Céline, but not executed by her. A consistent air of sweetness and sentiment hangs about Thérèse both in her own writings and in all the pictures that illustrate her life. It is important to see those glorious curls, all the loving and longing, the tears, the sacrifices, the intense sisterly affection, in the context of the time and its contemporary language, otherwise you could miss the undoubted mental discipline, and incredible courage that you feel Madame Martin handed on to her daughters. Although Thérèse was only four-and-a-half when her mother died, her older sisters, who then, especially Pauline, virtually became her mother, must have been influenced by this brave woman who worked right up to her death.

The house is very compact. The most striking thing as soon as you go into the little parlour, is the marvellous quality of the photographs of Thérèse. Her great vitality survives being first bunched up into pleats, satin bows and button boots, to be exchanged later for the uncompromising, rough and most unflattering, swaddling, lumpen shape of the Carmelite habit. In every photograph without exception there is great determination and considerable humour in her expression. There is such a spark of life about her even when she was dying.

The strange thing about saints is that although their lives are one long hurled conviction towards God, submerging self, yet the devoted faithful seem to want most of all to get near in some way to their bodily person, to unravel the mysterious business of dedication and sanctity. The chair, the shoe, the bed, the beads, the toys, the spoon of the saint are the kind of objects hallowed and carefully displayed. Maybe some energy of the person remains with objects they have worn or handled. Or maybe we need these kinds of pegs to trigger our imagination to build a vivid picture of a time and a person that is past but nevertheless in some way present.

Looking at the neat, precise handwriting, Céline's paintings, the tiny dolls and games I was reminded of Howarth Parsonage. Céline was the closest in the family to Thérèse and an intimate childhood companion; she was the last of the Martin sisters to enter Carmel but she entered with her plate camera and printing equipment.

The Martin household, like the Brontë's, had been constantly bereaved. Both groups of girls had suffered the loss of their mother. And both made out of this melancholy terrain a new and boundless landscape to inspire them. For the Brontës it was the imaginary world of Gondal, for the Martins it was the spiritual desert, and the challenge there of a martyr's crown: both routes were intense, imaginative ways towards achievements of the highest order possible. For the Brontës, the ambition was to become poets, literary figures. For the Martins, saints. Both groups of isolated sisters, continue to fascinate subsequent generations.

Sister Philippe was in charge of the *maison natale*. Sister Philippe was very tall and unsmiling. She had been a teacher of French in various English schools. In careful measured tones, she decribed the Martin family, each object, each photograph, the miracles, the various stages of canonisation. She spoke of the sisters, Marie, Pauline, Léonie and Céline, rather sternly. They might have been her ex-pupils. There was nothing sentimental in her attitude. She was simply relaying the bare facts of an important personal history.

At the back of the house, I think under the chapel, there is a room in which you can buy medals, books, cards, prayers, tapes and every size of reproduction of Céline's photographs of Thérèse. There was a coachload of pilgrims from Alsace, eagerly scratting through the boxes of medals.

Sister Philippe asked me if I was on a pilgrimage of thanksgiving. I immediately felt guilty that I wasn't. I said that it was more of a quest, a general, rather random voyage of discovery. Sister Philippe looked immensely disappointed and disapproving.

*

The days continued with a bitter north wind and far less sun. I had now found two bars and a small supermarket where I bought powdered soup, fruit, tomatoes, bottled water and black chocolate. In the little kitchen I boiled water, cut bread, and mixed up the soup. The bubbling of the water in the small, white, enamel saucepan made a giant throbbing sound in the still, grey emptiness. I sat in the small dining room reading Thérèse's words in the final unexpurgated edition; her sister Pauline had tampered fairly extensively with the first.

It was an extraordinary life, the intensely close, bourgeois, family background, might have been such a sterile, claustrophobic home, but somehow, sadness, love and a christian fervour that sounds almost unreal today, catapulted Thérèse towards heroic levels of sanctity.

The soft silence in the little rooms of the monastery, marked with the charm and quiet of 'Lady Poverty', became so much more intense than the words on the page. I began to feel that, perhaps, simply by being as it were 'in silence' one might edge closer to the whole mysterious business of saints and prayer and faith. With books and places and things, it was easy to try too hard to see, and so see nothing. A cat mewed urgently on the window sill, outside in the monastery garden. She looked heavily pregnant, but I had only Evian water and black chocolate, I resisted her anguished demands for attention.

The next morning I woke with a splitting headache. The doves, which had sounded so beautiful, now seemed devastatingly melancholy. One's own company is perplexing. There is little natural diversion; mood, the subjectivity of one's responses are thrown into harsh relief. Nothing within you can really be relied upon. Mundane hazards or irritations may race out of all proportion, and conversely something extremely small and incidental may seem to be almost painfully beautiful. Within the fecklessness of mood, everything can all too easily seem like nothing but illusory rhythms.

It was market day, a Thursday, just as it had always been. A thriving, bustling, brilliant market, carpets of flowers both real and artificial, trestles of cheese, mounds of colourful fruit and vegetables. In the chapel of the *maison natale*, before the mass, I talked with two American women, they were togged up in very good boots and anoraks and jump suits. Were they pilgrims to Thérèse? They were indeed. They were devoted to Thérèse, and had made a considerable detour to visit Alençon. One was tall and thin, with sharp features, the other was square, dumpy, with a small cheerful head that just managed to peep out from the quilted hood. 'We are sisters,' they said. Very stupidly I remarked how unalike they were. 'Sisters in religion,' they replied. 'We are Catholic, but we both feel we have a definite vocation for the priesthood, Thérèse understood that. She felt that vocation herself.'

Later in the afternoon, to shelter from a sudden downpour, I found myself in a gallery of small, glutinously-varnished, contemporary, provincial paintings. Harsh, acrylic colours tried hopelessly to be poppies and corn and sunflowers, little cottages and dark forests. But it was very warm and comforting in the gallery so I gazed intently at the wild spread of images hanging four-deep in their gilded frames. Two young men came out of the office. We exchanged a few words. I said I was on my way to Lisieux. I was interested in Thérèse. As I spoke a much older man came forward into the gallery. He was very dark and slightly stooped. He had black hair, dark brown eyes and a sallow brown skin. He was very friendly. His name was Monsieur Le Boyer. He was a retired *garagiste*. The property was his, the two young men were his nephews. He paused. 'You mentioned Therese?' I said, 'Yes, indeed'. He came very close to me. His eyes watered. 'She is an angel. She is here, always here, by my side. Always. I don't have to go to Lisieux. She is here. But I love Lisieux. Once you could kiss it through a small handkerchief.' He sighed. 'They cut off her right arm you know when they disinterred the body, but it didn't preserve. It is now a skeleton.' He looked very sad. I said I would pray for his wife when I was at Carmel. I increasingly found this was the best kind of exit line from various emotional occasions, but I always kept my word. I thought with horror of the terrible mutilations that were done to the body of Saint Terese of Avila. One of her relics, her arm, was taken everywhere by General Franco, as his personal relic. I wonder if Mother Teresa's body will be allowed to remain intact when the time comes. One assumes so, but fervour seems to know no bounds.

*

By the evening Office the rain had stopped, it was far less cold and there was a warm light in the sky. The usual collection of ladies were there at the back of the chapel. There was one striking fresh face. A very elderly lady, with rouged cheeks and a heavily powdered skin, and cascades of full white curls piled high above her forehead, that were just kept in control by a colourful headscarf.

As we left the chapel she greeted me with a beaming smile and asked where I was staying. I explained. I asked her about Thérèse,

'A little angel', she cried, just as Monsieur Le Boyer had done. 'I am unmarried and over eighty now, but it was she who saved my life.' The lady said her name was Genveiève. At eighteen she had had typhoid. 'For six months I was practically dead. The doctors said there was no hope. A nun came to nurse me. She prayed ceaselessly to Thérèse. Her picture was beside my bed. Suddenly my dear . . . ' She put her hand on my arm. 'Suddenly I sat up. I was hungry. I was cured.' She beamed. 'I don't usually speak of it. People get very irritated and jealous about cures, you know how it is?' I smiled. I didn't really, but I thought Geneviève was marvellous.

It began to rain. We exchanged kisses – two – and waving madly to one another, we parted.

I left the Rue de la Demi-Lune the next morning 'clacking' the door behind me as asked. It was downhill all the way to the bus stop. I had given myself more than enough time, so there was a good wait at Alençon station. But somehow on this kind of journey waiting is not really waiting. It is simply being there. Destinations are simply names and the space between the places often influences one's feeling of the place itself. I was looking forward to moving on. I was going due north, but it was going to get me south in the end.

It had occurred to me that I might photograph the names of stations. Place names can be so evocative. Perhaps I was thinking of *Adlestrop*, of Edward Thomas's poem. I had imagined the word Lisieux with blue letters on white enamel. But there was nothing romantic, pleasing or evocative about Lisieux station. It was simply a bleak, functional place you want to leave as quickly as possible.

I waited over forty minutes for a bus to the city centre. The monumental white of the basilica is clearly seen from the station. A dome breeding drama. A great clamp of stone on to the high ground. It didn't seem to sing out towards the sky as some domes do. I was horrified by my downbeat feelings. All I could think of was what a drear climb it would be to go up there. It seemed such a lump on the skyline. Thérèse so loved nature, trees, pines. They might have created a wonderful park. She might have been 'larded with sweet flowers'. Being big, seems to be the only way the Church and the City Fathers felt appropriate honour was being given.

Eventually the bus came. I stared out of the window eager for the first impact of new place. Lisieux was a disappointing, dreary sad, modern, concrete city. It had been very badly bombed in the war. The rebuilding is drab and sterile, quite unlike Caen. In the market square, just below the Cathedral of Saint Pierre, there remain a few buildings of elegance and proportion. In the cathedral, which was not damaged, Henry Plantagenet was married to Eleanor of Aquitaine.

The wind was searingly cold, racing along the gutters and pavements. Thérèse writes about the bitter cold in the convent, and you could easily imagine how relentless it might be in an unheated building with a wind like this blowing from the north.

I was making my way to the Benedictine convent where Thérèse and Céline went to school. Everyone told me, keep going, the abbey bell tower is clearly visible from the road. Thérèse had been very unhappy at school, eventually she ended up at home having lessons from a governess. After crossing the river there was this mass of tarry, grey concrete and glass, a run of steps littered with beer cans, tons of paper, an old shoe and greasy gunge crowded into the corners of the steps. Every so often the wind roused the dirt and papers into the air, making an incongruous spasm of life against the relentless grey. The building above the steps was the rebuilt church of Saint Desir. Just beyond it a tall, concrete bell tower was clearly visible. I realised it was the Benedictine convent of Notre Dame du Pré. But something made me cross the street and go into a small bar for a glass of wine.

I was beginning to discover that a stick and rucksack has a very polarising effect on people. Some dash immediately in the opposite direction, they are often well-dressed, middle-aged people who dread the deadly time waste of giving tourists directions; others, the street musers, young or old, actually come forward to offer advice. Guy Neuilly was one of these. He came in off the street and insisted on sitting beside me and paying for another glass of wine. He was obviously well known in the bar, they were all his friends playing on the fruit machines. He was also an evident customer, his eyes swirled and swum about, uncertain of focus or direction. Did I need a place to stay? He had a good douche and an available bed. Much laughter from the lads. I thanked him but said I was making for the abbey opposite. He registered surprise and resignation.

The abbey is another severe, modern building. The original abbey was devastated by fire in the bombing, twenty nuns lost their lives. The abbey is built on three sides of a rectangle of tarmac. There is a covered walkway between the chapel and the main building. Perhaps it's meant to be cloister reminiscent. I rang the bell. I was greeted by Geneviève, who lives permanently with the Sisters and helps with the 'Welcome'. There is no longer a school. It is really a guest house for male and female pilgrims to Lisieux. My room was on the third floor. On this floor all the doors were green. My room was number forty-six. Everything was spotless. There was a small basin in the corner behind a curtain, with a great assembly of buckets and bowls, also a bright yellow, slim-line, plastic bidet, with its own folding metal cradle. *Tout Confort.* On the writing table below the window there was a typed sheet of paper, with the rules of the 'Welcome', the times of services and silence. No talking after nine o'clock. Douche extra, ask Sister for the key.

Downstairs I met another Sister Monique. She was in charge of the guests. The contrast between the Benedictines and the Poor Clares was very noticeable. Here the Sisters walked with flourish and verve. The Benedictine habit was much more fitted and flattering, it worked as an active ensemble – the deft gestures, sometimes almost theatrical bearing, the flashing positive smiles. The veils were longer and softer, the white wimple framed the face in a complimentary way.

Downstairs tea was being served. Apparently it was usually two francs, but the custom of Benedictine welcome, was that on arrival your first two 'petit beurres' biscuits were free. After the soft silence and timeless stillness in the little rooms of the monastery at Alençon, the abbey was completely different. Everything was light, modern and on the go. There were about twenty-six guests. All happened to be women, but this was chance not policy, two men arrived towards the end of the week. Several of the women had come especially for Holy Week, some were there for a pause and rest, and some were vigorous petitioners to Thérèse. There were many fine-looking, extremely frail, elderly ladies, and several younger women, rather sadly celibate, in fact quite apprehensive and lonely. Decorum, silence; consistent tidiness of papers, chairs, cushions etc. References to Thérèse were frequent. The peak Theresian experience was a visit to Carmel, where she spent her short, intense, religious life.

Geneviève was the bright spark, always around, friendly and cheerful. She was tall and very thin, with a rather childlike, Milly Molly Mandy bob and fringe of thick dark hair. I imagined her to be about twenty-five. I learned before I left that she was fifty. I still can't believe that. She had a great sense of humour and was shocked at nothing. She made a good ally. I went with her to the Office in the Abbey Church. She had a marvellous, sure, superbly controlled voice.

The abbey church is built in an L shape. The altar faces the choir which is behind a grill and hidden from the public chapel. At the back of the chapel there is an altar commemorating the spot where Thérèse made her first communion. The public part of the chapel faces a very large, stained-glass window. It seemed to be a D.N.A. spiral, in bright orange and red, flowing upwards against a bright blue ground. I asked Geneviève what she supposed it symbolised. 'It's very modern,' she said with a grin, 'I suppose it's joy ... yes, probably joy.'

The singing from the choir was clear and strong and even. This cold, high, concrete structure, with intermittent brick and reconstituted stone, certainly had marvellous accoustics. The dynamic, direct, very pure sound of the nuns' voices was full and lasting into the space. There was nothing hidden and tentative, as there was in the mousy, quiet sound of the chant of the Poor Clares.

After the Office there was supper. Each morning the menu for the day was put out, and eagerly scrutinised and discussed; two five course meals with red wine flowing right through Holy Week. If anything was overcooked or heavy, with the vegetables swimming in butter, the Parisian ladies would say, 'This is typically Norman.' The food was excellent country cuisine and lots of it; wonderful soup, salt beef, baked fish, endives, haricots verts; flans, tarts, salads,

Pont L'Evèque. Meals really mattered. And I discovered the huge importance placed on a good quality, linen table napkin, frequently embroidered. The cognoscenti brought their own, folded into matching linen envelopes. Those less prepared were given one on arrival; in between meals it was kept in numbered wooden cubby holes.

On my first evening, the other newcomers were Madeleine and Monique. Madeleine is a very intelligent, special person; a power-house of creative energy and sensitivity. She lives in Paris although her birth place and roots are in the Auvergne. Monique lives on a remote farm in the Auvergne, where for little reward she carries the burden of the considerable labour. For the last seven years, Monique nursed her mother, who has since died. I understood that her father was a difficult and tyrannical man. Madeleine had brought Monique on holiday. She was obviously delighted to be in Madeleine's stimulating company. She was a well-built woman, with a mass of thick red hair. Like Geneviève I assumed her to be in her twenties, apparently she was forty. Certainly the sadness in her eyes reflected considerable experience of real distress. Madeleine was full of passionate interests; but they all seemed connected to her deep faith as a Catholic. She was booked in for a symposium on pilgrimages in Lambesc. She was soon to visit Bulgaria, taking bibles to Sofia. She was retired, but she had worked and still works for the disadvantaged. She had adopted two orphan boys, one from Cambodia. She was continuously stimulated and stimulating. My life took on a new force and drive while Madeleine was there. Over supper we debated faith and the contemporary church of which I realised I was woefully ignorant. 'It is the epoch of the laity. Everything is changing. Thérèse is very important to us now. We are rediscovering Love. *Tous Responsables*. Thérèse understood that. 'Love,' she wrote, 'comprises all vocations, it embraces everything, all times and all places, it is eternal.'

Palm Sunday. The wind was still bitterly cold, but there was plenty of sun. I walked down to the Cathedral of Saint Pierre where the faithful were gathering. Maybe it was the wind, but it felt like a very dour occasion, a drab, dogged ritual. Not much hosanna to it. The palms were privet. After the blessing of palms, several families moved off up the hill, in the direction of the basilica. I went with them. The tourist shops were just starting to set out their wares.

There were certainly some sacred horrors. A mannequin Thérèse everywhere, looking pure, empty and doll-like, bearing no resemblance whatsoever to the wonderful, authentic photographs taken by Céline. There was a large 3D head of Christ crucified. The eyes opened and closed as you passed it, but you had to be very careful because there is a point when one eye is open whilst the other remains closed. It is very Monty Python then.

Things were certainly more lively up in front of the basilica. Groups of gipsy children were selling privet, they were full of chatter and quick repartee. But for me the basilica itself still loomed up like a great gloom of stone. Everything about it felt huge, heavy and uncompromising. Behind the basilica is a vast, ultra-white Way of the Cross. There is also the tomb of the Martin parents, who were, I was told, being considered for canonisation. I went in under the pine trees and had an apple. It is very touching how, in spite of everything, this intimate family feeling continues to survive. The pale apple core, lying in fresh, brown pine needles, looked very beautiful. I thought how soon that soft, white apple flesh would grow brown, losing identity; ready to rot back again into the regenerative earth. I thought how we resist unity, by always pleading identity. The procession below was in full swing, to be followed later by a mass in the crypt.

Inside the basilica it felt like a tomb, which I suppose it is in a way. There is a mass of bright narrative mosaics, and many side chapels, each one the gift of a nation. The little brown finger, or skeleton arm, is there, far away in a glass and gold casket, beyond banks of candles and plastic flowers. It all seemed so far from the voice and vitality of Thérèse. The 'Little Flower' of a 'Little Way'. Someone who understood the gift of littleness. Everything here was as big as you could get, without any feeling of joy or celebration.

I went back down the hill in the bitter wind. I had arranged to meet Madeleine and Monique later at Les Buissonnets, the Martin's home on the outskirts of the city. Everyone kept saying it was very far, but I seemed to get there in no time at all. Perhaps I was driven by the wind.

Les Buissonnets is up on high ground. There is a turning up a fairly steep cobbled walk, on the left there is a high, brick wall. A large sign hangs above the solid, wooden doors set in the wall LES BUISSONNETS. Large white letters on a ground of blue enamel. It is a very peaceful place, well away from the traffic and the feel of the city. Tall trees full of blossom, billowed out above the mellow bricks. Birds chattered and sang and flew about, criss-crossing the vacant sky. The house was not yet open, so I walked in among the other houses, up little paths, past orchards and large, overgrown gardens. There were several chickens; a dog barked; a small child pushed a squeaky swing. It was such a relief to be away from all those monuments and proclamations. Here one could easily imagine Thérèse walking with her father, or blackberrying with Céline. The birds and blossom were celebratory. I sat down on the broad step in front of the high closed doors into the garden. It was warm down there out of the wind. I could almost hear the two girls charging out of the house; perhaps a ribbon would fall, smooth and bright on to the cobble-stones. They would be making their way down to school at the abbey; full of gossip, plans and schemes; ways and dreams towards the heavenly goal they both so keenly sought.

Promptly at 2 p.m. one of the Sisters unlocked the doors. I was the only waiting pilgrim. The house is charming. It faces due south, with a good-sized garden front and back. Vita Sackville-West in her book *The Eagle and the Dove*, which contrasts the two saints, Teresa of Avila and Thérèse Martin, describes the house 'as precisely the sort of house we see standing in its own grounds at the approach to any of our large towns and according to our standards of taste, was both ugly and for its size pretentious.' She goes on to refer to this *chalet bourgeois*. I'm sure from the focus of Knole or Long Barn it would be extremely bourgeois, but any similar family house in this country, would I feel sure, not be read today in quite the same certain tones of tastelessness. It would probably be described as a family house of considerable character. It certainly felt sunny and family-sized to me. There was a mass of yellow pansies and various other flowers. Once inside the kitchen the Sister switched on the tape. A low, suitably reverent male voice then escorts you through the house, describing the family saga room by room. It was full of atmosphere. From the kitchen there is a glass window into the dining room, where you can see all the original, heavy, carved furniture, and the ormolu clock on the mantlepiece signed 'Martin'. Upstairs there is Thérèse's and Céline's room, with Thérèse's bed, where she slept when during her adolesence she became extremely ill, with a still undiagnosed complaint that almost threatened her life. Toys, books, paint boxes, a birdcage are all there. Very soon the small house was full of people, moving quietly and attentively from room to room. Outside in the garden there is a rather surprising, larger-than-life-size monument, flashing white once again, it depicts Thérèse seeking her father's permission to enter Carmel.

If there was any presence in the garden it was his, Louis Martin; this melancholy widower, pilgrim and fisherman supported the decision of all his five daughters to take up the religious life, but such sacrifice cost him his sanity. He was to spend three years in an asylum in Caen after Thérèse entered Carmel. He was unrecognisable to all who knew him. His mad condition was foretold to some extent when Thérèse, as a child, suddenly burst out crying one afternoon, when she saw from a window of the house, this figure in the garden; a stooped man with a cloth covering his head. She later came to realise it was her father.

It is fascinating to visit the homes of people whose writings have already made them vivid to you; Chawton, with the squeaking door that so disturbed Jane Austen; Howarth with Emily's minute bedroom, where all you can see is the brooding church tower and heavy, thrusting headstones; T.E. Lawrence's cottage in Dorset with the specially built, low mantlepiece, so that T.E. could stand there comfortably, with his elbow resting on it. The size of these spaces, the way the light works in them, precisely how they are in relation to roads and boundaries, finally, it is this composite picture that remains with you, leaving almost a particular smell on the mental retina. For me, Les Buissonnets seemed a blue-white feel of violets and jasmine.

Madeleine and Monique arrived. There was a plan to go to Honfleur. Monique had never seen the sea.

Although I had not really been long from home, it felt peculiarly exciting to be getting into a car. Honfleur is a picture-postcard town; wonderfully preserved timbered buildings, narrow streets, a magnificent stone granary just beyond the harbour, which was full of moored yachts when we were there. Monique, who was loving everything, was particularly thrilled by the clack, clack of metal against the masts, it reminded her of the cowbells at home. There was not really enough time, so we sped here, there and everywhere. A large timbered church, Saint Catherine's, the exterior hung with wooden tiles. The roof inside was coved, like an upturned boat. It was built to celebrate the departure of the English from Honfleur.

There was the belfry, the museum. Then suddenly Madeleine remembered the little shrine on the cliffs. Miraculous. A favourite place of pilgrimage for the Martin family. I should go there. Notre Dame de Grace. We set out in the wrong direction. But Madeleine would not be daunted. A brisk three-point turn, directly into the oncoming traffic and we were on our way.

The chapel is high up on the cliffs overlooking the Le Havre estuary. It is built in stone in the shape of a Greek cross. It was built between 1600 and 1615 by the citizens and sailors of Honfleur to replace a much earlier chapel founded in 1023 which fell down the cliff. There was a curious round porch and then the wonderful surprise of the chapel itself. The Madonna was black and virtually life size. The statue was rescued when the chapel fell down the cliff. This Virgin apparently grants many favours, but most of her favours are granted to sailors. There are several model boats hung from the deep blue ceiling; old sailing ships and battle ships from World War II. On the walls there are many colourful, votive paintings of raging, turbulent seas, with vessels barely surviving; but in the corner, in a comfortable cloud, there is always the Madonna to guide them. Besides the statue of the Madonna, there is an unusual, wooden statue of Saint Anne holding Mary in her arms, who in turns holds the child Jesus.

Outside all the trees were in leaf, the first spring green I had seen. We just made it back to the abbey in time to grab our napkins from their little cubbyholes. Grace had already begun. Grace is sung before every meal. It is a grace that the older ladies are very fond of because they remember singing it as children. In its last line it is particularly relevant to today:

> Vous qui donnez pâture
> Aux tous petits oiseaux
> Bénissez notre nourriture
> Et purifiez notre eau.

Monday April 9th and still bitterly cold. Each morning the ladies asked, 'When are you going to Carmel?' As Thérèse entered Carmel on Monday April 9th I felt that maybe that was a good day for me.

My little room was warm and light and comfortable, but each morning I found I woke in a kind of black panic, with a splitting headache and some sort of weird sense that I was doing everything wrong. I was looking, seeing, walking, talking, but there was something about all the order, the kindness, the silence; it leant on this profound drama of Christian faith. All the stories of practices, favours, trials, the way the saints, particularly Thérèse of course, were part and parcel of everyone's life. I would be listening to someone recounting an experience of distress and it would be followed by the certainty in some way of God's direct and loving intervention. It went on all the time. All these varied boats of vivid human adventure bobbing about on this sea of certainty. Faith. Everyone assumed I was bobbing about on the sea with them. Why else would I be there? That was part of the panic. Why *was* I there? In a loose, wide way, I have never doubted Love to be the central, unifying force that in some mysterious sense connects all nature, man and beast, insect and stone, to the greater cosmic good of God. Atman. Nirvana. Heaven. Some source of liberation. A sum of transposed, live reality, that is intelligent beyond intelligence, and must remain within mystery. I had given up looking for exact words long ago.

I had given up proclaimed Catholic practice when the twins were born. We then had six children under seven, and a foster son of fourteen, and no coherent livelihood to speak of. The general cry was, 'sterilise her'! It seemed to me both sensible and responsible, but to the Church, in the way it was available to me, that was Sin, a sin that would reflect on our married relationship for ever. Jacob and Joseph were not baptised. With the help of an Anglican uncle, who was a Franciscan, we evolved a catechumen ceremony of blessing. I had the relevant knots tied and tried to go on from there. All of that was a long time ago. But access to a considerable amount of silence, with no external demands or particular relationships reminding you who you are, or what you should be doing, has a strange way of melting the shape of time. There is simply 'being' and its uncomfortable, intense incoherence. Somehow I was rather dreading Carmel. Being truly alive to my honest responses was becoming very hard. Before I set out I thought the problems would be practical: losing glasses, catching the wrong bus, not being fluent enough with the language. But these were not problems. The problems were odd, perplexing knots of disorder within myself.

I made my way up to Carmel immediately after breakfast, after

Sister Jeanne with her usual smile, had brought to each table, in a shining metal jug the 'Milk of Normandy'. Sister Jeanne presided over all the affairs of the kitchen with great calm and humour, combining the considerable, active organisation needed for her job with precise human skills with all concerned.

The 9 a.m. mass is the one attended by the Community, who are clearly visible in the choir; brown veils, short skirts. It is a popular mass with the pilgrims. Immediately inside the chapel you feel very definitely that this is a place of prayer for a contemporary community, not simply a mooching site for staring pilgrims. There is of course the big 'Snow White' glass and gold casket, with a life size wax model of Thérèse in her nun's habit, lying above her actual remains. but the emphasis is very much on the proper purpose of prayer. There are lots of notices about this. There is a light airy space at the back of the church for confession. Table and chairs, no musty curtained box. The method of preparation for confession is displayed outside on the wall. It is all expressed in very definite terms; the language is uncompromising and fairly fierce. Perhaps it is designed to put off casual tourists, it would certainly succeed.

A large group of extremely small, elderly persons were struggling in and out of the cold, with sticks and stoops and gammy legs. Each one wore a small crocheted circle of white with a blue centre, presumably so that they wouldn't lose one another.

Outside the chapel, beyond the shop, is the crypt. Here in a series of windows, all the Theresian memorabilia is displayed. For one franc the windows light up in turn, while the voice in the language of your choice fills you in with the relevant details; there is her habit; her paint box; clogs, hour-glass, the exercise books in which her life was written; the long, golden ringlets of hair, with a little wreath of flowers embedded in them, that were ceremoniously cut on her entry into Carmel. They are wonderful Cordelia tresses, preserved apparently at the specific request of her father. Poor Louis, you feel there may have been many Lear moments during his period of incarceration and insanity. There is a heavily embroidered priest's chasuble, made by Thérèse from a velvet dress of her mother's. On the back there is an ornate cross; in the centre, the painted head of Christ; at the base of the cross are two white roses symbolising the Martin parents. Five open lilies symbolise the five religious daughters; four closed lily buds symbolise the Martin children who died.

As I walked slowly back to the abbey through through the drab city of Lisieux, stopping in at various bars, a bank and a pharmacy. I thought how central to the lives of so many saints, artists, poets was the dynamic discovery of their own vast, miserable inadequacy against the pull and summons of their inspiration; some quantum leap has to be made; a leap into the dark. This brave leap forward seems often to fetch a circle back to their own centre. From there, in touch with God, Buddha nature, higher intelligence, various unnamed strengths. Finally the resources necessary are often found to be available, although this does not mean an end to suffering. Thérèse writes, 'If with faith alone Jesus teaches me so well, then surely he will teach others? We need only Him, not scholars or theologians.' Emily Brontë, out of her intense isolation discovered limitless energies within her own powerful nature. She wrote:

> No coward soul is mine
> No trembler in the world's storm-troubled sphere,
> I see Heaven's glories shine,
> And Faith shines equal, arming me from Fear.

> With wide-embracing love
> Thy spirit animates eternal years,
> Pervades and broods above,
> Changes, sustains, dissolves, creates, and rears.

> Though earth and moon were gone,
> And suns and universes ceased to be,
> And thou wert left alone,
> Every Existence would exist in thee.

In the same poem Emily refers to the formal religions as: 'Vain are the thousand creeds, That move men's hearts, unutterably vain; Worthless as withered weeds.'

Thérèse's vocation of Love, at the end of the nineteenth century, couldn't have sounded remotely political. Now, a hundred years later, we are witnessing the experience in Europe of an artist as President of his country. Vaclav Havel of Czechoslovakia wrote in 1979, 'There are times when an artist must put his art aside in order to do something positive in life, something modest that may not earn him a place in history, but which is the the expression of a moral imperative or simply a love for people.'

Plato expressed it, and the Beatles. 'All you need is Love.' The desire and pursit of the Whole is Love. 'Love is all you need,' seems to be the message, but the manner of achieving the necessary transformation to put such conviction into action, to put it beyond desire; that seems to be the challenge.

Every God-geared conversation, every kind of theological debate, always seemed to end with the word mystery. *C'est un mystère*, that, and Rue du Bac, were phrases that kept ringing in my head. Rue du Bac crops up in convents as frequently as Appleby does among Travellers and the Carlton Club among Conservatives. Rue du Bac is in Paris. It is the birthplace of the Miraculous Medal.

Fond farewells to Madeleine and Monique; three kisses and two kisses. A miraculous medal from Geneviève, who lent me her hair dryer on my last night, and got me into the douche free. After the Silence, we whispered together in her room. She was orphaned at two and was brought up by nuns. She has spent her whole life going from convent to convent. She has one battered photograph of her parents set in an album which is full of photographs of Thérèse and Rue du Bac, and various fawns and rabbits. Referring to the nuns she said, 'You know them, but you never really know them. Their life is really with their silence and themselves.' We discussed whether she should grow her hair or cut it short. The final decision was to grow it. Eventually I went back to my room, tiptoeing down the dark corridor to my green door. Every life is touched with such individual threads and subtleties of suffering. But also every individual is gripped and enthralled by possibilities within themselves, even if to the outsider they represent something extremely straightforward and simple. Everywhere, always, such mind-blowing variety.

2

Holy Week in Paris

Le Christ est Ressuscité. Il est Vraiment Ressuscité.

MAUNDY THURSDAY: Saint Jules.

I woke at last clear-headed. Perhaps it was the hair wash. I remember reading in Dorothy Wordsworth's journal how after sticking peas, she had a bad headache which was instantly cured by washing her hair. I remember thinking then, what a universal trial a headache is; a small thing, but common to all ages and peoples.

It was dreary and grey and very cold waiting at Lisieux station. The train to Paris was crowded, nevertheless everyone seemed to find a seat.

My idea was to spend the Easter weekend in Paris. I was to meet my greatest friend in the buffet of the Gare Saint Lazare. Almost thirty years ago to the day we had been in Paris together. Sitting waiting at the café tables, although you are under cover, there is still that marvellous street feeling. The café pause; an onlooker at the centre of things. I was fascinated by how many odd and rather ugly dogs there were; their idyosyncratic shapes seemed only to add to the considerable sense of importance and self esteem they demonstrated in their bearing. Being an absolute 'one off' is possibly much more rewarding than being an expected clone, however stylish and pedigree. Maybe 'one offs' before God are crucial to the energy of the beatific vision. Seeking to conform in order to confirm, liturgically or otherwise may simply encourage division and disorder.

It was wonderful just to be in Paris and a part of the nomadic,

27

colourful variety of its people. Even in the dark, greasy Gare Saint Lazare, there was the smell of coffee, bread and Gauloises; the weight and play of iron work and great bowls of lights on gilded stems.

The metro seemed much the same as I remembered it, full of evocative sounds, the surprise was the length of some of the *correspondances*. On and on, up hill and down dale, all over the place. We made our way to Simplon in the Clignancourt area where a small apartment had been organised for us by a friend. It was on the ground floor, light and airy, with extremely flamboyant covers on the sofa, that pulled out into a bed. It all felt a far cry from linoleum quiet, the blues and ochres and browns of the convent spaces. We unpacked and discussed plans. Rue du Bac of course, then, where and when for the various ceremonies of Holy Week. But all the time, niggling in the back of my mind was a sort of grey, rather pungent anxiety. The instinct was to think I was getting a cold, a bug, sore throat maybe. But although there were suitable symptoms admirably interrupted by glasses of wine and interesting victualling, in my heart I knew I had this dread of Holy Week. How could I get it right, because in a sense I didn't really believe. The facts of course, the traditions yes, and the idea of the person. But it was a remote idea of the person. A baffling, unnerving idea. It didn't seem part and parcel of the kind of belief that had got me going on this journey in the first place.

It was odd, because my recent experience of cancer, and the subsequent treatment, radium and chemotherapy, and after that all the obvious and necessary looking at life and death in a new way, I had found that very rewarding. It had seemed clear, that I had for some time, been voting myself out of life. I had been diving for the dark. Feeling driven, of course; but there is always choice. Considering *Death* had meant considering *Life*. I knew that now, I had made a firm decision towards life, not for length of time, that wasn't the point, but to find fresh ways of liberating its quality. Instinctively that seemed to mean going back to base. Considering roots; the depths of things. Go on Pilgrimage. The outward journey may be an inward one. Find out where the other seekers are. What are they doing and saying? Visit medieval stops, those ancient places that in their art and architecture, husband for us the images and archetypal energy of our collective European soul.

It had felt like an upbeat idea, all directly within the orbit of what I can only call 'Divine Regard'. Nothing complicated. Just a

Pilgrimage. Nevertheless I felt curiously unnerved.

We decided to plan a day at a time. We would go to Notre Dame for the major Maundy Thursday spectacle; washing of the feet, mass, procession etc. The ceremony was at 8.30 in the evening.

The great facade of Notre Dame looked far lighter and cleaner than my memory of it. Because of the cold there were few people sitting on the benches by the privet hedges in front of the cathedral. Those that were there were mostly tourists, who were obviously finding it hard to believe that they were 'in Paris in the Springtime'.

Inside, the cathedral was packed with people. The vast huddle of dark bodies under the heavy haze of incense looked like a stubby growth of heather in a huge forest clearing. The incense, like clouds of druid mist, blew past the magnificent, grand candelabra, that lit this stone cave of giant church space. The building, in proportion to the people, is so high. As we edged our way forward down one of the side aisles, we caught a glimpse of the tribe of thurifers and twenty or so priests, dressed in white, who were grouped round the central altar. We couldn't see the washing of the feet, we could only sense it happening. Every so often there was a great blast of sound from the organ and the voices would begin in unison to lap and echo through the smoky vaults. Suddenly there was a hymn, surprisingly to the tune of 'While shepherds watch their flocks by night'. Nudging our way closer and closer towards the seat of action, you could see how varied the congregation was; young, old, rich, poor, religious or camera-slung foreigners; people clutched babies and bags of food.

Again and again I heard the phrase I had grown to love in the convents, sung here with such solemnity and power ... *Maintenant et toujours dans les siècles des siècles*; somehow, unlike 'forever and ever' *siècles des siècles* sounds palpably like the passing of time, rolling soft and smooth over stones and streets, all landscapes and structures.

Gradually we became aware that the crowd was sloughing off into great lengths of people, all easing their way forward. At the front there were rows of sick and infirm. These slow-moving cords of people moved on past the altar. It was the Blessed Sacrament procession that was to make its way slowly round the church and up beyond the high altar into the Lady Chapel. As we were in a side aisle, we were divided off from the main body of the nave by a carved, wooden petition, however we were quite near a small fretted gate through which many people were passing. We attempted to follow, when suddenly an elderly lady firmly closed it in front of us. 'It will come this way,' she said with considerable authority. But it didn't. It went went in the opposite direction up the other side aisle. We pointed this out to her. 'But it never goes that way,' she said furiously. 'Never.' Then she flung open the wooden gate and walked past us still huffing and puffing until she vanished through a doorway marked *Tresors*.

We caught up with the procession. Every age and stage of life was there: cameras flashed; small children looked anxious; a cauliflower fell from an old lady's shopping bag. The Sisters of Mother Teresa were very distinct in their blue and white saris. The final hymn and the Blessed Sacrament was left in the ciborium on a long altar table among a mass of candles. The procession of priests and deacons began to file out past us. Wonderful faces, very Umberto Eco, like carvings, no characteristic fudged or small, all very individual, marked and made, one presumed by the weight and purpose of their vocation, unlike stockbrokers or estate agents who often seem remarkably similar. The priests were followed by the choir, led by two girls with long, thick plaits. Then it was all over and the greetings and meetings immediately begun. There were frantic cries of 'Julia, Julia', a small English child had become separated from her parents. She was retrieved from behind a pillar. The smell of the incense was still in the air, but the great whirls of grey-green smoke had cleared. We passed a band of stalwart cleaners waiting with long floor mops. They were dressed in bright yellow jump-suits, which gave them a vaguely heaven-sent aspect, their faces, round and rugged, were in complete contrast to the sallow, pale faces of the priests.

Outside in the bitter cold, the tall, thin gothic figures of saints and apostles seemed to smile down on the faithful, with an air of detached, almost snooty disdain.

So it was done. Worship. Prayer. An assembly of Witness. I didn't know. A poignant gathering in a magnificent building certainly. I had longed somehow to connect with that marvellous Mantegna painting, or simply the narrative sense of a man alone, unbelievably burdened. Something big. Something important. But it had felt to me like a tired, laboured ceremony. Perhaps that was right. Probably all responses are subjective and illusory. Where and what is meaning

I wondered, as we walked across to look at the magnificent charger bearing Charlemagne away from the cathedral. The great, acid-green streaks of weathering on this bronze statue seem to add to the sense of energy. Maybe energy is the means of meaning. Endlessly transforming, never able by its very nature to finally unlive.

Food and wine in St Germain, then back to Simplon on the metro, past sleeping, crumpled figures; rather Mantegna. On the crumbling walls of many of the stations there were colourful posters of Christ in a blaze of light with the words ... *Le Christ est Ressuscité. Il est Vraiment Ressuscité.*

Vendredi Saint. Once again, bitterly, bitterly cold. On the way towards the Sacré Coeur we visited Notre Dame de Clignancourt. None of the statues were shrouded in purple. There were flowers everywhere. There were a great many plaster saints. Side altars and small shrines to Saint Joan, Saint Francis, Saint Rita and of course, Thérèse. Several people were making the stations of the Cross. The only sound in the church was the voice of a well-dressed, quite portly, oriental gentleman, I felt he might have been Vietnamese. He was sitting before the statue of Saint Francis, some sheet music in his hand, and he was singing aloud, quite beautifully. The phrasing was complicated, his voice was most assured. His presence and devotions animated this dark, cold church for everyone. The altar was a long table in front of a huge dark, wooden crucifix, a thick red cloth was draped across the figure. On the table there was round of bread, a bunch of grapes, a silver pitcher and a basin of flowers. I remembered Anne at Lisieux, a graduate teacher, 'Liturgy is just *fantasie* these days,' she had told me, 'it has no structure. Everyone just does their own thing.' The gripping, biting cold seemed to overwhelm the symbols, as if they were simply forgotten objects in a freezing pantry. I'm sure this wasn't so for the oriental gentleman.

High up in front of the Sacré Coeur, the wind felt like a perishing howl off the dense, white stones of the columns and steps. Everywhere there were signs about the Way of the Cross due to start fairly soon from the square, below the basilica. There were purple tickets with all the information. Cardinal Lustiger will carry the Cross. The procession will start at 12.30 during the *pause du travail*. The procession used always to be at 3 p.m., the time Christ died, but now, as the majority of Parisians are definitely unbelievers, the lunch hour is the only possible time, on this perfectly ordinary working Friday, as far as the commercial life of the city is concerned. We and a great many others were preparing to look down on the procession from the good vantage points, directly in front of the basilica.

A mass of T.V. and radio technicians were setting up their apparatus. The place was strewn with cables and high, metal ladders. Police were organising the crowds, cordoning off and uncordoning various areas. Tourists rushed around, grabbing hectic children in bright anoraks, as they darted about the place, climbing and jumping, doing just about anything to keep warm. The atmosphere was of a fête, some sort of spring festival that must have chosen the wrong day. Rather like the Easter parade in Battersea Park when the weather is against it.

In order simply to get out of the wind, I found a suitable spot between two pillars round the side, where there were fewer cables and no children. Sitting there, huddled up in layers of rather ineffectual clothes, I was trying to make notes, but my pen seemed to be frozen, it made nothing but empty, glazed marks on the paper. Then an extremely attractive, young woman, dressed suitably in a long black coat and fur hat, began asking me questions. 'Why are you here? What does Good Friday mean to you etc.?' She was working for a radio station. Radio Tour Eiffel. 'Would I please do an interview?' Comforted by the knowledge that no one I knew would remotely listen that evening to Radio Tour Eiffel, I went on about not being sure of anything, having had a Catholic education, but finding the Church too rigid and dogmatic. I was not in any way a practising Catholic. I was on an idyosyncratic pilgrimage that would end, I hoped, in Compostela. Catherine smiled. Her parents were both Russian Orthodox. She played the tape back to me. I was surprised it didn't sound cold. She seemed pleased. 'There is a foreign accent,' she said, 'but everything is very clear indeed, completely comprehensible.'

From the basilica there is an amazing view of Paris. Far below us we could see the crowds gathering. There were really two crowds. The active Faithful, following the Archbishop and the large wooden Cross he carried, and the voyeurs, waiting up at the top and all along the balustrading that curved round the steps, and down towards the streets far below. Beyond the procession the city roofs spread out in a vast fan, like a scatter of broken biscuits in the cold watery light.

Little scraps of brick and stone, boarded finally by rather stubby tower blocks.

At last there were the faint strains of the Stabat Mater to be heard. The procession was on the move. Gradually the words became more distinct; the figures could be clearly seen, the crisp white of a nun's veil every so often punctuating the sombre blacks and browns. Round us the crowd strained to see the Archbishop. Every so often we were rewarded by a glimpse of his bright red skull cap, and beneath it his kind, intent face, the small, fine hands clasping the broad piece of smooth, dark wood. The cherry-red skull cap made me think of 'Poor Cock Robin', the nursery ballad when 'all the birds of the air fell a-sighing and a-sobbing, when they heard of the death of poor Cock Robin' and on reflection, all found they had some share in his death. As the Cross came closer, pigeons, police, cameras and crew kept scattering and then re-aligning. There was a sense of yearning for something that didn't seem to be there. There was none of the fervour and primitive passion of a similar, Spanish procession. Well-dressed, calm people repeated prayers for the forgiveness of sins. But the connection to contemporary suffering and abuse of human dignity, the contemporary Calvary as Mother Teresa refered to the famine in Ethiopia, any such 'contemporary calvary' felt absent, unknown. Of course, this is a subjective response. You are thrown back all the time on the lame limits of personal impressions.

Easter Saturday. We were very excited to wake to real sunlight, and every so often, patches of bright blue sky. Several people had told me that Notre Dame des Victoires had been, and was still a frequent place of pilgrimage, particularly for artists, and those with problems in affairs of the heart. This Notre Dame was certainly well loved by Louis Martin and Thérèse.

We discovered that the cult since 1836 had been for the Madonna to be a 'Refuge for Sinners' (maybe artists and lovers come all too easily under that banner). The church was built in 1629, but the cult of the 'Refuge of Sinners to the Immaculate Heart of Mary' was purposely set up by the *curé* in 1836. Apparently conversion, as well as forgiveness, was a strong suit.

The little cobbled place in front of the basilica was full of police cars. There is a police station beside the basilica. I had become increasingly confused by what constitutes a basilica. I vaguely thought that perhaps it had to have domes. Apparently a basilica is any church, that has, by papal authority, been officially recognised as a place of pilgrimage.

The church was dark and not particularly large. The actual Madonna is a very handsome, fairly buxom, fecund figure, swathed in flowing robes. A rather 'Cow and Gate' infant Jesus, rests beside his mother. The child is standing on a large globe, embedded with gold stars. Both mother and child effortlessly support huge gold crowns on their heads. As it was Holy Saturday, the lights above them were unlit, and the tabernacle door on the altar below them was open. As with all the pilgrim churches and chapels of the nineteenth century and early twentieth century, the walls are covered from head to foot with marble tablets of thanks; for protection, healing, guidance, and favours received. But the tablets here were most particular. They filled the church with vivid ghosts of many unusual people, whose lines of gratitude tantalised one to know more. For instance, in English:

'I thank thee my Mother for having preserved my wife's life.' Madras, India 1868.

'For my return to God May 25th, 1855.' Gustave Bizot, painter, pupil of Ingres.

'Mary O tender Mother! You have saved our family from a horrible situation!' (The exclamation marks are on the tablet.)

Then there is a brave, public figure: 'To Our Lady of Victories. Ant Loriol Advocate at the Imperial Court of Paris Dec. 1864. A converted sinner.'

There are many, many more; they make fascinating reading. Ex Voto and three large embossed and pierced hearts. Thanks offerings from three English converts: A R 4th May. I A 1st June. I.G. 2nd July, 1864, and prayers for the complete conversion of England. You wonder why it took I.G. so much longer than A.R.

At the back of the church there is an incredible organ, resting on a flowing flourish of buxom Cow and Gate angels. Looking at these happy, but discreetly swathed cherubs, I couldn't help being reminded of a current film concerning angels and sexuality which was being widely advertised and much discussed. Apparently there is a sequence when a jolly cherub has an unmistakable erection, as he pursues an ecstatic female cherub through the billowing clouds!

Although the decorative impact of these churches is very gothic and nineteenth century, much yearning and sentiment, what is going on in them now is very different. There is more about Love than Sin; communication rather than judgement. Images of the risen Christ, rather than gory, bleeding figures of the crucified Christ. Everywhere there seems to be some flavour of Byzantium. At the back of this church, there was a pamphlet advertising a weekend seminar. *Rencontre Juifs-Chrétiens-Musulmans. La Création et la Responsabilité de L'Homme.*

We went on by bus to the Opera, from there we walked down the Madeleine, across Concorde, until eventually we were there, in Rue du Bac. At school, we had had a particularly kind and affectionate Irish Sister who worked in the linen room – Sister Kiloran. In her tins of pins and spare buttons she had an endless supply of miraculous medals, which she insisted on pinning to our chilprufe vests. I remember feeling surprised, a little ridiculous, but on the whole rather happy to be so protected.

Rue du Bac has a positive, no nonsense ring to it. Somehow a country feel, like a clod of earth, or a hunk of cheese. The word *bac* actually means ferryboat or fish tank. The street is a very long one. The landmark to direct one to number 140, is the large shopping emporium of the Bon Marché. The little turning into 140 is directly opposite a double doorway into this marvellous period store.

The striking of the miraculous medal is another nineteenth-century story. Once more a pious little girl of humble origins loses her mother at an early age. The little girl was Catherine Labouré, her home was on a farm in the little village of Fain – Les-Moûtiers in Burgundy. Catherine, who was born in May 1806, finally entered the religious life after various trials and difficulties, in 1830. She joined the extremely active order of the Sisters of Charity founded by Saint Vincent de Paul. They were the Sisters with the wide 'butterfly bun' flyaway, large, white veils, that are often seen in the street paintings of this period.

140 Rue du Bac was the Mother House, so Catherine came there to begin her training. Very soon there were apparitions. This time the Virgin, very beautiful and wearing a silk dress – Catherine distinctly heard the sound of silk rustling – this Virgin appeared seated in an arm chair in the chapel. Catherine was led to her from her bed by a small child. The chair was no ordinary chair, it was the

Father Director's chair. Apart from some secrets to confide and a great sense of happiness for Catherine, the Virgin had a practical demand to make. The second time the Virgin appeared, she was dressed in white silk, her feet rested on a globe and she held a smaller globe in her hands. Then an oval shape appeared round the Virgin with these words in gold lettering.

'O Mary, conceived without sin, pray for us who have recourse to thee.' And Catherine heard a voice say to her, 'Have a medal struck like this. Those who wear it will receive great graces.'

The first medals were struck and distributed in 1832 and soon afterwards there was talk of many cures, comforts and conversions. The rest of Catherine's life was quiet and humble. She left the Rue du Bac and worked up until her death in a hospice for old men. But the medal's fame went from strength to strength. The demand for it was continuous and considerable.

Today you turn off the busy, narrow street into a little courtyard. When we were there it was full of pilgrims. Most of them were crowded around the medal-vending machines. The atmosphere was rather like a Women's Institute outing; everyone was very friendly and full of chatter. Many were coach loads of pilgrims on their way to Lourdes. Rue du Bac is obviously a cheerful, reassuring stop for pilgrims. There were people from Scotland, Ireland, Portugal, Spain and Japan. If the pilgrims didn't find the medal they wanted from the machines, there was a small room close by, where the Sisters sold the medals in a great variety of packs and sizes and metals. The Sisters made sure that with every medal sold there was an explanatory leaflet in the appropriate language for the customer. The way the medal is worn is all important.

At the end of the courtyard there is the chapel. It is very bright and light. There is a sort of Mabel Lucy Attwell nursery feeling, of sparkling creams and blues and pinks, with gilded stars and angels everywhere. The director's armchair is no longer there, but the heart of Saint Vincent de Paul is there, and the body of Catherine. Fifty-six years after her death, her body was exhumed and found to be completely intact, with supple limbs and the pupils of the eyes a clear blue. Catherine was given a clean change of clothes and then her body was placed in an ornate casket in the chapel, below a side altar, suitably far from too eager pilgrim eyes.

I found the feeling in the chapel bright, uncomplicated and very peaceful, but my companion fled in horror, without being too specific as to what the feeling of horror was. Places of devotion and constant pilgrimage seem to amass energy. Presumably people bring, and in some way transmit, their own energy, which turns into the energy present and reflects back to each one, at many levels and in a variety of ways. Variety. The subtlety, the quite intoxicating, infinity of variety. Whether it is grains of sand or sparrows or stars, variety seems beyond apprehension.

One thing quite beyond doubt, and easily apprehended, was the wonderful, clean, fully working quality of the loos in Rue du Bac. In constant use, but kept, perhaps miraculously, in excellent order. The same could not be said for the terrible loos for women in the Centre Pompidou, when we went to see the paintings of Rouault in particular. In this wonderfully extending place of culture and experience, only two loos at that level, one quite devastatingly blocked, with, as a result, queues of anxious, uneasy women; practically a procession. Sheets of paper had to be taken out before you went in to the lavatory. The number of sheets taken by the person in front was carefully noted. The glamorous and chic seemed to take a great deal, and so those behind them followed suit, but the supply seemed to totally exceed need; as a result there was a speckle of folded sheets floating about everywhere; a confetti deluge.

When we made our way back to Rue Beaudalique from Rue du Bac, Holy Saturday was rapidly drawing to a close. The choice of where to go to celebrate and witness the Easter vigil, the greatest, most important feast in the church calendar, was very difficult indeed. You must go to Saint Sulplice, some said. No, Notre Dame. Why not Sacré Coeur? What about an Orthodox vigil? For once the two calendars coincided.

On the metro, the vigil seemed far and near. Being in such diverse crowds made me feel closer to the meaning of phrases like 'all nations' and the exciting, continuously challenging truth of Love, and one's neighbour. At one level these ancient cries reverberate through you like some archetypal command. Love the Lord your God, Creator of Heaven and Earth. Huge idea on its own, just the concept of a creator. Love your neighbour as yourself. These phrases could sound intoxicating in the giant summons of their truth, but on the other hand, the same words could as easily fall away from sound and meaning, and seem simply like a great pile of washing up that has accumulated over the ages and simply can't be tackled; then you are back to hopeless, grey, anxious unease again.

*

In the end we decided simply to walk out of our door in Rue Beaudalique, and go to the nearest parish church. We made our way along the glistening pavements towards the church of Saint Vincent de Paul, which is near the Gare du Nord. Discussing churches, their various attributes both architectural and liturgical can become a little like discussing restaurants. Going blind as it were, unrecommended, into an unknown restaurant, is always an adventure. The number of other customers is probably as true an indication of quality as Michelin marks. You are alert to everything: it could be a wonderful find, or a complete disaster. I thought of this as we made our way in the dark, up the steep broad steps of the church. On the right of the steps was a small park. The street light by the gate was the last one. The huge porch ahead of us, with its rows of giant columns was in complete darkness. An enormous white cross swung between the columns, it creaked in the wind. We were in between showers, but there had been so much rain that the sound of running water, drips and bubbles, trickles and hard slow splashes on to tin, these sounds were everywhere. On the Cross the words *Par Amour* were written. As we pushed our way through the heavy, dark doors we realised that the service had already begun.

The church was simply bursting with light. The building is a simple, strong shape. It is very high; the stones are a warm naples glow in colour. The congregation half filled the space. There was a dome at the far end beyond the sanctuary. Behind the altar there was a huge, gilded figure of Christ crucified, with two figures on either side of the Cross; from a distance they looked liked women. From afar the effect was of a high bank of rippling gold. The rest of the church was divided by simple, very broad columns, reaching straight up into the roof.

The congregation all held a lighted candle. Above these small, individual flames were magnificent chandeliers, great bowls of light. All cities, places, countries, seem to give you consistent marks of identification that maybe you haven't anticipated. For me in Ireland, it was, and is, the marvellous, handpainted sign writing on bars and shops. Here in Paris I was consistently thrilled by the lights, churches, bars, restaurants, bridges, both old and new, sang out with these great clusters of light. From brass or iron stems, rigid and angular, or the twisting and turning rhythms of art nouveau, or complex baroque bunches of branch and foliage, from places of faith and feasting everywhere, these great cups of flame and brightness flow out.

The feel in the church was intimate. Only ourselves and possibly one other couple, who came in after us, were probably not part of the regular congregation. It seemed like the spontaneous celebration of a very real community. As Madeleine had said to me earlier in Lisieux, 'One benefit, now that believers are such a minority in France, is that everyone is in church because they want to be there. They have really chosen to be there.' It felt like that, a freely committed gathering.

The celebrant was an incredible character, not tall, but ebullient and forceful. He was a positively bounding figure, bursting with vigour, determined to transmit and share with everyone, what was obviously for him the thrilling, live dynamic of the evening's liturgy.

On the left of the altar in the front of the choir, the singing was being directed in turn by two young women. With strong, clear voices they would lead solo, then bending out over the congregation, their hands extended, they would draw the rhythm in the air, like dancers or mime artists. They coaxed the congregation through various phrases and responses. There were some older, cowled figures seated beyond the choir close to the altar, and several choir boys, one very small indeed, his diminuitive size was compensated for by his immense seriousness and sense of occasion. The tremendous difference in size and age of those vested, underlined the general family atmosphere.

Various lessons and passages from the Bible were read in turn by members of the congregation. All the time there were interruptions and interjections from the celebrant, who simply couldn't contain himself.

'Now wait ... just listen to this ... Listen, Listen.' He was so enthusiastic, repeating and underlining the joy of it all in his own words. 'New heart. New Energy. New Love. If you haven't got a book it doesn't matter. Come on. Come on. Give us, God, a new heart and a new spirit.'

When the time came to take a taper to the very tall paschal candle, to light the rest of the candles, the young man chosen to do so, couldn't reach the flame, even on his toes. A much taller priest came forward. With a great deal of bowing and smiling the taper was finally lit.

On and on, lessons and litanies, and then at last we were there.

The moment of the Resurrection. The earth trembling. The stone rolled away. This is it. The celebrant practically took off with excitement as he prepared the congregation for the Alleluia. Alleluia. Smiling the congregation really responded. There was a burst of Alleluias. The asperges took the celebrant down the aisle, where very personally, with great warmth, he greeted and blessed everyone.

The two young women had sung and nurtured the congregation throughout the service quite magnificently. Communion had been distributed, the kiss of peace, greetings, we must be nearly at the end. Suddenly the tall priest, the one who could reach the candle, was standing at the front of the altar, obviously ready to intone. He held the book high. He took a deep breath, this was going to be a wonderful, rich male sound, then suddenly, there was a loud burst and flourish of fortissimo from the organ. Helpless giggles from the congregation. A look of considerable disappointment and dismay from the would-be cantor. But nothing was missed by the celebrant. He would redeem the young man's chance to intone. The celebrant turned to address the congregation. He thanked them, the servers, the lesson readers, the choir, everyone, and finally he warmly thanked the two young women 'who sang so excellently, so well, but ... before we go one last huge Alleluia ... with all your hearts ... ' The celebrant turned to catch the eye of the young priest but he was preoccupied. He missed the opportunity. The congregation, greatly amused, rescued him with the biggest blast of Alleluias imaginable.

It was a wonderful, live, very immediate experience. Liturgy leaping the bounds. Someone told us that the celebrant had lived in the parish as a boy and that he was paying a special visit. We were very glad to have been there with him.

It was well past 11 p.m. We walked on towards the Gare du Nord. Before midnight, we wanted to celebrate if possible, not only Easter, but also a particular occasion we had shared on this same day twenty-eight years earlier. The bright lights of the Brasserie Européenne in the Boulevard Denain, beckoned us. Glistening oysters in the window. The smile of the maître d'hôtel just inside the doorway. The rain had stopped. The sky had cleared. We went inside. We ordered and waited. In silent, happy anticipation I looked outside towards the Gare du Nord itself. Water glistened on the cane chairs stacked up outside against the tables, large drops of rain gathered and hung like strange night flowers about to fall, from the green enamel of the balustrade round the entrance to the metro. Out there in the bright dark, I was reminded of Van Gogh's evocative painting *Café Terrace at Night*. Chairs, tables, street emptiness and stars. 'The night is more alive, more richly coloured than the day,' Vincent once wrote.

Escargots. Brouade of cod with masses of garlic, light strawberry cake. Lots of Beaujolais. There were few customers. The waiters had plenty of time and were very friendly. I loved their waistcoats, the small, multi pockets, stitched three layers deep in a slight curve. I remarked on the pockets. 'Very French,' the waiter said, 'each pocket for a particular coin.'

Maybe believers, non believers, one and all, maybe we are like so many varied coins slipped in and out of our appropriate pockets all with different attributes, but of the same currency. All one within the Divine Waistcoat. *C'est un mystère.*

3
Bussy-En-Othe. Monastery of the Protective Veil of the Mother of God

'Work inside the darkness – love and trust.'

MOTHER MARIA

S⊤ ANICET. I had said goodbye to my friend. I was once more
on my own. At last I was heading south.

It was still April, but with the bitter cold of winter. Chaucer
in the first lines of the *Canterbury Tales*, speaks of the 'sweet
showers of April'. He goes on about 'quickening forces which will
engender flower, life in every wood and field ... birds make melodies
... and people long to go on pilgrimages.' The feeling is full of joy
and hope, the anticipation of full adventure. I suppose it is this
feeling that makes travellers say that ... 'when May is in bud you
must get the wagons on the road.'

But there is another April engraved far more intensely on my
mind. Lines that I read and memorised long ago without any particular understanding, except the strange, compelling truth of the
human condition which they seemed to embody. From *The Waste-
land* T.S. Eliot begins 'The Burial of the Dead:'

April is the cruellest month, breeding
Lilacs out of the dead land, mixing
Memory and desire, stirring
Dull roots with spring rain.

42

The strange sense of desolation in the poem seems also to engender the kind of darkness, where Resurrection and light may belong . . .

> A heap of broken images, where the sun beats,
> And the dead tree gives no shelter . . .
> And the dry stone no sound of water. Only
> There is shadow under this red rock,
> (Come in under the shadow of this red rock). . . .
> I will show you fear in a handful of dust.

The recognition of emptiness, may lead forward. Such random, somehow certain, thoughts, can come at you suddenly, with perplexing strength, but they often leave behind them a peculiarly disorientating anxiety. It is knife-edge all the way. Stability may be some kind of fearless recognition of this.

I had wanted very much to visit a Russian Orthodox monastery in Burgundy that I had been told about. A monastery of nuns. The name of the monastery was the Monastery of the Protective Veil of the Mother of God. It was at Bussy-en-Othe. Eventually I found Bussy on the map. It is about ninety kilometres south of Paris, beyond Joigny. There was a train to La Roche Migennes, a terminal about three kilometres from Bussy, which is just below the ancient forest of Othe. But the telephone number I had been given was wrong. Although I was getting on well enough with the language when I had direct eye contact with the person I was addressing or listening to, the telephone remained for me a very unnerving business. I longed to hear a sharp voice cry out '*ne quittez pas*' instead of all the recorded messages that I could never make out in time. However with nervous and dogged perseverance I eventually got through to a human being. A man who was intrigued by the name of the monastery and was determined to trace it, which he did.

I telephoned and spoke to Mother Olga. She was Russian, but she spoke English. Because of my difficulties in tracing the number, I had to ask if I might come immediately. It was no problem. Take a taxi from the station. Mother Olga said, 'They know us well. We can't meet you as we're taking our car to the supermarket.'

I was beginning to find all the journeying, the waiting as well as the travelling, very important. These times were a necessary slack in the rope as it were. A chance to pause and reflect. To gather myself together in order to present myself on the next doorstep. I boarded the train south. Everyone was blue with cold. It was definitely Eliot's April. The wind was still in the north; not the west wind with any 'sweet breath' at all.

On the train, looking out on to a cold uncompromising landscape, I kept hearing the poem in my head.

> What are the roots that clutch, what branches grow
> Out of this stony rubbish? Son of Man,
> You cannot say, or guess, for you know only
> A heap of broken images, where the sun beats.

Maybe *c'est un mystère* was recognition of this wilderness. The dry stone and no sound of water. The dead tree with no shelter. And yet somehow among the heap of broken images where the sun beats down, there is a curious sense of hope. There is truth in the pastures of emptiness.

Quite apart from the April weather, temporate or otherwise, pilgrims must have been drawn by the post Lenten, celebratory season of the Easter Octave.

The train was on time as usual. I only had to say the word *'monastère'* and the taxi man knew instantly where I was going. It was a short drive, small villages, smooth, wide roads, open cornfields and then Bussy, with the forest heavy and dense above it. A very quiet village, a small stone church, one bar, and then set in high stone walls, directly on to the street, were the open gates of the Monastery of the Protective Veil of the Mother of God. The gates opened into a courtyard of lime trees. At the end of the courtyard, beyond the trees, there were high steps up to the front door of a typical Burgundian manor house. Agricultural buildings flanked the courtyard on both sides leading up towards the house. It was very quiet and still, then a dog barked. A young woman in short, brown gumboots and a muddy skirt, her hair tied back into a blue-and-white check cotton headscarf, came towards me, a large alsatian dog on a lead beside her. 'He's fine,' she said as the animal smelt into me and my baggage. 'He's soft, but he barks well enough.' She went ahead of me to put the dog into a run under some trees that were just below the front door of the house. There was a great sense of balance and symmetry in the courtyard; the strength of faded elegance, where proportions remain, while exteriors may crumble. Two flights of stone steps curved up towards the front door of the house.

After Paris, and trains and crowds it was so quiet, so still, such a gathered presence; you felt you might hear the snap of a spider's web. There is something very welcoming simply in stillness. It forces you to touch down, to go deeper into yourself. But then that in itself can be unsettling. I felt increasingly like some traveller grazing the theological 'Long Acre', pausing, attending, but needing to stay without the walls of any finite, dogmatic commitment. Being with people whose whole lifestyle is a demonstration of their certainty and focus can be unnerving if you are unsure yourself. I noticed a stone well, with various large bells of different sizes hanging above it. A short rope hung from the centre of each one. I was longing to hear their sound.

The young woman had gone inside one of the long barns that flanked the courtyard. Very soon, she came out again followed by a tall, elegant nun. Mother Elizabeth. She was Russian, but from Canada. She spoke perfect English. She was effusive, positively glamorous in her gestures of welcome. I was beginning to find in religious communities, that although the habit would seem to shroud and hide personality, in fact, body language from within it, becomes more expressive and particular than ever. The walk, the gestures of the hand, the tilt of the head; all became a subtle dance of personality. Mother Elizabeth was flowing, refined, ultra feminine.

My room was just inside one of the long farm buildings. It was on the ground floor looking out on to the courtyard and the lime trees. Outside the room was a high open area, curtained shelves and cupboards with labels pinned to them with clear directions not to touch or take away. Everything is needed for the chapel. I imagined flowing damask chasubles, but when I dared to peep several days later I found yet another spotless, highly organised, convent broom cupboard. From this stone flagged area, there was an open tread staircase up to more cells and loos, and douches.

Mother Elizabeth showed me everything. 'In a minute we will have tea, but first let me show you the chapel. Are you Orthodox my dear?' No. No. Sort of seeking Catholic Christian. I was determined to be honest, but my increasing, complete uncertainty, made even this feel very difficult. There was a long appraising look from Mother Elizabeth. 'Will you join us for the liturgy?' 'Oh of course. Yes please.' I understood very soon that the magnificent, long and varied liturgy, was the root and strength of the monastic day. It was the blazing fire at the centre of the house; its life and flame was the way of the house, all other activities led to it and in some way supported it.

We went out into the courtyard and then into the church. It was the door just beyond the well and the bells. Nothing outside prepared one for this beautiful, barn-cave of byzantine light and dark. It was breathtaking. The smell of incense, the mass of flowers, the glorious clutter of icons, on every beam, in every corner, small and large, and in front of them all, candles. Candles everywhere. On the lectern there was always an icon connected to the liturgical season. Of course that day the icon was an image of the Resurrected Christ. It rested on a white, embroidered, damask cloth; crowded around the edges there were the blooms of fresh white flowers. Beyond the icon screen, there hung the largest images of Christ and the Madonna. There was a small altar; a curve of votive candles hung above it; more embroidered clothes hung from it.

Crosses, images, those penetrating eyes, the curves and swoops, the rich colours, the musty dark, the smell of wood and beeswax and incense and all of it aflame; all of it breathing with particular intensity. It was the kind of place that would be utterly magical to any child. In fact I was suddenly reminded of our children's 'camps'. Wherever we lived, and that was in a great variety of places, they made them; secret cave spaces, where they often put candles and flowers. They would run there after school to be hidden, secret and undisturbed; in tree roots, or thick hedges, or in old stone ruins, or under high, overhanging banks. One had to know the password to go there, that was unless you were bringing food, then the password would be freely given. You could be invited, then there would be shared food. A genuine 'agape'. You never visited without bringing some gift. There were always particular rituals and orders to be strictly observed. There was always some kind of magic, some stone or feather, some secret space that had properties of transformation. There must be a link between children's camps, and hermits and churches and liturgy.

*

I unpacked in my little cell. A low bed, a chair, a wooden table. Small paper icons pinned here and there on the bumpy walls. Hooks on the door. I put my notebooks and things out on the table. Every so often, especially when a place and the people particularly interested me, I felt overwhelmed by my lack of scholarship and general knowledge of the background of things. Everything and everyone represented so much fascinating history. How could you just come in off the street and have responses of any validity? But I suppose, knowing nothing very much was half the point of being there. It would never have daunted Margery Kempe, she would simply have gone on, open-eyed and open-hearted towards it all, making her way as best she could, spurred on by some kind of longing for a fragment of truth; a morsel of consolation. Her passion and her sense of need seemed to keep her going and inspired her wonderful honesty. Maybe that was it, an unedited, open heart to all experience.

As I walked across the courtyard towards the house I experienced a pang of acute discomfort round about a tooth. I thought I had felt something like it on the train, but as the teeth in question were capped and plastic, with supposedly dead roots, I had persuaded myself that I must be mistaken.

There were many people gathered around the front door. Mother Olga, Mother Ann and several other nuns, their habits full and long. Some wore a tight, white veil that closely framed the face, ties just behind the head, on a level with the ears, kept it in place. The veil fell down over the shoulders and chest in a mass of soft folds. Some of the nuns wore similar veils in black. These veils were, I gathered, working gear. In church for the liturgy the long black veil was worn, flowing down from the flat-topped, black, monastic hat, worn also by Orthodox monks.

In the little hallway and in the vestibule on the right of the front door, continuous greetings were in progress. There were visitors from Switzerland and Paris. There was a rather shy priest from Bulgaria and a Russian professor and his wife, well known at the monastery.

This week immediately after Easter is called *La Semaine Radieuse* translated rather unsympathetically as 'Bright Week' for the English-speaking community. This is the time of continuous joy and celebration of the Resurrected Christ. The greeting is two kisses with the cry, *Christ is risen*, and the response, *He is truly risen*. It is made on any first encounter throughout the day.

Tea was just about to be served in the dining room. Two long, wooden tables; on each, a high-domed cake, with thick, white icing sugar cascading down the sides, red cherries on the top, and round the base a mass of dyed and hand-painted, hard-boiled eggs. The cake is called Koulitch; it remains there fresh on the table, one after the other throughout the Easter Octave. At supper each evening there was the delicious Pascha pudding, again, a particular dish for this time of celebration; a sort of sugary, cheese cake mixture of butter, cream and eggs – delicious.

Most of the visitors were friends of the Monastery known and loved by everyone. Tea was informal. A very pretty young English postulant, black skirt, black stockings, short black headscarf, poured the tea from a silver samovar on a small table by the window. Her name was Æmiliani. I found it very hard not to say Emily. There was a very ascetic-looking, young Rumanian priest who lived in the monastery. He had dark, dark eyes, and long, black hair, there was a feeling of great detachment and sadness about him. He was called Father Theophane. Continually he would say ... 'It is very, very sad in my country.' The two major topics of conversation were the long, exhausting Easter liturgy, which had just been completed, and all the great changes going on in Russia and throughout Eastern Europe.

I understood that there were fifteen women in the community, their nationalities included Russian, French, English, Spanish, Danish, Swiss, Romanian, Egyptian. Soon after tea a small car drove into the courtyard. It was the community car returned from the supermarket with supplies of food and the clean laundry. All hands rushed to help Mother Xeinia unload, she and Sister Magdalena both looked exhausted after their expedition. Mother Xeinia noticing my trainers, proudly showed me her black trainers bought from the supermarket on an earlier expedition. 'What a boon they are,' she said. Mother Xeinia and Sister Magdalena were both English. It was strange suddenly to hear so much English spoken and from Orthodox nuns.

Mother Xeinia had been an Anglican nun for many years, one day she found a book in the library, which showed clearly to her the pure origins of the Orthodox Church, their teachings direct from the Apostles. 'We are getting closer to one another all the time,' the Anglican writer stated. Mother Xeinia, a practical, no nonsense person, felt that simply wasn't true and to waste no more time, she became Orthodox and joined the community at Bussy.

The heart of the monastery is the choir. It is through the voice of the choir that the liturgy is most keenly expressed. There are chores, guests, meals, and various literary commitments, but all is secondary to the liturgy; the mystical life reaching out towards God, to experience on earth a little of heaven by the tireless purification of the soul. A pure heart must find God. That was how it was expressed to me by several of the nuns.

I was more and more fascinated by the route of the individual vocation. Æmiliani simply came by, and then she stayed. 'I don't feel I made any decision,' she said. 'It just happened.' Sister Magdalena was widowed. She has three grown-up sons. She told me, 'I just couldn't read the Bible and live with myself unless I did this. It can be very hard, very lonely. Then suddenly you are given strength.' She described how after she had made all the arrangements to come to the monastery, sell up her house in England, all her possessions etc., just at the end, for the last few remaining days in her home, suddenly every object became intensely beautiful to her, in a way they had never been before. Things she had taken for granted, hardly noticed; a cushion, a cup and saucer, the view from the kitchen window, suddenly they were all unbearably beautiful friends. As she spoke I thought how a religious life is really a poem continually being made; continually being refined, synthesised, pared down, reborn, re-worked; a poem loved back to life, again and again and again.

After tea there was the liturgy. Very soon the little church was crowded out. The choir stood in a group round a high sloping surface like a desk, on which the musical texts were laid out. Above the texts was a low electric light, all the dark, veiled heads were bent together under the light; they looked like a painting by Rembrandt or de la Tour. Æmiliani, Sister Magdalena, Mother Ann, the young woman in her country-check headscarf and boots. In the centre of the group was a young Russian nun, Sister Tatiana. It was Sister Tatiana who wielded the tuning fork; it was she who controlled the tempo and pitch. Just behind the choir there was always an elderly, very small nun. I learnt later that she had been the choir mistress for many years, before the young, dramatic Sister Tatiana took over. To me Sister Tatiana was dramatic; her presence, her gestures, her general intensity; she had wonderful smooth, sallow skin and a dynamic, creative drive in her dark eyes. All the other nuns made a point, at various times and in various ways, to make some contact with the guests. Sometimes it was a tentative, rather wistful smile from a doorway, or across the kitchen. Sister Tatiana seemed powerfully aloof from such contacts. Any painting whether on the napkin rings or in other parts of the house were hers. The planting and lay-out of the gardens was her work. She was obviously an intensely gifted and a naturally creative person, a rare force in any household. To me within this small community she seemed a dramatic one.

For the liturgy the special, long veil is worn. Most of the nuns arrived in the church with it on. Mother Xeinia flushed from the kitchen, Mother Ann from the office, telephones, typewriter and photocopier. Only the Mother Superior came into the church in her working headgear and then whisked on the long veil and circular black hat with its distinctive flat top, when she got to her lectern.

On arrival in the church everyone makes for the decorated icon of the day, bending to touch the floor as a sign of humility; kissing the icon three times in between each bend. The Mother Superior was Russian, she had not wanted to be made Abbess. She was over eighty, but she fasted every Friday and all through Lent. Until several months before my visit she had walked every evening to the outskirts of the parish where the cemetery, on a little rise of ground, looks back down to the village roofs and the central and most distinguished building of the monastery house itself. In the cemetery there are the graves of various members of the community, a Russian priest and several friends. The Mother Superior was small in height, but fiercely present and all-seeing. She reminded me of a singularly alert woodland creature, peering out at the passing world, listening for every crack of twig or thump or screech that might sign to her danger, the need for further acute vigilance. She stood effortlessly throughout the hours of liturgy. Her bows before the icon were deep, her hand always hitting the ground. It was not so with everyone else.

The Offices are sung in Slavonic. Repeated rhythms again and again like fine spears to pierce the dividing clouds between heaven and earth. During the liturgy people come and go, sit or stand. All the time the small, yellow, beeswax candles blaze on before the icons.

Sometimes they burn dangerously low, too near to the dark wood. Then there would be signs from Sister to Sister. Busily, dangerous flames would be extinguished and fresh candles lit to replace them.

At the end of the service, the community process to the priest for blessing. He has already processed among the congregation, leaving his domain behind the icon screen. He comes forward, during this Easter season, with three lighted candles in his hand encircled by flowers. The flowers were so bright and unusual. I thought they were extraordinary peonies, but they were in fact tulips, the heat from the candles made their petals fall wide open. With this bouquet of flame and flowers, Father Theophane blesses one and all, with cries of, 'The Resurrected Christ. Christ is risen from the dead. He is risen indeed, trampling down death by death. And to those in the tombs he has given life.' Having passed the priest for blessing, each member of the community passes the Mother Superior, to be greeted, warmly kissed and blessed.

The ceremonies were all so live; so human; so present. A real sense of awe persisted; there was this feeling that a belief in the presence of God, his incarnation as man, his death and resurrection from the dead, really was the breath in the church. It was quite unlike the Holy Week services in Paris, that seemed to me, tired, struggling ceremonies, weighed down by the patterns of time, shifting rituals, of a static, inherited order. Here at Bussy there seemed to be this immediate presence. Not just a memorial shape tied to the perplexing structures of history. Of course you never forget how subjective and personal impressions are, nevertheless if you are to proceed at all, towards any uncertain area, you have to use all the antennae at your disposal, rational and otherwise. Dazed after the journey, all the greetings, the silence, and then the sound of the choir in this stunning Byzantine cave, the impact was considerable.

After the bell for supper we filed into the dining room. There were many guests, some permanent, others newly arrived. Two full long tables. The Mother Superior was at the head on one table. Father Theophane and the young Bulgarian priest at the other table. The community ate separately from the guests, apart from the Mother Superior.

The far wall of the dining room was hung with icons, a Greek Cross and on the dark mantelpiece various plants and flowers. Before the meal all turned towards the icons. Grace was sung. When we sat down there was still an air of formal quiet and recollection, quite unlike the informality of tea time. Æmiliani served the soup. In silence everyone passed one another bread and water. I took a mouthful of soup, then felt this strange, hard pebble in my throat. It was my tooth, my front tooth! Fearful of choking I fled. Outside I soon realised that those pangs of pain had been real. There was nothing dead about the cavity. My heart sank. How could I return to the dining room. Then I decided that if you had to drop a front tooth, a Russian Orthodox monastery was a good place, because surely everyone's mind would be on higher things! I returned to the dining room. It wasn't necessary to explain my sudden absence, it was all too obvious!

A lady from Paris who was sitting beside me, clapped her hand over her mouth in horror and looked steadfastly in the opposite direction. She told me later that her greatest dread was that such a thing should happen to her. She couldn't handle it. I told her it wasn't that bad. It made speaking French a little harder, that was all really. Everyone was very kind. I was promised a visit to the dentist in Migennes after the liturgy the next morning. Mother Olga who is very, very tall, with a wonderful soft round face, and always the kindest, most attentive expression said, 'My poor dear, but you have beautiful eyes.'

The next days were mild, even and warm. There were bolts of real blue in the sky. The garden was a mass of lilac and cowslips. Æmiliani showed me the little oratory the nuns had built, far down at the bottom of the garden. It is a small, wooden structure, with a large Greek Cross on the door. Inside the penetrating gaze of Saint Seraphim instantly greets you; an old man, huge halo, long white hair and beard, his hand on his chest. He stares out rather fiercely in what seems to be every direction at once. There is no place where his beckoning, ascetic eye doesn't seem to meet yours. Æmiliani told me that distressed by his loss of contact with God, he went into the forest and stood for three years on the same stone.

'Outside the oratory,' Æmiliani said, 'there is a big pine tree, in the wind it creaks and sighs, you can really feel then that you are in the forest as Saint Seraphim was.' I longed to know how Saint Seraphim felt when he left his stone.

At last it was Chaucer's April. Warm spring days, tender shoots; a quicking force, engendering many, many flowers. It was very hard to plan to move on. I began to long for the liturgy. The day felt like a painting, every mark in it was needed, but every mark would be nothing, pointless and empty, without the central colour; the constant seeking and praising and being with God.

The monastery was founded in 1946. The manor house and grounds were presented as a gift to the founding Abbess, Mother Eudoxia by a Russian Professor. Mother Eudoxia had been secretly professed in Russia, in 1927, shortly before her monastery in the mountains behind Yalta was suppressed by the Bolsheviks. Some time later she herself was arrested, when she refused to make reports to the secret police on pupils who came to her house. However her father was French, and after vigorous protests by the French consul, she and her parents, and her sister – also a nun – were expelled from Soviet Russia.

Although in the beginning there was more livestock on the surrounding land than at present, the monastery has had from the start an important literary and printing tradition. The major work, of translating into English the original liturgical texts from the Greek, was carried out here at Bussy, by Mother Mary who died in 1980. She was the daughter of the Russian pianist, Mark Hambourg. She read history at Oxford, later she moved to Paris and became editor of the Albatross Press. She was married to the Romanian sculptor Mircea Bessarab. During the German occupation of France she worked with the French resistance. Two volumes of her work were revised in collaboration with Father Kallistos Ware and were published by Faber and Faber. Many more of her translations remain at Bussy still unpublished.

I felt increasingly sad to be moving on. It made me realise why places of pilgrimage give rise to shops full of terrible souvenirs. There is such a temptation to take something tangible from a place with you. But such instincts probably signify a too rooted, earthbound ego, and not sufficient trust in the transient unity of things. I suppose it's like learning to look at, rather than pick, wild flowers.

One evening I spent some time with Father Theophane. 'The East is a mystical Church,' he said, 'the West is a pedagogical Church.' All the time I was with him I couldn't forget Romania and that priest in Timosora, who suddenly became a catylyst for so much unimaginable change. There was such deep sadness about Father

Theophane. He explained to me that he was a monk. Priests may be married in the Orthodox Church. Monks are celibate. I think he was missing his monastery.

He spoke of the logic of God. The varieties of interior states. To be alone with God. To be against sin, but never against the sinner. The sinner is blind. Divorced couples may remarry. Real faith is to accomplish the commandments. I asked him about the veneration and kissing of icons.

'We need to kiss them. I love them. I need to kiss them.' He spoke with great emphasis. 'They are not only a presentation. They are a manisfestation of Divine Light and Grace, but this could only be found by those who have been penetrated a little by the Divine. It is forbidden to have an icon of God the Father, because we cannot see him.'

I remembered that I had been told that you should pray for some while before an icon before you would venerate it. The whole thing made me think again of children, small children, that real, quite extraordinary comfort and security they can invest in a rag, a length of ribbon. Once the rag has become the comforter, its powers only seem to increase, nothing short of complete disintegration can reduce its strengths. The patient, loving dirt from sweaty fingers, seems to create and increase its validity, maybe like prayer. Maybe it is the Divine in the soul, projected via prayer towards the icon, that becomes, in turn, a registered, increased Divinity, that can play itself back, increased and transformed, to the beholder.

Visitors came and went. A new tooth after two long visits to a brilliant dentist in Migennes was securely in place, with cement that I was assured would be a strong enough mix to keep the temporary cap in place until the end of August, and, therefore, safely until after my return home from Compostela.

On my last day, Anna arrived. The nuns had kept telling me that an English lady was coming from London. Anna had only recently become Orthodox. She said that she had definitely seen herself as an atheist. She was studying for a degree in anthropology at London University. Her thesis was on funeral rites. She followed an Orthodox funeral as part of her research. 'After the funeral,' Anna told me, 'I knew instantly that I should become Orthodox.' She talked so intelligently about bonding, gesture, man's natural need to express himself with his body. Anna had no problem with the bows and veneration of icons.

'We need to manifest our relationship with God, involving the body enables us to express our humanity. Ritual is a way towards the Sacred . . . ' 'What is the Sacred?' I asked. Then the same answer came that I had heard so often, 'It's a mystery.'

Anna lived in London, but she was on her way to stay with a hermit nun in Provence. Mère Thais. 'I know I'm not a Desert Father. I want to find my way as a woman. The vital aspects are qualitively different from that of a man.'

On my return to London I telephoned Anna. As I had anticipated she had not returned. Now in November as I write she is still with Mère Thais. They had run out of water when she last wrote and were walking two kilometres a day to fetch some. Anna enclosed a photograph of the little corrugated tin and rock dwelling, and from it a marvellous view of the mountains. 'Basic chores for survival take so long, but I feel much closer to God,' she wrote.

I tried not to feel intense disappointment that during the liturgy on my last morning, Sister Tatiana was absent from the choir. Mother Mary, the little nun who always sat behind the choir came forward to wield the tuning fork. The result was a slower, quieter, much less gathered, more uncertain sound. I confess I missed very much the verve, almost 'fado' of thrusting, energetic voice under Sister Tatania's direction. Later, while washing up the lunch I heard Mother Xeinia say loudly to the other nuns, 'What a relief in choir this morning, as it should be, no more of that dreadful shouting.' She was horrified when she saw me. I said that I definitely loved 'the shouting'.

Just before leaving I was given permission to take some photographs. 'The full habit please, the rest is so untidy,' Mother Elizabeth said. I had assumed that Mother Elizabeth was the sacristan as she was always there attending Father Theophane by the altar behind the icon screen. I asked if I might photograph her in the church, and was I right, was she the sacristan?

'No. No. Not sacristan. Something more than that my dear.' Then very secretively she said, 'I assist the priest. It is a special blessing given only to those past the menopause.'

I was amazed. That seemed to infer something unclean in female rhythms of sexuality. What about priests, fertile every day of the year, almost all their lives night and day? Certainly the inherited female position seems wildly weighted against and historically mis-trusted. Apparently Thomas Aquinas felt rape to be more natural than masturbation. Strange to mete out such disregard towards the vessels that conceive popes and priests, every bishop, even the Son of God. Maybe part of the way forward for women is for them to feel confident that Divine Revelation is offered as much to them, as any male. They may in the future become such obvious vehicles of wisdom and revelation, that the great forest of patriachal priesthood, brought to heel so often by Christ, may be forced to turn truly towards them and begin to acknowledge their qualities before God; they may find their blessings sought, and also their forgiveness, for so much banishment.

It was with definite sadness that I left the monastery at Bussy. The feeling was rather like after a magical picnic: as you drive away you are sad simply because it went so well, but in a manner that is circumstantial and cannot be repeated.

I was sent on my way with a shower of blessings, a handful of chocolate eggs and a medal from Jerusalem from Mother Elizabeth. All those candles and chants; all that darkness and light; the pace of fervent longing towards God, so evenly matched with the pace of ordinary human life; being, loving, cooking, caring; struggles with the bare darkness of isolation and with the daily irritations and foibles of so many diverse personalities under one roof.

Soon there was nothing but the empty road ahead. The station platform was deserted. I was unsure where I would sleep that night. I was almost sure that probably I would never return again to where I had just been. In everyday emptiness and ordinary waiting, you are suddenly back simply with yourself, which feels to be nothing more than a pool; some empty space that fills and empties, is calm or angry, dark or light, grasping and clawing, or quiet, almost stable and content.

Mother Xeinia had been most insistent that I should go to Auxerre. But I had this ache to go again to Vézelay, visited once before, but all too briefly.

4
Vézelay and Nevers

'What is God? He is at once the breadth, and length, and depth and height. Each of these four divine attributes is an object for your contemplation.'

SAINT BERNARD OF CLAIRVAUX

T HERE WAS A slow train that went from La Roche Migennes to a small station about five kilometres from Vézelay. The train was not crowded; one old man and several students. The lady opposite me was a visiting grandmother, she was replaced later by a local, knitting grandmother. It was late afternoon. There was the forging, determined feel of spring throughout the landscape. The countryside became increasingly wooded and undulating. Masses of cowslips and rape; neat rows of just-planted-out lettuces; lilac in full bloom hanging out over the station platforms. Many clean, well-tilled, small patches of ground, looking eager and ready to be custodians of summer produce, under the protection of old stone walls; the single apple tree, a froth of blossom; a washing line full of small, spotless, white garments; yard dogs tethered to rough posts; roaming geese and ducks and hens.

It was a beautiful, still evening when I got off the train. A sharp, unexpected cold, after the warmth of the train, gave a certain bite to the sunlight and the shadows. I noticed a beat-up, yellow car and a smiling, somewhat dishevelled individual leaning up against it rolling a cigarette. Full of shame I walked towards him. The vigorous thump of thousands of years of pilgrim feet rang in my ears. But I knew with my one and only back, I couldn't possibly contemplate the walk up into Vézelay. The man grinned when he saw the rucksack, bag and staff. 'Taxi?' 'Yes please.' He suggested that I should sit in front beside him to see better the church on the hill as

we approached it. It was a spectacular approach, definitely reminiscent of the way Assisi lies on that hilltop, way ahead, beyond the
station. From a distance, the two strong towers, the calm, solid form
of the church, is like a heavy, guardian crown, keeping the small
town pegged down, on this isolated peak of high ground. 'Bitterly,
bitterly cold up there in winter,' the driver said. It was easy to
believe him. 'Just drop me in front of the church.' I had no plans of
where to stay, but I instinctively felt that first I should pay my
respects to the Magdalene.

I know many people are critical of the young architect Viollet le
Duc, who at twenty-six was responsible for the restoration of the
basilica from 1840–1841. I had read, with reference to Vézelay, that
on arrival you should remember that, 'The beauty of the King's
daughter was within.' But standing there in front of the restored
tympanum, there was this power of a physical presence. The state-
ment of the building just being there, on top of this high hill. Against
all the odds the Church of the Magdalene is here, still standing after
years and years of terrible, turbulent history; you feel intensely
grateful that she is rescued, rebuilt and ready to receive you in 1990.

There were still several cars and a straggle of visitors preparing
to leave. Rather like good wine, or a great painting or poem, I was
beginning to realise that you must come slowly to a place; wait a
little, before feverishly resorting to guidebooks or information. Place
has a mighty tongue of its own. You can become an aspect of it,
simply by being there, if you lose the sense of yourself as a passing
outsider. You can gather up the mystery of yourself, and with it
confront all the other wonders and mysteries.

I thought I would just go into the narthex of the church and pause
there, before thinking of a bed for the night. I went in through the
small, side door. The damp dark of that extraordinary space,
instantly seems to still and shelter. The huge, spread hand of Christ;
the whirling, pulsating, fine gathers of His robe. At the thigh, it
races into a single circle, as on the far knee. You feel that Divine
creative energy courses this fabric, and that all the diverse, throbbing
world of saints and sinners ranged about it, are in some way caught
up in the vitality of the threads.

From the sheltering dark of the narthex, where penitents and
pilgrims probably ate, drank, rubbed their feet, were shriven and
exorcised, you hardly dare to look beyond, past the elegant, forest
balance of the nave, towards the clustering, pale columns that spread

and peak out in a fan of light over the altar. I felt content to remain in the narthex on that first evening. I would gradually make my way forward up the nave tomorrow.

When I came out of the church most of the cars were gone. Vézelay was retreating back into itself. Shops and bars were closed. I wandered down the hill, sad even to have my back to the church. I had banished any thought of perhaps not finding a place. I simply imagined shelter and became sure that shelter would be available. Just a little way down the hill, on the left, I came to an open door into a small courtyard. It was a substantial, double doorway, painted white, with an ornate M carved in the half circle of wood above the door. There was a bell chain and a brass plate, which said Centre Sainte Madeleine. I rang the bell twice. Nothing stirred. I went into the courtyard. In the corner under an arched walkway, there was a small, white, china basin and brass tap. I hesitated to ring again. I called out. An old man came to one of the open doorways into the courtyard. He simply said, 'Come in,' so I followed him down some steps into a warm kitchen. There was fresh bread and some biscuits on the table. 'You a pilgrim? Is it for the one night?' I was surprised to find myself so expected. It was like those children's stories, when the traveller, anxious on some mission, is always accommodated by people, who, in some way that is never made clear to the reader, seem to have advance knowledge of his or her arrival. 'One night would be wonderful,' I hoped to stay several, but thought one would be good for going on with. A few moments later a short, business-like woman came into the kitchen. She was dressed simply, in a brown skirt, yellow shirt and dark cardigan. 'Are you a pilgrim?' 'Yes. Yes I am.' She smiled and consulted a large diary that she took from behind a brown teapot. 'The one night?' 'One night is marvellous.'

In fact, I stayed four nights. I discovered that the woman was a Franciscan Sister, and that the buildings had been housing pilgrims to Vézelay for hundreds of years. There was a small, very dark crypt chapel, where the Office was chanted morning and evening. A single Cimabue (photographic reproduction) crucifix above the altar, the rest, dark stone walls. There was a big communal room full of long tables and a large, modern kitchen available to the guests. The Sister took me a few doors up the street into the labyrinth of dark, wide corridors and curved stone steps that were the rest of the building. The first night, I was in a strange, lozenge-shaped room, that seemed to be halfway up the stone staircase of a tower. For the following nights I had to cross a flat roof and then go through an old, battered door like a barn door. Across a few flagstones, opposite the door, there were two small rooms that looked down over tiled roof tops to the vineyards and fields beyond.

For about thirty francs I had a bed, two blankets and the use of a communal wash house; piping hot water at all times. It was a wonderful feeling to hurl down the baggage, try the bed, usually good and hard, and then make for the door, with the cold feel of a key in your pocket, representing the secure space that would be waiting for you to return to.

The monastery at Bussy seemed far away, but the greeting: *Christ is risen. He is risen indeed* still rang in my head. I had no provisions so I wandered down the street in search of lights and an open door. About three-quarters of the way down the steep hill, there was a small, inexpensive restaurant; very pink and enticing. There was a roaring log fire. The *patron* looked extremely unwell. He had a sore throat and a temperature, so he said; certainly unshaven and with swimming eyes, he looked fit only for his own bed. He said that because of the cold, perhaps I should sit with my back to the fire.

There were various families and their children; several who refused either to eat or sit. One had to be taken out into the street and slapped. On his return, the rather worried father looked anxiously round the room for some kind of approval for what he had just done. I remembered so well our travels with small children; all the excitement; all the anxiety. The knowledge that you could never please everyone; there would always be one with an excess of exuberance and energy, and another too flaked out to make any sense at all. It was odd to find myself alone at a small table, with notebooks and pencils and a pichet of rouge, while around me mothers struggled and scolded, admonished and praised.

Towards the end of my sixty-two franc menu of soup, rabbit and flan, a tall, grey-haired, very well-dressed man came into the restaurant. He was most solicitous of the rough condition and general state of health of the *patron*, whom he obviously knew well. He came over and sat at the small table beside mine, enquiring first if I minded. The fire was so tempting. It was not long before he was asking me a variety of questions. I realised early on that it was the notebook and writing that intrigued him. His name was Jean Marie. He lived in Paris. He too was writing a book. He rented a small tower in Vézelay where he came most weekends. Writers love Vézelay. Did I know that Romain Rolland, Nobel prizewinner, had retired to Vézelay in 1938?

It was when Jean Marie heard me describe the general gist of my book and travels, that he excitedly asked if it would be too presumptuous to push our tables together. The *patron*, highly amused, assisted Jean Marie in this.

Jean Marie's book was the story of his own life. He had been born a Catholic. He had been active in the French Resistance at nineteen. One morning he had pulled open the drawer of a bureau in the family library, while looking for a paper knife, and he had discovered a loaded revolver. It belonged to his much older brother, who had been in the room when he found it. His brother had simply taken up the revolver and handed it to Jean Marie saying, 'Do you want to help?' He had helped. His brother had been killed soon afterwards, following appalling torture. The body was returned to his mother's house; just left there on the front doorstep. Jean Marie had become atheist. He had been analysed, a Freudian analysis. He had been married with dramatic and difficult results. He had followed Tran-scendental Meditation, becoming a Master of Siddhi Meditation (the one where the meditator may bound into the air). Then suddenly during his final initiation as a master, he had felt, out of the blue, the overwhelming sense that he was denying Christ. He experienced a compelling re-emergence of faith in Christ.

The fire behind our tables had died down to less than embers. All the struggling families were gone. The suffering *patron* and his kitchen staff had just finished their own meal. They were obviously longing to shut up shop and go to bed. I pointed this out to Jean Marie. But there is more so much more for us to discuss. May we have dinner tomorrow? I agreed. Neither of us was properly fluent in the other's language and so the esoteric 'franglais' that had developed over pichets of rouge was very exhausting for both of us. Jean Marie was well muffled up in a camel-hair coat, long woollen scarf and brown hat. It was very cold outside. The hill is so steep that you are forced to take the climb at a considerable angle. Suddenly round a bend there was this flood of light and the Magdalene was there towering in front of us. Buildings, if possible, should definitely be experienced in all the twenty-four hours of light and dark. Structure seems to use light and shadow as if it is its breath; smaller and stifled in full sun, deep and expanded with the depth and incision of rich shadows.

In the bitter cold there was a clear, starry sky. We walked round the basilica. Just beyond the end of the church there were two small tents pitched bravely on the open ground. Looking back to the building it seemed that this great monument stored, and was, energy. Like a tree it seemed to pull force from the centre of the hill, up into its strong, solid, challenging form. Jean Marie's elegant tower was almost opposite my Franciscan doorway. I found myself saying goodnight in a firm, singularly Anglo Saxon manner, with the promise of further discussion tomorrow.

The next morning it was bright, but still bitterly cold. I went into the small bar beside the church. In the morning light the Magdalene looked rested and attentive; not the dramatic, deep creature of the night. Strong black coffee, fresh bread, apricot jam. Opposite me there were two very brown and healthy men. I was fascinated by one, because I was sure I had seen his legs and feet under the door of the shower in the communal wash room. The next day I met him in the corridor and knew I had been right. He was travelling alone, on foot from Holland. He had a tent, but he had decided the night was too cold, so he had sheltered with the Franciscans. In the warmth of the bar, resuscitated by the coffee, I was able to catch up with myself from all the notes taken at Bussy. Then with that marvellous feeling of having all the time in the world, I went back into the church. There were only a few people. Everyone was looking up to the carved capitals, and beyond to those precisely placed port-holes of clear light. From the ambulatory, looking back down the nave, the alternating dark and pale brick, in the high curve of the arches above the columns, seem to spring out, a sheer 'Hosannah' of celebratory sound. The building seems to rise into this great chorus of perfectly pitched, palpable sound. A sound that vibrates within you, while remaining earthed, it still seems to be reaching effortlessly to heaven. It is impossible to describe the peculiar joy of walking and being in a place of such tangible harmony.

There was mass at ten o'clock in the Chapter Room, it was considerably warmer there than in the main church. The little Sister from the Centre Sainte Madeleine read the psalm and lesson. There were about twenty people in the congregation. A family from the restaurant of last night were there, their children at the beginning of the day calmer and more biddable.

It was such a privilege to feel that cold key in my pocket and to know that my visit could be as long as I cared to make it. A journey makes such a particular shape; up or down; hills or valleys; busy, peopled, modern buildings; or empty, calm, ancient stone spaces. But the shape doesn't feel like a line outwards. Strangely, it feels like a series of circles; smoke rings. Perhaps it is because all the experience is rooted in you; the choice and manner of the journey must be yours. It is you who keep experience on a long or short rein. No amount of fatigue or pleasure will rid you of choice.

I went down into the crypt. There always seemed to be a waft of expensive scent down there. I wondered if it was the low, vaulted ceiling and general airlessness as people came and went. At the back of the crypt, behind glass, there is a coffer; in it there are the relics of Mary Magdalene. There is nearly always someone praying in the crypt. As I write this, I suddenly wonder, maybe that scent was hers, the generous unction still playing about her bones!

Remaining in the quiet, candle-lit dark of the crypt you think of Mary Magdalene. There is an Eastern proverb which says of places of pilgrimage, 'No bones, no miracles – no pilgrims.' It was the sheer numbers of pilgrims to this spot that inspired the first church to be built for their shelter. It was Mary Magdalene's relics and subsequent miracles that brought the pilgrims.

In 858 Girart and his wife Berthe founded a convent of nuns. The Benedictine monks came later. There were fires, invaders and a variety of destruction. The crucial turning point for Vézelay, its real birth, was the arrival of Mary Magdalene's relics from St Maximin at the beginning of the eleventh century. From then on, thousands and thousands came to this holy hill to pray to the repentant sinner whose own sins were forgiven 'because she loved so much.' Vézelay became a major stop for pilgrims from Europe bound for Santiago in Spain.

In 1146 Bernard of Clairvaux preached the second Crusade on the north slope of the hill where a thousand warriors and peasants were assembled. The young King Louis was there. It was in 1166 at Vézelay that Thomas à Becket, Archbishop of Canterbury, pronounced the excommunication of King Henry II of England. In 1190, Richard the Lionheart led the third Crusade. But resources had been squandered. The entire body of Mary Magdalene was discovered at St Maximin. Pilgrims soon forgot the way to Vézelay.

Wars, bloodshed and turbulence continued. By 1790 the Magdalene legally no longer existed. Statues were mutilated, furniture sold. The whole building was near to dangerous and complete collapse when the restoration started.

For the greatest number of visitors today, it is the sheer beauty of this supreme example of Romanesque architecture that attracts them. The extraordinary vitality of the stone carvings, their human depth, the wonderful way they reveal to us our own humanity, as much as they did to the medieval pilgrims, who were seeking the Risen Christ; forgiveness of sins; assurance of the Love of God, and a place with Him in heaven.

We may live in a time that is predominantly sceptical of religious faith, but if we are moved by the truth of these carvings, we must acknowledge that it was from a background of faith that they were made. The live eyes, the vivid, spontaneous gestures, the flowing robes and hair, the abundant clarity of every kind of human emotion – lust, despair, attentive gentleness, pleasure and terror – mundane work; battles and legends; and the mystical narratives, as in the Mystic Mill. The mill is Christ, symbolised by a Cross, who grinds the grain of the old testament, which is then gathered up by Paul to represent the teachings of the new testament. At a technical level having to move the story on round the capital develops this quality of action; in plants and humans; feet and foliage.

I was finally driven from the church by the dank cold and an aching neck, but I knew I would return. I threaded my way down the hill, in and out of smaller side streets; many old buildings, Jean Marie's tower; glimpses of bright gardens, down the hillside, the seventeenth-century hospice, still sheltering the old, infirm and mentally handicapped. A small Orthodox chapel, with an icon painter working in the room above it. Galleries, a second-hand bookshop, various hotels and restauraunts. I found a group of students standing on a low wall, singing in four-part harmony: a young girl, similar to the women at St Vincent's in Paris, was conducting them. It was nothing serious, simply for fun, they told me. Basic shops with food, fruit or vegetables seemed hard to find.

There is a little sandy path that girds the hill. Below there are neat rows of vines, and above, wild, overgrown gardens; crumbling high walls held together by the sinuous strength of ivy, lichen, moss, lilac, sweet alyssum, wallflowers, iris. Bushes of bay, long wild grasses

with, every now and then, purple orchids. The path winds from
below, up to the grass and trees and stone wall that gathers in the
town on the highest side of the hill beyond the church.

These few days seemed wonderful, long stretches of calm. In and
out of the church. In and out of the wind. Coffee, a *coup de rouge*
and each evening food in front of the fire in the little pink restaurant.
The *patron*'s health improved daily. He was clean-shaven and much
more cheerful. His claim to fame, Jean Marie said, was that he had
been a steward in the restaurant car of De Gaulle's private train. It
didn't seem in retrospect to be an impressive memory for him.

Jean Marie had calmed down considerably. He apologised for his
excessive *chaleur* on our first meeting. It was, he said, the excitement
of being able to discuss his work with someone. His work seemed to
be gripped more by the mind and force of Rudolf Steiner than
anything else. I know very little of Steiner, only the reputation of
the residential schools. I had no idea that the laws of Karma operated
in the Steiner canon. I was soon reeling from details of angels and
spheres, Lucifer and Arihman and the possibility that Lazarus was
in fact John the Beloved. All Jean Marie's study was to prepare him
for the next life, when he would be available to serve mankind.

In the little room that was out over the roof I had the most vivid
dreams. I was with two pilgrims in the narthex of the church, one
was small and crippled, but a happy master of his fate, his companion
was a large person in a hopsack cloak, with a cowl that was tied close
in to his face. I can see his profile clearly, very round, ruddy cheeks,
bright blue eyes, soft lips and a bulbous, rather fleshy nose. He was
exceedingly cheerful, full of talk, stories and anecdotes. Every so
often to emphasise a point, or out of sheer exhuberance, he would
crash his thick staff on to the stone floor of the church.

On Sunday there was a sung mass in the main church. That
morning in the communal wash house, a big lad, with tight, curling
black hair had become most embarrassed because his friend in the
shower, assuming no one else was there had continued singing in a
loud voice. 'But he's got a brilliant voice,' I said. Pause. Silence.
And then nervous giggles from within the shower.

During mass I saw that the curly-haired boy was taking the
offertory procession with a young friend, whom I guessed to be the
hidden singer in the shower. Later in the afternoon, as I made my

way down the steep track towards La Cordelle several boys came bounding up the path towards me. 'I'm the one with the brilliant voice. It was me. It was me.' I congratulated him again, this time face to face.

As I continued on down the track I heard the cuckoo. The wind had dropped. It was much warmer, the sun was bright with real midday heat in it. There was a feel of the presence of spring, not simply a struggle towards it. Orchids, cowslips, bees and butterflies. Outside the little stone chapel at the bottom of the hill, there were lizards darting and pausing on the smooth stones and many pairs of beetles with distinctive red and black geometric markings. The chapel – La Cordelle – is so named to refer to the cord worn by the friars who lived there. But a chapel on the same site preceded the Franciscans. The first chapel was built in 1150 to commemorate Saint Bernard preaching from the hill at the start of the Crusade. A little above the chapel, about halfway up the hill, is a tall wooden cross set into a pile of huge stones. It marks the spot Bernard preached from. Now it looks across a calm, well-farmed, peaceful countryside; a peace that feels as if, at last, it will be sustained.

I knew of course that these full, empty, silent days must end. I couldn't bear to think I was making my last visit to the church and the crypt. I kept being there for lengths of time, in a strange state of recognised 'unknowing'. Somehow, 'unknowing' becomes a considerable peace, and silent, focused attendance to it, the greatest possible activity.

I chose a cold, rainy day to leave Vézelay. *Auto-stop* didn't work. There were few cars. After a several hours waiting, I was forced to take a taxi to Clamecy, where I could catch a bus from the station to Nevers. There is never any difficulty in France travelling north south or vice versa, but a stone's throw east or west is another matter. Such a journey is almost bound to be a straggling, roundabout, long-winded affair. But all the railway stations are a mine of information about the times of the cross-country coaches.

Finally the bus dropped me out in Nevers, directly beside the high stone walls of Saint Gildard's Convent, in the rue Saint Gildard. The impact was of a huge, extremely well-ordered place, maintained to the highest standards. Various signs said 'Welcome.' I met a Sister who directed me towards a pair of heavy, wooden doors. On a large, stone pillar, a typewritten piece of paper covered with cling film gave details of 'The Shrine of Bernadette' in every imaginable language. There was something rather authoritarian about the tone, that, and the vastness of the building, the endless shining black asphalt; it all felt decidedly overwhelming.

Inside the heavy wooden doors I was reminded of a modern Irish hotel. Thick pile carpets, an incredible blast of central heating, large, rather lonely pot plants, a glass cabinet full of carved African animals (later I learnt that these were left over from the missions), a huge, green leather armchair, in which a small nun sat chatting with another Sister who was behind a large, leather-topped desk.

Yes. They could have me. There was a retreat for visiting Sisters starting, so silence would be appreciated. Signature. Keys. Lifts that way. As I walked on through the spotless, carpeted corridor, with my staff and baggage, I realised I was leaving marked indentations in the pile, from the excellent, indented, leather soles of my trainers. I did catch the nuns at the desk speaking of the Little Sisters of Charles de Foucald, but as their conversation obviously didn't concern me, I paid little attention.

The convent is huge. It is built on three sides, there are five or six floors. There is a wide, covered cloister round three sides of a formal garden. Regimented tulips and spotless shapes of gravel are seen through large plate-glass windows.

Spotless, even unto death, were the words that occurred to me as I made my way to the lift at the far side of the cloister. I was on the second floor, more glass doors off a dark landing, leading into a long corridor of squeaky, thick linoleum. Downstairs, the Sister had asked if I needed a towel. Stupidly I had said no, that I had one. I now regretted this. In my room there was a large, piping-hot radiator. I had one small towel, now would be a wonderful opportunity to wash and dry it. In fact I could wash and dry everything. On the landing outside I saw a pile of clean towels on a chest of drawers. I longed to take one, but felt foolishly guilty about the idea. Somehow, the whole place, was threatening and stifling, there was such a towering sense of enclosure. The dark, dust-free stillness, felt steeped in guilty, fear, loneliness and scruple. Subjective impression of course. In the end I grabbed a towel, because I could suddenly hear my daughter's shrieks of laughter at my hesitation to do so.

There was a series of bathrooms and showers on the floor above; irons, ironing boards, deep, spotless clay sinks, but nowhere a mirror – instead, neat precise notices about cleaning up after you. Downstairs, there was a separate dining-room for those guests not on retreat. Plentiful food and wine, but I had only one thought, how soon could I leave. I was here because of Bernadette Soubirous. Bernadette the humble, sickly child from Lourdes whose apparitions of Our Lady changed utterly the life of that region. She became a nun and took the name of Sister Marie Bernard, remaining here at Saint Gildard's until her death.

Bernadette was born in 1844. She, like Thérèse, had to be nursed outside her family to survive infancy. But her family, unlike the Martins, were very, very poor indeed. They lived outside the small village of Lourdes in the south-west of France, in the foothills of the Pyrenees. In 1858 Bernadette went wood-gathering with her sister and a friend. She was undoing her stockings in preparation to wade through the water when she heard a great gust of wind, but she noticed that the trees were still. The noise came again. She looked up and saw in a grotto, in the large, overhanging rocks above her head, a lady. A shining lady, who wore a white dress, tied with a sky-blue girdle. On her head was a white veil. There was a rose on each foot.

That was the first apparition. What followed is, of course, the history of Lourdes. A hundred years later it is a prosperous town, a vast centre of pilgrimage visited by over forty million people a year. There were seventeen more apparitions. After them Bernadette's life became intolerable. She was besieged by questions and accusations; continuous offers of wealth, which she steadfastly refused. Her poverty embarrassed the authorities. But Bernadette insisted on remaining poor. She went to live in the hospice in Lourdes that was run by the Sisters from Nevers. Then she decided to become a nun herself. She was far too frail to enter Carmel so she joined the novitiate, here in Saint Gildard's. The convent at Nevers was then the mother house for the order. The present building had just been built when Bernadette entered. Bernadette suffered considerably at Saint Gildard's. Although naturally humble and modest, and by all accounts with a great sense of humour, her superiors felt it incumbent on them constantly to humiliate her. Her job was to help in the infirmary, but more often than not she was the patient there. Tuberculosis and bone cancer were discovered. Bernadette died in the infirmary in 1879.

Originally she was buried in the grounds in the little chapel of

Saint Joseph, which is just above the extensive south-facing, walled vegetable gardens. The vegetable gardens now are nothing but a great expanse of tilled soil with very little growing, only leeks, lettuces, parsley and lavender. Apparently the professional caterers who cook and clean for the convent, will not peel.

The body of Bernadette is the pilgrim currency of Saint Gildard's. It lies in a glass casket in its own chapel, where throughout the year coachloads of pilgrims pause, to stare and pray, and whisper among themselves about how real or unreal it is. The general consensus among the visitors while I was there, was that it must definitely be a *poupée*.

Poor, poor Bernadette. What an ugly lack of faith it seems to be, to need to display her. How remote from her life this macabre celebration seems. There is various small print displayed to say that the state of her body didn't influence her canonisation. Her body was exhumed three times in front of various important people, bits were reported to be broken, blackened, stiff and sunken. Relics were removed: two ribs, part of the liver and diaphragm, two kneecaps. A Paris firm made a mask for the face and hands from a wax model taken from the body. Then the whole terrible nightmare was washed and brushed and re-dressed by the nuns and laid out for all the world to gawp at.

What horrors! What an unmitigated travesty of love and respect for any human being, most especially a country girl, who had tended sheep on the open hillside and would surely love to have been buried under some rich clod of earth.

I realised I had to visit the chapel. It was, after all, the reason for my visit. As I was sitting in the cloister plucking up the courage to go in, a Sister came by and said, 'Have you had your little moment with Bernadette?'

The nuns at Nevers seem very active, independent people. Some do professional jobs outside the convent, teaching in schools or at the University. Few wear the habit. 'One doesn't have to be provocative.' The rest of the community run the considerable business of the 'Welcome' to the pilgrims. There is little, if any, shared prayer or liturgical life.

In the chapel, between coachloads of Germans, I stood and closed my eyes, as a mark of respect to Bernadette, trying not to stare at the glistening pink nails and the plucked eyebrows. I tried to imagine a deep earth grave; thick grass above it; cows munching; bees and butterflies and weeds; weeds full of spider's webs. Then suddenly I felt that I just had to get away. It was pouring with rain. I longed to be drenched in it. I had to stay because I had given the Saint Gildard telephone number as a possible place to be contacted from home.

I ran across the smooth, black asphalt and down the hill, away, just away from those high walls. In a small, crowded bar I had a coffee and bought a copy of Le Monde. The smoke of cigarettes, the constant 'ding-a-ling' of the space invaders and fruit machines, the talkative, friendly exchanges of dripping-wet shoppers, it was a great relief. After about half-an-hour there was a pause in the cloud burst. I made my way across the park towards the cathedral, possibly it was an important stop on the way to Compostela. When I got there it was a great, dark lump of a building, full of scaffolding and polythene, unsuccessfully bucketing and spilling the torrents of rain that were pouring through the roof. Little solace here. Outside there was a clap of thunder, another roll or two and then it was torrenting down again, pelting great slabs of water. I noticed a small stairway that was under cover. It said Archaeological Museum. I ran up the stairs. Suddenly carved stone; strange creatures; ancient images. It was really closed but they took pity on me. I stayed for an hour or so drawing the figures, and winged creatures. There was a slightly stooped, carved, wooden Virgin. She had large, almond eyes, a wide, soft mouth and a broken nose. She was cracked and dry with age. She was beautiful.

I returned to the convent in time to make excellent use of the piping-hot water and the deep, clean bath. Just as we went in for supper I heard the telephone ring. I knew the time was exactly right for my call. I hung around listening, hoping for a summons. I heard the English Sister being sent for. Then I heard her say. No. No. There is definitely no English woman here. The only person who came today was a little Sister of Charles de Foucauld. You are wrong, I thought, so wrong. It was no little Sister, it was definitely an English mother. Eventually we had things sorted out, and I received my call.

There was a couple and two of their close friends from Versailles at the table. It was their holiday. They were retired country people. They were amazed by the central heating and the large colour television in the library and horrified by the *poupée* in the chapel. There was another place laid. Suddenly the door flew open and a very weathered and exhausted Dutchman came in. It was Kees whom I had met briefly in the washroom at Vézelay. We greeted one another. He had walked from Vézelay, with one night's stop on the way. He was obviously starving. We told him that the soup was good. He began to eat. He was a married man with children. He was walking alone from the Hague to Compostela. He had to do it. There was no religious motive. He simply had to walk in the footsteps of other men. It was really doing something. By things like this we preserve our culture. He told me how anxious his wife had been that he was going alone, then he said rather shyly, but I have this extraordinary feeling that I am accompanied. Last night in my tent I was not alone. Suddenly he asked me what I had paid at Vézelay. I told him. Too much, far too much. 'Well, it'll be far more here,' I said. 'Pay here.' He was furious. 'But I'm a pilgrim.' He immediately got up and went and threw the rest of his soup back into the pot to the amazement of the family from Versailles.

The next day the English nun, Sister Marie Noël, was eager to talk about her life in the missions, teaching in Tunisia. She had also worked in Japan, where she was interned. She was in Nagasaki when the atom bomb went off. Interestingly when she returned to France, very unwell, she was sent to the Pasteur Institute; she never visited Lourdes.

All I could think of as she spoke was how much I longed to to move on, out of Nevers. Marie Noël was both persistent and insistent, her life was long. Later she did show me round the rest of the convent, other rooms, and the little chapel in what had been the infirmary where Bernadette died. I followed Sister Marie Noël down yet another long linoleum corridor. I felt I might have been in Blue Beard's Castle. There could be horrors in any room. Lowering her voice, Sister Marie Noël opened the door. A clean, small, quiet chapel space. Sister Marie Noël pointed and said in a hoarse whisper, 'Over there she died.' But my feelings were numb, glazed, peculiarly indifferent. I knelt and could only think Sister Anne. Sister Anne. A pile of dust. An endless open road. Just a journey. Everyone's journey. Never ending. Deeply mysterious.

There was one good moment I cherish, when I suddenly felt curiously close to Bernadette. There was, of course, the usual gift shop of leaflets and pieties, beside it there was a museum of photographs and memorabilia concerning Bernadette's life. Priests and nuns stare out from heavy frames. And there is Bernadette herself.

The headscarf, the shawl, the high forehead, the dark, tired eyes. Then behind glass, her worn, faded, work apron and slippers, and then a pair of long, black woollen stockings and in one of them, very near to the glass, this huge darn. A perfect circle of calmly woven thread, no bobble or tug, no tension, no rough knot. Only someone very special, stable and peaceful could make that kind of darn. To me it was a work of art. To do the smallest thing so supremely well, it had to be done with Love.

5
Paray-le-Monial

'The City of the Heart of Jesus.'

I T WAS WITH relief that I made my way down the hill from Saint
Gildard's Convent to the railway station. I had left before
breakfast, with a good two-hour wait until my train to Moulins
was due. I wanted that wait. There is something rooting and stable
about a crowd of transitory people. Faces look out anxiously towards
clocks and timetables; baggage is checked; but primarily the traveller's attention is inward. In the staring faces, worries, plans and
hopes and schemes seem to float about in the air. In this pause
there are few external demands, no personal definition, simply your
internal self; a minimal, biding presence in the company of strangers.

At Moulins there was another long wait, and an excellent bar on
the platform, that served the local people as much as the travellers.
The train to Paray-le-Monial was just two carriages. It was bound
only for Paray, stopping frequently on the way. Tiny halts. Vegetable
gardens; lilac and apple trees, right up to the edge of the platforms.
Many of the small station buildings were boarded up and for sale.
Huge dead clocks staring out full of rust and spiders. Paray was a
small station and quite deserted.

I made my way through the town. It was the sleepy, quiet of
midday. Over the river, past the usual alimentation, small bars and
closed shutters. It felt unremarkable, like any small agricultural
town. But I knew that Paray-le-Monial was different. It was 'The
Heart of France', 'The Blessed City of Heaven', 'A City of Visions
and Pilgrimage', 'The City of the Heart of Jesus'.

Just past the river and up towards the centre there was a sign 'To the Basilica'. Much road building was in progress. Very soon across a broad sweep of still water the sharp, pointed towers and Romanesque arches of this magnificent church. The first monastery was a foundation from Cluny made in 971. The construction of the church from 1090–1109 was a faithful, far smaller replica of the grand church at Cluny.

Here, by the basilica, the whole aspect and feeling of a small market town alters completely. There are very fine gardens laid out in front of the church; from there, broad sweeps of steps with balustraded walls, lead down to the river. The basilica today presides over a grand vista of wonderful parks and gardens on both sides of the river. Magnificent, green spaces for campers, most of whom will be pilgrims; thousands and thousands of them. Paray-le-Monial, seriously boosted by a recent Papal visit, proudly boasts greater numbers of pilgrims now than Lisieux. Lourdes still easily maintains the real lead. The contemporary pilgrims here are organised primarily by the Community of Emmanuel, who work in conjunction with other Charismatic groups, like 'Young for Jesus' or 'Presence and Witness'. All over Paray there were leaflets and advertisements for the summer sessions, 'et vous ... trouvez La Joie'. From the photographs all was joy; clapping and singing, guitars and dance, carefree children, relaxed parents and a tanned, expansive priesthood.

Everywhere tremendous building work was going on in preparation for the summer season. At the back of the basilica there was a very large shop of pieties. Here icons and Byzantium are less in evidence. The most striking replicas are the rows and rows and rows, in different sizes, of that Christ, with long flowing hair, a red robe and a finger pointing to a fleshy, furnace of a heart, bleeding and crowned with thorns. The sort of statue that is in nearly every bed-and-breakfast and boarding house in Ireland, and in so many schools and homes, hospitals and orphanages throughout the Catholic world. This cult of devotion to the Sacred Heart sprang directly from Paray-le-Monial. Here in the convent of the Visitation just behind the basilica, in the late seventeenth century, a young nun, Sister Margaret-Mary Alacoque, was the recipient of intense visions. Her visions demanded a devotion to both display and honour the Sacred Heart.

Margaret-Mary came from the countryside close by. After

experiencing considerable difficulties in getting her family to support her, she finally entered the convent of the Visitation when she was twenty. Once a nun, her life, despite consistent attempts on the part of her superiors to subdue her, was a life of ecstasy and vision, mortification and suffering. Once she wrote out her resolutions for the spiritual life in her own blood. The community were extremely sceptical of her continued ecstasies. Among other things they noted that she sometimes felt overwhelmed by hunger which was then followed by a complete disgust for food. However, although her visions might have been mistrusted, her virtues of obedience and humility, were always widely recognised by her superiors. In the end, after considerable suffering she triumphed. The Sacred Heart was honoured by a particular feast in the church's calendar, increasingly devotions and dedications to the Sacred Heart abounded. The turning point for Margaret-Mary was a young Jesuit priest, Father de la Colombière, who, for a short while, became her confessor. In some of her visions, the heart of Father de la Colombière, was joined with her own, within the Sacred Heart. Father de la Colombière felt Margaret-Mary to be holy and completely genuine.

Against this background of ecstasy and fervent devotion, Paray-le-Monial has made its way from the first monastic beginnings from Cluny, to the huge Charismatic Centre for Pilgrimage which it is today in 1990.

It is very easy to shudder. Suddenly it all seems too much. A sort of rampant, crazed devotion. It is not so much the first tale of the life and convictions of one, obviously sincere, person, however strange and deviant she may sound to contemporary, post-Freudian ears; it is the fierce, physical way subsequent generations seem to have capitalised on the initial experience, making such terrible solid objects out of an intangible, mysterious experience. Of course Margaret Mary herself did stress that an image of the Sacred Heart must be displayed and honoured. A furnace of sacred flesh and flame, is hard to capture. Paul Klee might have done something wonderful with the idea, but I suppose it would never have caught on.

A kind lady who ran the pilgrimage shop of pieties directed me to the House of the Sacred Heart. She stressed that I should avoid at all costs the Foyer of the Sacred Heart; hopeless. The Foyer of Nazareth was good, but so far out. Go for the House of the Sacred Heart was her emphatic advice. Extremely grateful for any advice in this labyrinth of sacred situations, I left my baggage in the shop and went on my way to seek a room.

I passed the Hotel de la Basilique, which even sells pieties in the bar, and the convent of the Visitation itself, which had a very calm, low-key exterior. Not far up the road was the House of the Sacred Heart. Small, cheerful and most welcoming. Soon I had that wonderful feeling of keys in the pocket.

I felt extremely nervous about quite where to begin. I suppose one of the things that is unnerving, is accepting kindness and hospitality from people who assume you to be an ardent believer. They say things like 'I'm sure you'll receive great graces here in Paray.' 'Great graces' might not be bad, but it felt oddly unnerving to be on the verge of them.

There was an evening mass in the 'Chapel of the Apparitions' as the signs said. I made straight for the basilica in order to return later for the mass. The basilica is a marvellous example of Romanesque architecture. Once again your gaze is ever upwards. The spaces spin with the rhythms of the pointed and broken arches, the gathered attached columns, the strong, rough curves moving round and up, ceaselessly harnessing the emptiness into such complex patterns that, nevertheless, remain calm. But there is a great deal of clutter from other epochs. There is a fine, stone-carved font; long-necked birds weaving into leaves and flowers. Although the guidebooks go on about light, the whole experience is one of darkness. It is miserably dark in the basilica. Recent stained glass, like great bruises, club the spaces where you long for light to be. The darkness feels like some kind of suffocation of the intended experience. I kept going in and out, hoping to find my first impression of the darkness wrong, at least less intense. But each time it was the same. The whole is much more gathered in and complicated than Vézelay. Maybe I was just thinking too much of Vézelay. But arches and height, moving with the solidity of stone, are an extraordinary experience of space, creating by its very vitality a particular, pulsating kind of stillness.

The contemporary Visitation nuns are very laid back. The black, iron grill is the same one that Margaret-Mary prayed behind, from the nuns' choir, looking out towards the altar. The nuns chant the Office, work and pray, light candles and sell holy pictures. They seem quietly intent on the business of God, hardly involved at all with the constant flow of emotional or dazed pilgrims.

I had been expecting a real horror of hearts in the chapel, but there is a very recent, large mosaic above the altar. The colours are subdued. There is a strong figure of Christ suspended in circles of light, more glow than anything else. Below him Margaret-Mary is kneeling, calm and attentive. Various saints surround these two figures.

It is dark in the chapel, several brass sanctuary lamps hang from the ceiling to light the public part, they give a flickering, intense, shadowy light. The evening mass was attended by many local people, both young and old, and a variety of foreigners. To the right of the sanctuary there is the chapel of Margaret-Mary. In a very ornate glass case, with bronze angels and coloured enamel, studded into the metal frame of regular arches, the calm, elegant, undisputed *poupée* of the saint lies there in a black habit, her head resting on an embroidered, white and gold pillow. There is no talk here of miracles or any stories of exhumation. The saint's true remains rest below the *poupée*. Above in mosaic there is a colourful heart and crown of thorns, some flames and substantial rays.

After the mass a steady stream of pilgrims came up, one by one, to the shrine. A tall, portly Franciscan with a gleaming white cord round his protruding, brown stomach, ushered his flock forward, one by one, by pointing a long, pink forefinger gravely towards them. He had very bushy, black eyebrows and a thick, well-groomed beard. His somewhat theatrical air seemed to make his flock a little nervous. If they hesitated in coming forward, the pink finger would wag ferociously.

There was a sense of devotion and prayer in the little chapel. Many would kneel for some considerable time with arms outstretched. There was one large, black lady, who had been over-come with emotion during the mass. After the mass, when there was a pause in the flow of people, she knelt in the central aisle, arms outstretched, and then, with great courage I thought, she prostrated herself on the ground. I remembered how Margery Kempe had frequently done the same thing in holy places, when she felt over-whelmed with the sorrow of her sins. She would weep and wail, which often irritated priests and fellow pilgrims, although some were drawn to her on those occasions.

Later, out in the road, I saw the same lady who had prayed with such abandon, being berated by her husband and children for being so long. Where were you? What on earth were you doing? They kept screaming at her. I'm sure she must have received 'great graces' for her prayers and courage.

The convent has its own small shop. There were little pictures of the saint for sale, with, in the bottom right-hand corner, a small circle of brightly-coloured moiré silk: pink, green, mauve and violet. On the back of the picture it said that, 'This material has touched the bones of the saint.' I was intrigued to find out what the colours signified. 'Oh nothing,' the Sister said smiling, 'it's just for a little fun, just to be pretty.' I still keep wondering how they do it. I have a vision of the Sisters out there in the sunshine, bones on a trestle table, and great rolls of fabric swirling forward and back, this and way and that, over them. Or maybe the material simply lies there folded, until the time to cut and paste comes. Anyway, the result *is* pretty.

Further down the road, just behind the basilica, is a little house set back in long grass. In the front room there are models of the saint in her cell, and various other memorabilia. There is a large display of many, small, handstitched scapulas, in felt and cotton, of the Sacred Heart, which were worn by various, illustrious people. The names are written below each one in faded, brown ink. Then I saw a painting of General de Sonis, (his scapula is there). As a child I was brought up on stories of his sanctity as my great aunt married his son. After the Franco-Prussian war the General headed a great pilgrimage from Paris to Paray-le-Monial in honour of the Sacred Heart.

That evening over a Plat du Jour in the centre of the town, well away from the sacred quarter I was intrigued to hear the citizens' reaction to the progress of their town. There were many complaints that the large pilgrimages were too well-organised. They brought all their food with them, there was little local business from the crowds. Then several of them said, with great accord and vehemence, 'Some of these movements are very fascist. We worry about that.'

The next morning I had breakfast with Madame Hill. 'I know it's an English name, but naturally we pronounce it "eell". Madame "eell" lived in Nancy, she visited Paray fairly frequently as she had a great friend who was a Jesuit priest in the town. Madame Hill had a very smart, embroidered, cotton envelope and matching napkin, which she had brought with her. She was full of interesting obser-vations on all mankind, contemporary France and the Catholic

Church in particular. Nearly every observation ended with laughter. She invited me to come and stay with her any time in Nancy; I think to improve my French. She took delight in correcting my endless, grammatical mistakes, wrong genders etc. I told her what I had heard in the town about a fascist element in the charismatic movements. She would ask her top Jesuit at lunch and report to me tomorrow.

In the night there had been thunderstorms. I had watched the lightning clashing about the basilica tower. I could just see one tower from my bedroom window. Everything seemed softened by the rain; damp and full of smells. In the basilica there was a large, coloured postcard of a Madonna, that I felt very drawn to, but could not find. She was a solid, gentle, rather lumpen Mother, her crown might almost be a woolly hat. Her face was very round, with a straggle of long hair. The Child rests on her hip, snuggled close in to her body. He is very plain, with rosy cheeks, her right hand is under his bottom, her left hand cradles his bare feet as if to keep them warm. He holds, what looks like an orange, but it must be an orb. She is a true, country presence. Her gaze is quiet and direct; no heavenly, upward stare. I was determined to find her.

In the bookshop they told me that she was Our Lady of Romay. A miraculous Madonna, that was out in a tiny chapel in the hamlet of Romay, about four kilometeres on the Charolles road. By midday the sun had broken through. I decided to take a picnic and walk to Romay.

It was a relief to be out of the town. At last spring was much more than a promise. Abundant, wild flowers in the long grass. Walking and warm days; springs and small roadside shrines, that was how I had imagined it might be. Just a little way out of the town I heard a bell ring the angelus. Below the road there were some red brick buildings that spread out down a yard. I went into the yard and poked my nose into an open doorway. There was a smell of cooking and warm bread, and on a small table, a replica of the country Virgin. Then a tiny, little figure came towards me in the unmistakable habit of a Dominican nun; at her waist, her smooth beads glistened and jangled, with her scissors and keys.

I asked her if I was going in the right direction for Romay. I was. I suppose I had really come, not to check the way, but to get some

79

taste of these quiet, enclosed spaces, where small groups of people carry on a religious life in buildings that were once thriving large monasteries and farms. Now they seem to be almost hidden, out of the centre of the time, like underground streams. Large houses struggling to keep going, with a handful of frail, elderly people. Once such places were central to the structure and vitality of European culture. We owe them so much in terms of art and music, let alone threads of wisdom and consistent compassion. Maybe just to say 'Hello' is to acknowledge in some way those links with the past and the fact that they are still here for us to tune in to.

The little Sister was delighted that I was English because, 'We have Barbara from Liverpool with us. She can't speak any French. She would love to speak with you.' We looked for Barbara in the chapel and in the gardens. Bells were rung and messages were sent to find Barbara. We went into a tiny office to look up the timetables of jobs. Then suddenly the Sister leant across and threw up a wooden hatch, into a very small room, well below the level of the room in which we were. Two Dominican fathers were sitting opposite one another at a small round table having lunch. Their rough, white habits and white hair was in such contrast to the dark panelling of the little room. Broken bread was beside each one, very bright on the worn mahogany surface. From a large, central blue bowl, they ladled out thin soup to one another. Sun from a high window just gave a rim of light to their cuffs and knuckles and the edge of the bowl, and the broad, curved handle of the ladle. The careful, quiet way they spoke and ate, made me think they were monks from San Marco in Florence as painted by Fra Angelico. The Sister asked them if they knew where Barbara was. They did not. Although Barbara could not be found I was happy to have this small, midday, monastic second so firmly fixed in my memory.

After the convent there were only fields and trees; a broken blue gate, wild, long, uneven grasses, damp, gnarled logs, some huge, stone wheels thick with moss, and beyond, down the hill, a view of the river. Every so often the cuckoo. Sitting on a log, I ate my bread and orange in the warm damp of buzzing and crawling softness, and the keen smell of a generous, opening earth. I was careless of saints, or dogma, miracles or faith.

Beyond more fields, cows and crows, there was a sign off the road to Romay. Just in sight, was the unmistakable open door of a very small chapel, beside stone farm buildings.

Inside the chapel it was very dark. One candle flickered. I lit another. Above the altar was the small figure of the Madonna, it was made of stone and quite crudely painted in colours that were fading. Beside the box of candles was a damp leaflet which told me that the sanctuary to the Virgin was established from Cluny in 973. The statue is thought to be twelfth century. Twice it has miraculously escaped destruction. During the usual stories of wars and general disaster, it was hidden in a river and then much later miraculously found.

The little Virgin's favours seem to be many. The chapel is filled with tablets of thanks. But there is one particular miraculous favour for which she is most renowned, with many contemporary witnesses.

Stillborn children could not be baptised or buried on consecrated ground. This situation caused untold distress to many, many people. Apparently if the stillborn child was placed on the steps below the Virgin and urgent prayers made, the child would regain sufficient colour, life and breath, for baptism to be allowed and so Christian burial.

Cardinal Boyer who became Archbishop of Bourges, remembered vividly as a child with his mother, witnessing such a scene. They were in the chapel when his mother noticed a farmworker, standing awkwardly in the shadows with a large bundle hidden in his blouse. Realising the situation she took the dead baby from the distraught father and laid the child on the steps below the altar, then together with the father they fervently prayed. After some while, a little arm waved, the skin grew pink and the lips moist. The child was baptised.

While I was in the chapel a great deluge started. Thunder and lightning flashed and pounded. While sheltering, with the help of one of the candles, I read all the votive tablets and the complex indulgence that might be granted for praying here. There were also contemporary graffitti written in felt pen over the white, nineteenth-century marble. For 'Passing Exams', for 'My happiness'. One read, 'PLEASE may the boy I am going out with come on Saturday.' I thought it was interesting that no one had wiped away the contemporary petitions.

On market day it was a great relief to look at round cheese, tomatoes, flowered aprons, and a great knot of brown galoshes hanging from a hook in the sun as if there to ripen.

Whenever I thought that I had looked at every colourful display and diorama of Margaret-Mary and her visions, there always seemed to be more. Bones and relics, chapels and cloisters everywhere.

The last bones I visited were those of Claude de la Colombière; they were in a small chapel in the Jesuit compound. It was heartening, at last, to see a real skull and femur, and definite other bones, all a rich, greenish-brown. Here at last one was honestly confronted with death and with it, 'Alas poor Claude', the recollection of a real life. Those lips, that had prayed and consoled and encouraged Margaret-Mary. Claude must have prayed fervently, when in England, as chaplain to the Duchess of York, he gave help to Catholics and was thrown into prison. He did return to France and was able to give strength to Margaret-Mary and assure her superiors cf the value of her special vocation.

Madame Hill reported back to me from her Jesuit, that while there was absolutely nothing fascist or political in any of the Charismatic movements, elements of fascism definitely were trying to muscle in on the movements and make this new-found energy their own. 'It is very worrying. We must be attentive.' I was to hear this said by many people, over and over again.

I was bound next for Taizé. Everyone in the shops and bars, market stalls and convents agreed Taizé is different. Taizé is not commercial. Taizé is spiritual.

For a long time I had heard about Taizé. Most of all I had heard of the vast numbers of people that were always there, people from all over the world; most particularly young people. I knew Taizé was a recent Christian foundation. I had heard the music of Taizé. I knew that it was a broadly-based community that welcomes every kind of Christian with or without denomination. But I was apprehensive. In a way I definitely felt stronger and more certain than when I had set out. It is a baffling kind of certainty to try to express. I felt more at ease with myself; less at bay; less run to ground. The landscape felt less dark, less devouring, which was how it had felt before the cancer was diagnosed. Although I had voluntarily put myself on a route, which was full of the words and gestures of belief and faith, I did not want to meet them head on. I was discovering one thing that definitely didn't work; truly objective travel. I had thought it would be more simple, just being there; seeing things and remembering them. But all experience must be gauged via self, that sum of body, mind, feelings, and senses. Occasionally there is mysterious certainty and many odd, intrusive shadows. Self makes some kind of choice, second by second. That is the truth. Grasping experience as ideas, to be pursued, delved into, clarified to find their origins. That doesn't really work, because it leads too easily to making judgements. The true caste of phenomena is vast and transitory. But you can keep a definite focus, uppermost within attention, which may then influence all responses.

The small practical things like washing clothes and hair, making notes, waiting in silence, just being alone; all of that became something very tangible. But the most consoling, rejuvenating imperative was going on again. Every night I had a sense, to consciously pitch the tent of my being in a definite place of 'unknowing'. Bang in the pegs saying, I do not know anything. Inside the tent it might be dark, or maybe there were spins of moonlight. But in there, somehow or other, you know that there is Love. Love is, and may proceed from wherever you are, without you knowing anything very much.

6
Taizé

'In our era, the road to Holiness necessarily passes through the
world of action.'

DAG HAMMARKSKÖLD

I CAUGHT THE bus to Mâcon from the market place; it was a
meandering country bus. It was a brilliant day. Vigorous, white
clouds moved fast in a strong, blue sky. There were rolling hills
and deciduous forests, white Charolais cattle, and dark brown goats,
in meadows of rich, long grasses full of flowers; cowslips, and buttercups, but no primroses. Everywhere leaves were unfurling fast.
Their fresh brilliant green was in keen contrast to the dark grass. A
real Vivaldi spring day. Piping energy in everything except perhaps
the cows.

The country buses in France are so good, but so empty. On this
particular journey there was only myself and a young girl who was
going to Mâcon to buy a christening robe for her sister's baby. I
told her that I was going to Taizé and the driver overhearing this
said that I should get out at Cluny, where there were three buses
every day into Taizé. Grateful for his advice I got out at Cluny. It
was really hot. There was the sense of full, still, midday heat; closed
shutters; cooking smells and snatches of conversation coming from
behind open doorways, the dark, cool interior hidden by a beaded
curtain. There was no one about. Beside the bus stop there was a
very handsome, five-storey building that the bus driver had rec-
ommended to me as a cheap hotel. I walked into the cool shady
grounds. Boules were being played under some trees on the left of
the gardens. On the glass doorway of the building, a large notice was
displayed. Vacancies. Open 5 p.m. Although it meant lumping the

84

baggage about for a while I felt reassured by the notice and would return at five.

In a small bar, the proprietor said he would mind the baggage for me, so, wonderfully unencumbered, I was able to make my way up the hill towards the ruins of the great Abbey of Cluny. Throughout Europe the vast spread and power from this place in Burgundy was extraordinary. There is hardly any monastic ruin or ancient foundation where the name of Cluny does not figure somewhere in its history. The first foundation of monks here was in 910. By the early twelfth century the great church was completed. Until Saint Peter's in Rome was rebuilt, Cluny was the largest ecclesiastical building in Europe.

In the heat and brilliant sun there were few tourists about. Little remains today, but the scope of the vastness and subsequent power can still be imagined. There is one tower still standing, the Bourbon Chapel, vast grounds, the granary and many wonderful fragments of carved stone. You have to go with a guide which means lots of standing about, but the insignificance of man against the huge height of the remaining tower helps one to imagine the extent of it all. Many of the early abbots were remarkable people, several are canonised as saints. They were frequently from grand, well-established families and enjoyed the confidence of Popes and Sovereigns. Peter Abelard, lover of Heloise, the wandering and frequently protesting scholar of the Middle Ages is buried at Cluny. Twice condemned for heresy he was on his way to Rome when he became sick and was nursed and subsequently died at Cluny. By the middle of the twelfth century the order embraced 314 monasteries, but the power of Cluny, of the abbot in particular, held sway over them all which was the very antithesis of the Benedictine ideal. Benedict stresses the unique role of the abbot in each monastery as crucial to its well being. In the end, the great buildings were deliberately destroyed, after colossal wrangling and infighting between the reformed monks and the unreformed monks. By 1790 there was nothing.

Standing beyond the ruins in the well-maintained grounds, which seem to reach out towards the hills beyond, it is very easy to sense the supreme power that this place became. The thirst for authority and supremacy, raced like a giant tide, swelling the fortunes of the monks. It seems extraordinary that again and again men, assuming they serve God, reach towards extensive earthly power and possessions, even though the message of Christ seems so clear. No home. No place to lay His head. Bread simply for today. Don't be called Rabbi or Father. There is only one Father who is in Heaven. Serve. Serve. Simply Love and Serve. And yet religious man finds no problem, so it seems, in continually inheriting massive wealth and power; places of grandeur and positions of extreme authority. The giant hierarchy grows and grows, mitre upon mitre, it heaves its way ever upward, further and further from the feet they might wash, certainly from the brotherhood they might serve. The hordes may be gathered for blessing, but is that the whole extent of service?

Sadly many of the stone carvings were closed from view. But it was an interesting pause in the heat of the day. It is fascinating the way history so often seems to lap forward and back over the same terrain. The benevolence and force of Cluny in the Middle Ages, and now in the 1990s, a few miles north of Cluny, the tiny village of Taizé, where thousands and thousands come from all over the world, to camp out on this wide, open hillside and share with the monks there, the seeking and praising of God.

I was still apprehensive of all this for myself. The crowds. The certainty. The fellowship.

I gathered up my baggage from the bar and made my way back to the great building by the bus stop. The notice 'Vacancies. Open 5 p.m.' was still there on the door. The clack of wood on to wood, and sometimes applause and laughter still came from the boules game under the trees. I walked round to the back of the building. There was a grassy slope in the sun just below a hedge. I lay there in the rough, warm grasses. The sun was bright on to weeds and wild flowers: speedwell, dandelion, buttercup; bees, spiders, butterflies, all manner of intense insect activity over every inch of ground. The sky was a brilliant clear blue, now and again pale wisps of white steam-shapes, passed across the wide emptiness. When you stare up from the ground towards high, warm blue above you, it feels so wide, so full of nothing. Beyond the low bank there were more forested hills and fields bright with cows.

In my scruffy, dented blue notebook I wrote, 'Pink shutters, noisy sparrows, purple vetch, clover, sorrel. All is warmth and damp. To lie on a bank in the sun if you have no idea where, and with whom, you will be in an hour or so, is different to a pause between known destinations. Because you know nothing of your immediate future it is easier to become saturated in these instants. There is more quality because nothing is known beyond them. There is no schedule, no parking meter, no meal in mind soon to be prepared, no telephone call to make or to receive.'

At five o'clock I wandered round to the front of the building which was in the shade. I sat down on the stone steps immediately below the glass doors and the large notice about Vacancies. Suddenly I heard behind me the clatter of high heels on stone. A sharply-dressed, blonde Madame opened the glass doors. She looked at me with some irritation. 'There are no vacancies. I'm expecting fifty-two Germans any minute.' I felt she longed to sweep me and my baggage briskly from her doorstep. I pointed to the large notice on the glass door. Swearing furiously she ripped it off. It was all a mistake. By now I had come inside and sat myself down opposite her desk. The building was vast and cool. I knew there were no other beds in Cluny as I had enquired earlier in several places. Madame fussed with forms and papers hurling her unfortunate notice into the waste paper basket.

I told her that I had waited all day and had specially returned here on account of the notice. There were no more buses and no rooms in Cluny. She then started to rail eloquently against my incredible lack of *prudence* in not making sure in advance.

I suggested that my lack of *prudence* might be very similar to her own in leaving the notice declaring Vacancies on the door all day. She huffed a bit, but acknowledged the point with almost a smile. I remained sitting there. I have often discovered that if there is a problem, sometimes just by remaining in position without saying anything, the person in question seems more often than not to find an answer. I had heard a great deal about 'prudence' in France. It seems to be a way you can call someone a complete idiot, while remaining within the bounds of polite, socially acceptable language.

A large family arrived. They had made all the right bookings. Madame asked, please, for payment in advance. It was only 'prudent'. The father of the family asked for the keys first please. Only prudent!

A single middle-aged man came in. Madame said how annoying it was because he had a double room, why couldn't she put me in with him? She laughed heartily. Neither of us even smiled. Time passed. People came and went. I just sat there. Madame was becoming increasingly concerned for me, telephoning here and there. There was a Gite farmhouse further on, a mile or so out on the road towards Taizé. Should she ring? There was a vacancy. I thanked

Madame very much and heaved the baggage up on the back and happily made my way out from Cluny.

It was now considerably cooler. There were rich, long, evening shadows, wide, soft verges. I crossed the main road, gradually Cluny became a distant cluster of roofs and that one predominant tower. I felt now truly bound for Taizé, and once more sad that my damaged back prevented me from a true pilgrim walk all the way there.

The Gite was a small modern house, with grand views north and south. Madame to my surprise asked if I would like to have an evening meal. I was delighted. I had expected an enforced fast. There was a young family from Alsace staying there with two small children. Together we shared a generous meal. Endives salad, beef, local beaujolais, goat's cheese and piles of fruit. The family offered to drive me over to Taizé the next morning in time for mass. Maybe one facet of prudence, is simply waiting, just letting things happen.

The next morning, at breakfast, I met Jacqueline. She was bound for mass at Taizé. with her friend Marie-Danièlle, a brilliant academic, who had found a bed in Cluny. Jacqueline said we should meet. I felt, however, that the mother of the young family who had offered me a lift earlier, really wanted to go there. So I declined Jacqueline's offer saying, 'See you there.' 'Don't be ridiculous,' she said. 'Sunday mass, there'll be thousands of people there.'

Together with the family from Alsace we made our way towards Taizé. Below the hill the road is straight and wide, Chalon to the north, Mâcon to the south. Taizé still has a little railway station, although the line is not in use. The battered, peeling board saying Taizé on the disused platform is evocative, unlike Lisieux or Nevers. We crossed the railway line and began to curve round the hill, cows and sheep, several goats, signs of honey for sale, no hint of any crowds. But once past the little church and on to the real back of the hill, then the great migration is suddenly evident. The road seems almost to vanish; wandering, slow-moving crowds, crossing this way and that from one sandy space to another, seem to arrest its purpose. To the left, large car parks, a children's play area, two ultra-modern telephone boxes, and beyond, tents and cars and more tents. On the the right-hand side there are ranch style, timber buildings, open-sided huts and other barrack lengths of buildings. Under the trees there are low, wooden benches, arranged in circles. High above it all, a dark metal canopy houses a peel of five bells. On the ground below the bells there was a mass of blue forget-me-nots.

Crowds and crowds of people moving this way and that, predominantly young, although every age was visible somewhere. The children of the Alsace family instantly made for the play area. The mother was intrigued and amazed, she wanted to go into the church, but her husband was horrified, utterly bewildered and dismayed. He couldn't take crowds. He wanted to get away at once. We said quick goodbyes and they were gone. I stood alone with the baggage. I understood very well how he felt. I, too, was seized with a dull, numb kind of panic that froze me to the spot. But the immediate response which is hard to resist and which takes you a little out of yourself is a 'guess the nationality' kind of game. I wandered vaguely in the direction of a small house that said, 'Welcome'. Against the door was another sign saying 'Closed'. Just across from this little house there was a yellow house. Beside it there was a huge, black board saying on it 'Urgent Messages'. It was quite blank. It seemed wonderful that so many people could be here without a single urgent message.

By watching people come and go it was easy to sense that the yellow house was responsible and important. Inside in the cool, I saw several rucksacks. I left my baggage there. With no consoling cold key in my pocket I walked towards the church. The young seemed very friendly and at ease with each other. Like a giant insect swarm everyone was going towards this great hangar, a high building with a vast flat roof, that hangs over the base of the structure like a card house. Apart from its sheer size, it makes little aesthetic impression. It might be a vast grain store from which to feed the world. It is in fact the Church of Reconciliation.

I went with the flow of the crowd. The bells started. The footsteps hastened. Outside the church various young people stood about with large signs swinging from their necks, saying 'Silence' in a variety of languages. People gathered up worn sheets of music from a small table. In many languages on panels outside the church there was this notice:

Be reconciled all who enter here; parents and children, husbands and wives, believers and those who cannot believe, Christians and their fellow Christians.

The crowd was too vast and pressing to consider anything. Quietly and quickly once inside the church you clamber in the dark over

shoes and coats and people. I was reminded again of T.S. Eliot ...
'*O dark, dark, dark. They all go into the dark. The vacant interstellar
spaces* ...' I love the kind of phrases that remain clear in the mind
because they do not strangle and mark with any rigid, didactic
meaning. Simply image and flow, the sound of the sense curiously
unbounded; just resting within the rhythm and metre. Is this, I
wondered an interstellar space between stars of certainty? At first it
is so dark. All round you there is this huge narthex crowd of seeking
travellers; rough clothes, worn cloth, bare limbs, loose hair. Inside
the church there are various levels. Round the outer walls there are
benches; for the rest, people sit or kneel on low, wooden stools, or
on steps, or on the flat ground. As the crowd keeps coming in
everyone is nudged on, people shuffle up, making more space again
and again.

On this first occasion I couldn't work anything out very well.
There was just the impact of this huge, biblical crowd, somehow so
certain of itself. Every individual seemed an inward entity, quite
unlike vast crowds at a spectacle or great public event, who seem to
move out of themselves. Here there was the force of thousands of
separate souls reaching within themselves to make a powerful unity
of long silences, and the repetitive, simple chants, in Latin and in
many other languages. Then there was the mass. There seemed to
be two altars, one at the far end, was in front of a honeycomb wall
of side-on, chimney pieces, in which a mass of lights flickered. The
large central section of the church was divided by two low partitions,
made from sprigs of green privet. In various corners there were
icons. The mass seemed to be a concelebration at another altar at
the opposite end of the church, away from the of lights.

As things went on, I felt increasingly a kind of vertigo. I have
never before felt so acutely unbelonging. I seriously thought, maybe
I'll duck out of this one. After all neither my publisher nor agent had
ever heard of Taizé. Who would notice? The more these thoughts
pursued me, the more anxious and uneasy I became. I had to wonder
why I felt so threatened and distressed. It had to be ego in some
form. You get to recognise the ego's particularly loud, furious kind
of self-importance and wingeing bluster; the determined, neat sound
of its self-sense. By the end of the chants, after rows and rows had
taken communion from standing figures in white, presumably the
monks, who were dotted throughout the church. At last, the narthex
crowd began to pick their way over kneeling and seated bodies

making a slow procession towards the door. Still the powerful chanting persisted. Everyone sang, the chants are in a natural polyphony that suits any voice. People bent down searching for their shoes in the dark; smiling, thanking, and apologising. I was still battling with thoughts like, nobody need ever know I got as far as this. But why the fuss if it was only a church and a crowd of people? But my feelings of dread and horror persisted. To cut and run seemed the only sensible thing to do. I could hear myself saying later, I never made Taizé ... I could take in more medieval stops. As I thought, on and on, people picked a slow passage over my feet. Then suddenly I saw Jacqueline from breakfast. 'Jacqueline ...' I whispered. She was amazed that we could have met so easily in all the crowds. Outside in the dry sandy space I met Marie-Danièlle, Jacqueline's friend.

I had said almost nothing, when Marie-Danièlle announced. 'You can't take it yet. We are taking you to Cluny for a wonderful lunch, then we'll bring you back.' I couldn't believe my ears. 'But it's so far, it would be such a bore for you coming back', 'Nonsense. It's decided. Quick or we won't get a table. We invite you. Come on.'

We sped away down the hill and back into Cluny. Marie-Danièlle drove with the same kind of speed and panache as Madeleine in Lisieux. The restaurant was crowded, but we were just in time to get a table. I was back in the calm of pink tablecloths, thick napkins, and tall menus expressing delicious ideas. We talked of faith and disease, stress and harmony, London and Paris and food, over hake and spinach, a light rosé wine, sorbets and cheese.

It was such a brief meeting, but crucial for me. When we returned the hill was emptier. I did not know how to thank Marie-Danièlle for her spontaneous kindness. My consolation is that I think she and Jacqueline knew exactly what they had done for me.

In the hot, mid-afternoon stillness, people simply sat around chatting on the benches. Occasionally someone went past singing in competition with the vociferous birds. I gathered up my baggage and lay down on one of the wooden benches, as a few other obvious new arrivals were doing. Same sky, same self, but somehow now, a less muddled orientation. Maybe it was just the sun and the rosé, but that black panic had completely gone.

We were all waiting outside 'Welcome', but Welcome's doorway was still closed. I was reminded of a great friend, a healer, called by one and all Mrs B. She lived in Weston-Super-Mare. She had grown up in the Rhondda valley, but her true origins were Irish. To her tiny house people came from dawn to dusk seven days a week. There was an appointment book, but the times written in were more an idea than anything specific. I have witnessed people who came considerable distances, thrash about in fury and frustration as hours passed. They were often professional people with busy lives; lawyers, priests, doctors, and some very landed ladies, who were not used to being kept waiting. Apart from the fact that Mrs B. responded to the needs of each patient, giving them the time she felt they required, she also told me that the waiting period was very important to her work.

'By the time they come in to me they have got back more into themselves,' she said. 'They are closer to their true feelings. It helps my work considerably.'

As I lay waiting in the sun I felt that this pause did, in some way, disorientate one from the external world, although probably unintentional, it felt a good way to begin at Taizé. Instinctively you drop back from the busy, managed, structured world into some kind of more timeless space. The usual, fairly hectic processes of analysis, judgement and data piling that are often a significant mark of the contemporary mind felt more or less suspended.

Then 'Welcome' opened its door. The newcomers wandered in. Much of the practical running of Taizé is managed by young people who, for several months, work here unsalaried, they are a crucial part of the operation. They come from all over the world. A young woman from South America welcomed us. Is this your first visit? Yes. The requests rather than rules were then given. They are firm requests. Please stay on the site. Do not walk into the two neighbouring villages or fields, local people need to carry on their lives as normally as possible. No alcohol. Observe silence in the silent areas. Please dispose of money and valuables in the yellow house where there is a safe.

We were then given a detailed drawn plan of the site. It was rather like a Peter Rabbit Race Game kind of map. There were small line drawings of trees, cars, tents, telephones, people, children, bells, bowls and cutlery and the yellow house. I half expected to find an 'Eeyore slept here' sign. Armed with this plan and all the meal and prayer times you begin to feel initiated. Valuables are carefully put in a thin brown paper bag, which is then named, and sealed with sellotape. It is all done very carefully You feel sure that the paper bag will be used again. There is no waste at Taizé. I remembered my grandmother's kitchen drawers, full of carefully-kept paper bags, elastic bands, and lengths of string. Just seeing someone treat a crumpled brown paper bag with respect reminds you of all the waste in a consumer society.

I was to sleep in the next village, in 'Olinda'. We were off the map. I was to share a dormitory of four. Taizé which is predominantly a vast 'Welcome' of young people asks those over thirty to feed further up the hill in F Tent, which is on the map. In the fields surrounding F Tent, when weather permits, various groups meet for Bible study and discussion. The groups are made up of those who speak the same language. The washing up and the distribution and collection of food is done by the groups in a rota system.

The sound track of Taizé, for me, was footsteps, birdsong and silence broken three times a day by the choral voice of Taizé during the church services; morning prayer, midday prayer, evening prayer, and mass on Sunday.

The curve of the hill on which the road runs feels like the spine of a sleeping land-creature. On either side of this land-creature there are other ranges of hills. From both sides of the road, there are commanding views of the Burgundian countryside.

Living in Olinda means that you definitely leave the main Taizé site and move out into the depths of still countryside. That walk forward and back every dawn and dusk became a kind of hammock shape; something very quiet and assuring. The week was a heat wave. The days were incredibly hot after bright, cool excited dawns. The nights were very still, steeped in moonlight, making the the sleeping cows look like neolithic stones in the long grass. In the mornings, the sunlight on the abundant dandelions made them rich and creamy, in the moonlight, they were pale, shimmering silver saucers. By the end of my visit the dandelions were soft puffs, ready to be blown, leaving a meadow of straight stalks. What a short, spectacular life a dandelion has.

Olinda is a cluster of old farmhouses just down below from the level of the road. When I arrived with the baggage, Hannah from England was in charge of the 'Welcome'. She was cheerful and kind.

She had already been at Taizé for nine months. She wasn't sure what direction her life would take. Taizé was a pause, a chance to think and work things out. She told me that as a helper, your life was continually discussed and reassessed by the Brothers. But she added rather wistfully, 'It is much easier for the boys, they can get really close to the Brothers. We can't. After all they have taken a vow of celibacy and it wouldn't really be fair.'

The cottage was full of character, tiled floors, a wide stone stair-case. In the room numbered for me, there were two double bunks and a small bed below the window. Every mattress was covered in attractive, pale blue cotton. There were stacks of blankets. Most people brought their own sheets and pillow cases. There was no sign of the German ladies. I put bits of my baggage on the small bed. Out of the window I could see tumbledown, stone walls and build-ings, sheep and hills, apple blossom and wild flowers; you could feel the weight and strength of a deep, archetypal, rural stillness.

Taizé prefers people to come for a week at a time. Sunday after-noon to the following Sunday mass. Each week follows a particular shape. Friday is the day of the Crucifixion. Saturday the Easter Vigil and the joy of the Resurrection.

By Sunday evening the Germans had arrived and many others. A variety of English speakers met together over the evening meal. An Australian Franciscan, a rangy, tanned, easy-going man, but there was in his eyes the unmistakable focus of a particularly dedicated life. He was very much in mufti, open-necked shirt, cloth cap well back from the high forehead, but I had sensed he was a priest. In our English-speaking group there were several priests, and a variety of other committed people; an American theologian, an Oratorian, a female pastor from the States-Diane, David – an English Doctor from Winchester, Georgia, a wonderful lady from Jamaica, who had been encouraged by her priest to come and bring back home to the parish some reports and strength from Taizé. Hesitant and friendly, we all met in the soup queues. There were three young Dutch friends, who had just graduated from the youth section, where they had been last year. One of them was cheating considerably to be with us, she was definitely 'youth', but they were a great asset to the group, as they were continually amused by the intensity and hot debate of some of our company.

In the church the elderly tend to make for the benches by the walls, where they can find some back support. The young people fill up the vast central space, sitting or kneeling, heads bowed; whatever feels natural and appropriate to them. It is the great numbers and their naturalness, that makes such a vivid impression on anyone who belongs to a generation, used to worship being synonymous with rigidity of postion, stiff, often unfriendly clothes and a general feeling of 'must' or 'must not'.

The central space of the church during the times of public prayer is reserved for the Brothers. There are over eighty Brothers in the Community of different Christian denominations, the first Roman Catholic priest joined the Community in 1969. Only during the services are the monks seen in their long, white habit and cowl. They come in from the far end of the church led by Brother Roger. There is no processing. Brother Roger, his strong head, with his distinctive, neatly combed grey hair, is thrust forward, with him there is a child. Brother Roger walks purposely and practically, like a man striding the length of a row of potatoes. The child remains beside him with a lighted candle. The other Brothers take up various positions beside the low privet partition, most of them on the wooden stools, some on chairs. The shape of each service is divided into sections of silence, gospel readings, and reaching up out of the darkness, the chants, led by strong individual voices both male and female. The many languages very soon seem like one language. Sometimes the brothers face the far altar with the lights; then they turn to face the opposite end. This movment of altered focus, seems to give the whole giant space, a circular aspect.

There is a moment when the child leaves Brother Roger's side and with a lighted candle, lights other candles that are grouped on a single stand. It is very soon felt and understood that you and all these people are simply being welcomed here to the monk's hillside to share with them the seeking and praising of Christ. They seem to be saying, we are here, we are a community living the trust of Christ. You are most welcome to be with us. It is this simple truth that is made available to anyone in the world who cares to come. That is the extraordinary strength of Taizé, it asks no questions, makes no demands or assumptions, it simply welcomes the world. But there is much listening. 'Listen to the young,' Brother Roger says. 'Listen.' At the end of the evening prayer the brothers stand at various intervals throughout the church. People then come up and talk to them. The semi-darkness and the background chanting seems to give a natural confidence to the speakers.

Brother Roger has said that there has to be visible reconciliation, 'We are a parable of community. We must all, day after day, dispose ourselves inwardly to trust in the mystery of Faith.'

C'est un mystère. That phrase kept ringing in my head. I had heard it so many times. That night, looking out over the moonlit meadows, listening to the wonderful, frantic applause of the crickets, cicadas and frogs, it seemed to be a mighty phrase that effortlessly wrapped round all nights, and all nations, with an extraordinary dynamic of profound purpose.

Once again I pitched my utterly 'unknowing' tent of the mind. It was harder here in this sea of belief and Christ certainty. One German lady was asleep, the other bed was empty, but various black leather suitcases indicated someone would be there. The sleeping lady had a great family of matching brown leather cases, her own embroidered duvet and pillow cases; a kettle and cups and coffee.

Brother Roger was born in May 1915 in the Swiss Jura. His father was a Protestant pastor. From an early age he was aware of what in Taizé and elsewhere today is called, 'The scandal of separation'. His father was once seen to pray in a Catholic church. His maternal grandmother, horrified that Christians were killing one another in Europe, used also to visit a Catholic church, in order to achieve reconciliation within herself.

After periods of unbelief, illness and uncertainty Roger dreamt of finding a house to live with others the essential dimensions of the Gospel. In 1940, alone, Roger bought a small derelict farmhouse in Taizé, here he worked the land, milked his cow, mended the house and prayed. A few miles to the north was the demarcation line. There were people on the run, hungry, hunted and in danger. Roger gave them food and shelter. He asked no questions. Many were Jews. Later there were Germans. Roger was denounced and forced to flee to Switzerland. In 1944 he returned to Taizé. Gradually he was joined by others. The community grew. The Welcome grew. Buildings, church, tents and kitchens spread on and on, up and out over the hill. In the reforming Europe of 1990 Taizé is a focal point for Poles, East Germans and many others now free to move, and explore beyond their own countries. A tremendous building programme was in progress while I was there to be sure to have accommodation for all who might need it.

The week went very fast. It seemed sometimes a strange, suspended experience. So many people, so many voices, languages, ideas, themes. So many coloured plastic bowls, in so many different hands. There was an overriding sense of deep, positive involvement with the contemporary Christian Church. In the groups of F Tent, the life of the church, liturgy, social problems etc. were central to most people's experience. In this context I felt myself most definitely to be an outsider.

The younger people said that their groups were more inclined to silence, and then perhaps discussions, of deeply felt, far more personal experiences. The considerable degree of to-ing and fro-ing kept each day on the move. Meals, chores, groups, prayers, films and silence. The Brothers are assisted by the Sisters of Saint Andrew, a very old order originally founded in about 1231 to assist the pilgrims to and from Compostela with help and shelter. Sister Agnes, brown eyes, quick fine expressive hands, thin as a wraith. She flew up and down the hill on her bicycle. She seemed to be in so many places, but always gave the impression of having time for everyone; all the time they needed. She maintained an effortless flow of impeccable languages – English, French, and German – alternating them as easily as different notes of the same song, according to the needs of the group. She gave our group a bible study each morning, but whatever the biblical occasion, woman at the well, loaves and fishes, the gist seemed to be: Now is right, you are right and you are of God, but a choice must be made by you. With vivid imagery and clear coherent structures she seemed to be that rare phenomena, a poet and theologian. 'Brilliant theologian,' was the consensus of the ordained professionals.

The nightingales were unbelievable. I returned late one evening to find Leni listening to them in the little meadow beside Olinda. We shared the same room. Leni had just lost her husband. After his death, her son, who had been to Taizé before, begged her to go there with him. 'The nightingales are thirty years too late for us,' Leni said, 'No,' I replied, 'their song is the timelessness with which we are continually charged.'

I've not had much experience with groups. Ego down must be the motto. There were little snags now and then but overriding good humour. We had one late arrival, Brother Pascal, who although he sported a distinguished white beard, had been lost with 'Youth' for the first three days of his visit. He expressed great relief on discovering F Tent!

There was one afternoon when it all became too much for Leni. She asked me to drive her car and go with her to Tournus. I drove so anxiously on the right that I kept mounting the pavement, but it only seemed to cheer Leni up! Tournus has the most remarkable Romanesque church, built in a soft pink stone. There is the famous, gilded, black Madonna and Child; all hands and folds, and Saint Philbert's bones.

At the morning prayers there is no mass, but communion is offered and taken by almost all. I most mistakenly brought up the subject of the eucharist and interdenominational communion.

Later Sister Agnes said, 'We cannot impose on so many young people a problem that is part of the history of Christians, before these young people have decided that the risen Christ is the source of their own lives, therefore we are careful to give out information to all by personal contact.'

Taizé imposes nothing. Among all the sunlight and flowers, the jokes and smiles, the real friendliness, you are faced above all, with a manifestly celebratory and seeking Christian Church. If you are not at ease with that, there may be peculiar strain, the unnerving grip of alienating dark. Sometimes my back began to rage as if it would fall apart. I found myself retreating to hidden corners of ground to lie flat.

So many people, so many nations and histories, all coming to ease in, under the great robe of the resurrected Christ. In the church I was continually reminded of the narthex Christ in glory, in the tympanum arch at Vézelay; that wide hand and the thin thread rhythms in the robe. Maybe the confusion of history, tribes, wars, holy places and heresy, made the hierarchy and church leaders too greedy for coherent control; an organised face. Maybe they grasped too much and tore the robe and now, diverse, thin spins of cloth trail the globe, struggling to be united; perhaps Taizé is some kind of seamstress.

Awareness of the real, intense poverty and suffering throughout the world is central to the consciousness of Taizé. There are brothers from Taizé living with the poor in India and South America and other places. 'Be with them, share their lives. Listen to them.'

Perhaps there is an alchemy, that witness to suffering renders, an alchemy that may reduce self-density and expose the crucial unity within all living that must be the matter of Christendom.

Increasingly I felt drawn to this robe, its voice, its transforming hope and yet I remained very definitely without, increasingly tired and sometimes peculiarly dismayed.

'Of course all are saved,' Sister Agnes said in a talk I had with her on my last day.

'Well then, what is a Christian?'

She paused. Then she said with great emphasis:

'A Christian is one who knows he or she is saved, and is happy continually to bear witness of it.'

I began to look forward to swinging the rucksack up on to my back again, and being off alone down another road. Love and the brotherhood of man, that was no problem. God and Love was fine, but there was something scary about Christ. It wasn't the message. It was something else.

I had brought with me one English paperback. A battered Penguin. F.C. Happold's *Anthology of Mysticism*. A good 'dipping' book covering the wisdom of both East and West. Confused and tired I made a random dip just before I packed. It was the pages on Simone Weil. I had once read everything of hers I could lay my hands on, but not for years. With reference to herself and God she wrote:

> Yet I still half refused, not my soul but my intelligence. For it seemed to me certain, and I still think so today, that one cannot wrestle enough with God if one does it out of pure regard for Truth. Christ likes us to prefer Truth to Him, because being Christ, he is Truth. If one turns aside from him to go towards Truth, one will not go far before falling into His arms.

The next day, Sunday, there were crowds and crowds for the mass which was celebrated by Father Maroun, a Maronite priest who had been a hostage in the Lebanon. He now lives in Paris. He spoke in Aramaic, the language used by Christ.

After mass the migrations were in full swing. The arrival of a great number of Indians and Italians and the departure of a great many

Germans. Through the kind offices of Lieselotte, who shared our room and made coffee for us all every morning, Pastor Tetzlaff had been persuaded to give me a lift south of Lyons. Pastor Tetzlaff had brought his parish from Hamburg in a coach which was driven exclusively by him. After Taizé they were to visit various places of culture staying, so Lieselotte said, in the very best hotels. Taking me and my baggage seemed to be a dubious pleasure for Pastor Tetzlaff. He wore a dark beard which suited his dark bearing. He suddenly announced that if I didn't stop saying goodbye to people instantly, he would drive off without me. The Hamburg parishioners were all settled into their places. Lieselotte, who had made me swear again and again to write and thank Pastor Tetzlaff if he gave me a lift, now looked extremely worried. I cut short all goodbyes and climbed aboard. We left the hill. We left the sound of feet and silence and song. *Laudate Omnes Gentes*; the nightingales; the frogs and cicadas and sparrows and that field of straight dandelion stalks beyond the sheep and white cows; past the tents, but well before the nightingales.

The pastor's wife was several seats behind her husband, throughout the journey she managed to knit, very fast, an elegant and complicated pattern. I speak no German; several people spoke a little English. Everyone was very kind, but I had the feeling I was something of a curiosity. It was thought strange for a woman of my age to be travelling alone. It had been difficult to communicate with the pastor where I might be set down. Discussion wasn't his strong point. He was more at ease with declaration. Soon we were past Lyons, driving fast on the clear *payage* in the stifling heat of early afternoon. I was looking out for Givors which I thought was where we had decided to part company. Now and then the pastor drove with surprising abandon conducting to his tapes of Schubert, conducting with both hands off the wheel. His son is Christian Tetzlaff, a violin soloist with the London Philharmonic. The pastor himself is, as Lieselotte told me, a keen musician. Suddenly he stopped. There was a sign to Givors, but no verge or space off the motorway to put one foot in front of another. I expressed some dismay. We drove a few metres on, into the outskirts of Givors. The Pastor opened the boot of the coach and tried hard to persuade me that my rucksack wasn't blue. However soon all the baggage and staff were found. I waved a frantic farewell. Lieselotte, I knew, was still worrying that I might not write and thank the pastor.

I was finding more and more that alone on a dusty road was home. I felt like a dog back at last in its basket. The heat was oppressive, thick and humid. But the unknown street ahead was such a joy: a dirty river; blown papers; faded shutters; torn hoardings; stray dogs; voices from cool, indoor darkness; smells of food and urine. I made my way through the town following signs to the railway station. Three Arabs squatting in the shade called out to me 'Pilgrim?' 'Yes, Compostela.' They nodded wisely. Eventually under a bridge I saw the station. It was very, very hot and the back was really raging. Le Puy change at St Etienne. In the station it was almost cool. I didn't mind how long I waited. 'You've just missed the last train by four minutes. There's another station about twenty minutes' walk away from here, there's a later train from there in about half an hour,' The young man behind the guichet tried to deliver his miserable news to me, with the greatest tact. I stared out from the shade of the station towards the sizzling street. On your own there's no point expressing disappointment or frustration. I was just about to heave the baggage up on to the back again, when a young man who had been buying a ticket said he would drive me to the other station.

He was studying electricity. As an electrician there would always be a job. He was so kind and attentive. I felt immensely grateful to him. The other station was unmanned and completely deserted. Just three platforms and a view across industrial ground towards a football pitch.

In that drowsy, urban Sunday silence, the bustle and throng of Taizé seemed already like a dream. Huge storm clouds were gathering. I thought of the lush, Burgundy meadows, the marvellous, moist moonlight, the thrilling sound of the nightingales. What is time past? How easily the rich drench of memory, packs down those keen fragments of individual moments, and particular people. The knitting pastor's wife seemed to belong to *Babettes's Feast*. As I waited I remembered keenly all those varied pilgrims. Georgia from Jamaica who could not believe she had got sunstroke in Taizé! I could still hear her voice ... 'Oh my mangoes. I have a beautiful mango tree, they will all have gone.' Siegmar from Fribourg in East Germany, one little gesture with his tray of paper cups had made me certain he was an actor. In fact he was a mime artist who had been playing in political fringe theatre, bars and clubs, where if the officials arrived, he would effortlessly convert from political comment to the gentle pathos of clowning. Siegmar did a mime show for us, dissolving instantly every kind of language barrier.

I remembered all those travellers' tales from the two Australian priests. How thieves spit on your shoulder, then having diverted your attention, the skilled hand seizes the wallet. In Rome, Brother Pascal with another priest had his rosary pinched out of his pocket but it was quickly put back into the fellow priest's pocket. Most particularly I remembered Jimmy and his father David, the doctor from Winchester. David's outgoing kindness, his humour and wise humanity gave no hint of his anxiety for Jimmy, that could never have been far from his mind. After a life of difficulty and various major operations to deal with a congenital heart disorder, Jimmy had been forced to shelve his medical studies. Now he was urgently waiting for a complete heart and lung transplant. In the back of his father's car there were two oxygen cylinders. Jimmy had difficulty keeping going. He laughed when I said that he emanated such energy, but it was true. There was about him a great sense of vigorous, peaceful courage. Jimmy and his father, independently and collectively, gave one a glimpse of human qualities that it was a privilege to witness.

Jimmy had been to Taizé several times before. It was David's first visit. Together they had been invited to lunch with the Brothers. Jimmy sat beside Brother Roger. The meal was out on the terrace: trout, salads, fruit and wine. A sung grace before the meal the music of Bach and then a reading of Bach, on his relationship with religion. One of the Brothers was celebrating a birthday. After lunch he was given a book on trees and a hand-carved wooden bowl. The Brothers had a Labrador dog. This description was, for the rest of us, a glimpse of the calm, simple order of life that the Brothers maintain together, alongside their mammoth welcome of the world.

Gradually as the storm clouds increased, the oppressive heat became more manageable. A storm would be a release of the pent feel of the day. Great mood swings of weather, seem in their constant variety, fierce reminders of our own natural turbulence. Stability must be something very live; a poised fraction continually made, not an ordered clamp down. Rigid thought must be a denial of the reach of reason. Going on is the nature of things, perhaps that is why journeying feels so appropriate.

7
Le Puy – Saint Michel
d'Aiguilhe – La Chaise-Dieu –
Brioude

'The tall rock, the mountain and the deep and gloomy wood'
WILLIAM WORDSWORTH

B Y THE TIME the little train arrived the storm clouds were
immense, all those high, blue skies of Burgundy were quite
forgotten now. Menacing, low, purple-black whale spreads of
cloud gathered in the sky space, but still no clap of thunder, no feel
of rain.

From St Etienne the train winds with the River Loire up and up
towards Le Puy. Hal, the Oratorian theologian from the States, had
remarked on the wonderful diversity of the landscapes in France, all
coming so close, one after another, unlike the huge distances between
similar different landscapes in America.

Past Firminy the sky began to clear, storm clouds still gathered,
but with less intensity. The countryside was completely different.
Although I frequently felt sad that I was not doing my journey on
foot, at least a train plunges you deeper into the feel of the landscape
than it is often possible to do in a car. The noise and rhythm of the
train, the fact it is there to serve every part of the community, gives
it a pack-horse flavour. Even with the consistently smooth, rolling
stock of the S.N.C.F., there is still a rattling, foraging, animal feel
about a train.

Now the hills were dark. Below them, there were small stone
dwellings; rich, meadow land marched with little copses of poplar,

apple and lime trees, down to the banks of the river. The cows were dappled, brown and white, no longer the white Charolais of Burgundy. At first the river was wide and majestic, then there were plenty of fishermen. In Retournac a very fat man was walking proudly home, with a large flat fish flapping against his stomach. A great many of the small station dwellings were bleak and derelict. They were often boarded up and for sale.

There was this feel of following the river, up and up towards some kind of darkness. Gradually as the land grew steeper, the meadows became odd, mean, pocket shapes. They struggled against outcrop rock, fallen stone walls and the determined bound of narrow streams.

Travelling alone, enables you to go with place, to breathe into it, almost as if it were your own internal landscape. Silence of mind, by that I mean simply staring, being a collected quiet. Without seeking to amass or formulate any reponses, it seems then, that the giant, timeless quality of stone and shape and depth, become this unity, bonding experience into one single force, without the fragmentation, which continual identification of parts, brings to bear on most experiences.

Soon the slopes were steeper, straining up into dark pine forests. Huge grey stones, slapped now and then with the brilliant yellow of furze. Suddenly there was Voray, a smart, newly painted building, with a live, working clock. Then St Vincent Le Chateau; here a majestic, dead clock, derelict buildings and battered blue shutters. Everywhere the buttercups were fading; the dandelions were all stalks. La Voute sur Loire. Olive green shutters on an ochre building. The Loire was narrow now, no longer a wide sweep of water. A pulse of froth, stirring and stumbling over harsh grey rock and ruts of smooth stones; all bends and turns. A heron was the only fisherman. This gaunt, grey bird was extremely comfortable with the steep sides of jagged stone and patchy, rough, uneven banks, it monitored keenly the clear water as we trundled past.

It would be well past eight o'clock by the time we reached Le Puy. Grey stone, the height of ground, dark pine forests and a dark sky. I felt this deep sense of a summoning dark; it is hard to describe. Some mountainous regions seem lyrical, carefree, they seem to open up from their height into a majestic, celebratory, sound; but there was a perplexing, dour quality about these volcanic ranges.

Le Puy is a large, straggling town, very ancient in origin. Well before Roman occupation a town existed, clinging onto the slopes of the Roc Corneille. The Romanesque basilica stands on the slopes of Mount Anis, the modern city flows out from the old city into every available space below the mountain. Le Puy seems to sit in this basin surrounded by cold, volcanic peaks. From the train the first thing you cannot fail to notice is the enormous, red statue of Notre Dame de France, which was erected on the highest point of the Roc Corneille in 1860. It is a statue 22.70 metres high, cast from the molten iron of Russian canons taken at Sebastopol during the Crimean War. Apparently it was painted this violent terracotta, to blend in with the city roofs. It is a fierce landmark, competing with other high rocks for a superior, towering position.

My back felt extremely stiff and battered after the long day. Arriving at a new place is rather like turning up an unknown card. It says Le Puy. I knew it was a very old city and an important Marian shrine, one of the major stops on the route to Compostela. I knew also that there was a little village just outside the city, St Michel D'Aiguilhe, 'the needle' and that on a high, solitary volcanic peak there is a small Romanesque chapel to Saint Michael. Madeleine at Lisieux had made me swear to her that I would visit it. I knew that in the basilica there was a black Madonna. That was all I knew. Even though it was late, I had this sense that I should first climb to the place of sanctuary of the black Madonna, the basilica.

The sky was threatening, everywhere there was this weight of stone and dark. It is a very steep climb up to the basilica. There are many different approaches. I simply followed the first signs. But there was no life in any form to be found up there, in the bowel darkness of narrow streets, and closed shutters. The streets were cobbled in purple stones made from the frozen froth that had once been leaping tongues of fire. This dead-fire feel is very visible in the stone; it reminded me of cold clinkers. By taking fairly obvious short cuts, I arrived at the bell tower. The huge, cavernous, church building was closed. All the steep steps and courtyards were quite deserted. No bars, no lights. I made a hurried descent back to the exact spot I had started up from. It was a triangular *place* with a large, stone central fountain. There were high, battered old buildings, several bars and a *dentelle* shop, with examples of lace arranged in the window. There was a Logis de France sign; the Hotel

Verveine. Inside the hotel bar there were weathered men with caps and dogs, and Madame, whose manner and bearing somehow inspired me to feel that the cuisine would be generous. There was a room. Beyond the bar, and Madame's desk, at a vantage point between the two, there was the dining-room. The small tables, all laid with white clothes, were pushed together in rows. There were one or two couples, but mostly there were single men eating alone, glancing up between scoffs and sips to the large, coloured television set, just beyond Madame's head. Jokes and local references were called out from the bar to the tables, and vice versa. Everyone knew everyone else, and everyone knew Madame.

My little room looked out directly on to the fountain, which still played. Running water was a constant sound that seemed to console the dark weight of stone and grey. Just as I dumped the baggage down on to the narrow bed, there was a grumbling roll of thunder and then a triumphant clap and then, quite soon after that, the hard, pelting sound of heavy rain. Constant dramatic storms are a feature of this whole area and of Le Puy in particular.

In the dining-room I sat beside an elderly man in a faded blue shirt, the rolled-up sleeves exposed strong dark arms. His worn flat cap lay on the table beside broken pieces of bread. He greeted me and I him. Together, with occasional references to the storm and the television programme, we ate our way through a generous menu: soup, lamb, salad and flan and delicious, *fourme* cheese. A *coup de rouge* is a thin, dead creature here, after the same in Burgundy.

There is no greater consolation than to come in late, to a place you feel has almost anticipated your arrival. Nothing is odd or strained or difficult because it is a place, where the archetypal thread of commercial hospitality has always been local life and gossip; work and family celebrations; a blast of cooking steam and the crash of the swing-to kitchen door; the pulsing whoosh of the Gaggia coffee machine from the bar. There seems to be some kind of natural balance at work. Nothing goes unnoticed. But everyone is at ease.

I noticed in my diary that it was the feast of Saint Prudence, perhaps she had guided me here. It was a very uncomplicated, comfortable place from which to play the 'Le Puy' card.

The bedside light was small and shone a very yellow beam. Rain still pounded down overflowing the drains and gutters. Trying to make the usual notes I found myself wondering ... what was I really exploring? Place ... or self? And what anyway, in that context, is exploration? Is it standing back and sorting out, or is it moving on? Maybe it is all three at once. And maybe place and self share this curious, compelling unity. Perhaps going out towards places where there are others, or where many, many others have been before, perhaps such a journey reconciles our sense of impermanency, to the mysterious continuity we share and make and are, with all mankind.

Sometimes travel, people, places, sights and smells, all shift into a dream space. Then the mind feels enlarged, loose, random. You almost cease to have a place there; you are simply energy-choice within the universal current.

The next day the sky was clear. The atmosphere outside in the street was bright and busy. I decided to explore the town, doing a general bar crawl to catch up with my Taizé notes before visiting the basilica.

Down below in the bustling streets and squares of Le Puy, the basilica seems far away. A giant, ancient creature that is back from the life and style of the contemporary town. It is a very old town. A great many of the houses are extremely high; three to five storeys. The faded 'shutter-scapes' are wonderful, so many pale, weathered, bleached-out soft colours, that trace the life of the wood in the various grooves and knots. There are large and small squares, many modern shops and supermarkets, and a red brick church facade that is now a cinema. But wherever you are, any glance down any narrow street will reveal, the bright red Madonna, and her vigorously waving offspring. You never forget that Le Puy is a Marian city.

I was intrigued to find a Simone Weil street and school. At a local bookshop I enquired about her. Had she ever lived in Le Puy? Some said she had taught in the local school, all said that she had 'of course, worked here with the Resistance, as we all did'. 'This region is very good for hiding people.' Later on in my journey people confirmed that Simone Weil had both lived and taught here in Le Puy.

By midday and many bar stops later, I had more or less caught up on Taizé. I decided to make my way to the basilica in the afternoon. There was no need here to have the cold key in my pocket, it simply hung there on the board above Madame's head. I don't think she ever left her vantage point of management and authority between the bar and the dining-room. I'm sure even as I write, she is there now, round cheeks, tight curls, and large glasses that seem to magnify her commands and her cheerful comments.

On the steep and slow climb up to the great church, I took a slightly different route from the previous evening. I found a large building, with the bright yellow Coquille of Saint Jacques emblazoned on the wall. It was an Auberge de la Jeunesse. I could have stayed there, the *jeunesse* is purely nominal. The pilgrim routes to Compostela have been given cultural status by the E.E.C.; all the important stops have lodgings and shelter. At the Auberge de la Jeunesse I was told that I had just missed the departure, that morning, of a family who were making there way to Compostela via Roncevalles, on a horse. Mother, father and two small children. One horse? I exclaimed incredulously. One horse but very, very robust indeed, I was told. I have this vision now of some Suffolk Punch, bearing, I hope, a fairly thin family, over the mountains towards Spain. In Spain there is a statutory amount of water that must be carried per capita as well as everything else. I wished I had seen them leave, apparently the priest had been there to give them a particular pilgrim's blessing.

Just past the Auberge I heard the sound of water coming from inside a building. A sign outside said 'Car washing absolutely forbidden'. I peered in. It was a public laundry. Two huge stone sinks ran the length of this cellar-like stone space; streaks of brilliant green broke the dark of the curved ceiling. Various women, many young and colourfully dressed and surrounded by bright, plastic buckets, slapped and scrubbed their sheets and clothes against the broad edge of cold, sparkling stone. A high, single brass tap, continually poured clear water into the vast, soapy, grey mass in the sink. The women seemed very cheerful and in good heart, they were getting the kind of whiteness Persil has never seen. What an old rhythm: scrub, float and slap down; roll and fold and wring, again and again and again. I thought of women throughout the world, kneeling or squatting or bending by some edge of water and following these same gestures. There are so many strong marks, carved continually into the space of each day; digging, sweeping, scrubbing, stirring, rocking, wringing; the *mudra* of mankind. A simple scale of gesture that creates a continual chord of strength and purpose.

I came up to the basilica from the east entrance which opens out from a narrow, dark, cobbled street into a small patch of ground beside the bell tower. There are high stone walls on every side but the roof is open to the sky. There are some striking Roman reliefs of animals. Strong, thick, muscular creatures, reflecting in their quarters the weight and power of this local, volcanic landscape. There was also a tomb, the tomb of a Canon; on the side carved into the stone is a Madonna, holding a very carefree infant, who is pulling a little at the neck of his mother's garment. In her right hand, against her breast she holds the fleur de lys. The work is loose and crude, but full of warmth, it was carved in the mid fourteenth century.

Pushing at heavy doors, I eventually found my way into the cathedral itself. A very dark, mysterious place, utterly unlike anywhere I had been before. The ceiling of the nave is a series of stunning, twelfth-century, brick cupolas between the arches. There was to me this giant, waiting, cave feel. Gradually your eye is drawn to the dark, secret space beyond the high altar, here, amid hanging sanctuary lamps and several lighted candles, high up under a white gilded canopy, is the tiny black Madonna. Her face and the face of the child, are glistening ebony, that is all the black there is to see. A stiff white robe and veil accentuates their small, staring faces. There is something hypnotic about them. They are so small in the huge dark space, and yet you feel compelled to keep looking back to them.

There many legends about Le Puy and the Virgin. Sometime in the fourth century there was a widow, who lived near the stream of Borne, she was suffering from a malignant fever. It is said that the suffering widow saw the Virgin, standing on a large, flat stone, surrounded by angels. The Virgin told the widow, that if she were simply to come and lay herself on the stone, instantly, she would be cured. The widow went and found the stone, and was instantly cured. A bishop, presumably excited by the vision and cures that followed it, ran to the holy hill (the legends vary, but all say that the bishop *ran*) and he saw a stag come out from the nearby forest. Running in the snow, the stag traced out the plan of the basilica that should be built, according to the wishes of the Mother of God.

The stone was the top stone of a dolmen that had been on this spot since pre-Celtic times. Later it had been incorporated into a Roman temple, where it was thought to have been the stone of sacrifice. In the fifth century when the temple was demolished, the dolmen stone was rediscovered. The stone became known as the

'Fever Stone'. Many came for cures and favours to be obtained by lying on it.

Another miracle in the fifth century, curing a paralytic from Ceyssac, brought new pressure to bear on the church authorities to build a sanctuary to Our Lady on this spot. A bishop journeyed to Rome and brought back an architect and Senator called Scutari, who seems to have been responsible for the first sanctuary, his name is incised on a stone lintel.

At some point the 'Fever Stone' was brought into the Church and placed in front of the altar, where it could get the rays of the sun. The fact the Virgin had stood on it, would have completely exorcised it from its original pagan and sacrifcial function. Some time before the Revolution the 'Fever Stone' was taken out of the church and placed at the top of the great stairway, where it remains today. The vision of the Madonna, here at Le Puy was one of the first, and happened significantly on the eve of the Council of Ephesus, which proclaimed the Virgin Mary as Divine Mother. Interestingly Bernadette's vision at Lourdes coincided exactly with the pronouncement by the Church of the Immaculate Conception.

Le Puy celebrates many *Jubilées* which are the dates when Good Friday and Lady Day conincide. But Le Puy doesn't seem to have merited the considerable boost of a Papal visit. Cardinals, Monseigneurs, pomp, ceremony and the little black Madonna processed through the city; many, many pilgrims, but no recent Pope. The anthem to Our Lady the 'Salve Regina' came from Le Puy in the eleventh century. It was originally a marching song for the Crusades. I remember it as the general night prayer of the church, after compline, before the Greater Silence.

There are some colourful frescoes in the basilica, but they are quite hidden in the general cave-dark, until you happen to find the right button, then there are a few, ticking seconds of wonder. A very tall Saint Michael in a splendid robe of red and gold, the whole figure is on a sea-green ground, with various fronds and creatures. There is Saint Catherine on her terrible wheel, consoled by angels. There are the women at the empty tomb, with a very fit angel to greet them. All the images are full of Byzantine flow, and warm, earth colours. As you move from one corner of darkness to the next, you feel that any minute Harrison Ford might come crashing in, or that you could catch a glimpse of Tin Tin and Snowy vanishing into the cloister, or the Chapel of Relics, or the Chapel of the Dead. It feels like a place that hoards mystery.

Black Madonnas abound in France. Again and again you hear guides and sacristans or priests saying to groups of wide-eyed children 'Ah black, Why black? We don't know. Maybe it is years of burning candles, or that they have been hidden in the ground. We don't know.' Once again, *c'est un mystère*. There is various contemporary literature suggesting links with Isis, Artemis, Esoteric Schools of Initiation, the Dynasty of the Merovingians, Alchemy etc. Some wise, necessary anima image anyway. All of it is tantalising conjecture. The first black Madonna I ever saw was in Guadalupe in Spain. It was so small, but the impact of the figure on one was intense. An icon intensity. The black Madonnas seem to be about strength. They are not an attempt to portray pure, unsullied, virgin characteristics, like the later Madonnas.

As I sat in the great cave of the basilica at Le Puy, I thought that maybe this tiny, black stub of face, in her white robe, maybe she is some kind of plug, keeping in place the strange, hoarded energy that very ancient places accumulate. The Madonna's role is as an intercessor for mankind towards the Divine. Darkness, its possession of us, seems to be an essential part of the spiritual route. To the Sufis blackness is the final stage before beatific light. Maybe the black Madonna demonstrates for us the wisdom of this bridging darkness. A darkness her Son had to enter to fulfil His work for the world. In the same way we must in our turn know darkness if we are to be united with her Son. At a practical level, darkness slows the pace, it forces you to come to heel, and hear the sound of silence; maybe that is important.

In a dark and dusty corner I found a tired, rather dazed Saint James; his worn habit, his staff, belt and sandals, and his hat, with the wide brim upturned and a shell pinned on it.

Various signs kept saying that all the secrets of this ancient sanctuary would be revealed in the sacristy. Arrows and more dark doors. The sacristy was a very cheerful place, a combination of museum and cathedral shop. The parish priest was finishing the tour, for a group of extremely attentive school children. When he had finished speaking they all dashed to the medals and postcards. I was interested to see how many of the boys, between eleven and fourteen bought medals of the Madonna, which they instantly hung round their necks, over all the sports wear.

There were many paintings and various display cabinets of relics. Saint Bernard, Saint Hilary and the True Cross. A medal of Sebastapol from Queen Victoria and a very large, about size seven, black slipper, that legend says was dropped from the Virgin's foot when she stood on the stone surrounded by angels. It does say LEGEND in large letters.

I left the cathedral as I had come in, by the east door. I thought I would return the next day by the great stairway and main entrance. I wanted to have another look at the Roman reliefs and the Madonna on the Canon's tomb. There was a cold wind, and odd spots of rain. I was very surprised to hear sounds of singing. In the tiny area near the bell tower, there was a group of about fifteen, rather smartly dressed, young people. Standing on a square stone, there was a young girl leading them, with more of those elegant hands. The singing was beautifully modulated and controlled. 'Are you a choir?' I asked. 'No. No.' they replied 'We are simply friends, this is just for fun.' I remembered a similar, but not quite so elegant group singing on a wall in Vézelay. In fact I realised more and more on the journey, how singing, serious part-singing, is a very real and natural aspect of life in France. Everyone seems to be able, instantly, to sing well, and sing melodies known to one another. It reminded me of the non-singing, shy, absolutely unlyrical kind of voice that the actors roused from the eager supporters of Save the Rose Theatre in London. No one seemed inclined to sing and no one knew the same song. Eventually it practically ended with 'Here we go, here we go, here we go ... and the chorus from 'Where have all the flowers gone?' A sad reflection on the passing of something or other.

Next day was Victory day. I was woken by bright sunlight and the sound of drums. A small group of serious, uniformed, young men and women were drumming and bugling their way round the fountain, below my window. I hurried my *petit dejeuner* and with thoughts of Jackanapes and the General March of History, went to follow the band. They were regrouping and having cigarettes when I found them again. I suspect that it was all a practice for a greater ceremony later on. One old man, with distinguished bearing and a slight stoop, paused with me, no one else seemed in the least bit turned on by drums, white gloves, thick moustaches and flat hats.

I was on my way to Saint Michel d'Aiguilhe, the little village just outside Le Puy. Very little remains of the village below this extraordinary, giant obelisk of natural rock. In the twelfth century there had been an important hospital. There is a fountain and chapel, one bar, several houses and a carved, stone cross.

The rock is dramatic. It stands utterly on its own, a shaft of stone sprouting incongruously out from the surrounding countryside.

The light was marvellous, very clear, everything was washed and alert after the rain. From a good distance you can see rich, golden lichen on the sides of the rock, and there on the summit, the tiny Romanesque chapel complete with bell tower. The rock is eighty-two metres high, fifty-seven metres in diameter, one hundred and seventy metres in circumference at the base.

The first oratory to Saint Michael was built in the tenth century. It was then enlarged in the twelfth century leaving the first chapel very much intact. The guide books say that many authors consider the chapel to be the eighth wonder of the world. The building runs with the shape of the summit of the rock. Right from the beginning the sanctuary was said to *plaît a ceux qui le voient*.

After the compelling, dark pull of Le Puy, the walk out towards Saint Michel felt definitely like a pull to light. At the base of the rock, there is a little Roman arch and then you start the climb of 265 steps. It was hot, still and clear as I went. On the climb there were many places to pause, and look back down to the red roofs of Le Puy. I was amazed by all the abundant flora and fauna that flourished on the face of the rock; iris, wallflowers, star of Bethlehem, lad's love and so many lizards and butterflies. There always seem to be lizards on church stones, perhaps they are pleading entry and forgiveness for the serpent species; all those that slither near the ground.

Outside the chapel in the sun, there was a sense of peace and well-being. There were few people. Apparently pilgrims used often to sleep out on the rock, to gain even greater graces from Saint Michael. The stone of the chapel is warm ochre, it is marked with green and white lichen. There are many carvings, it has a decorated, eastern feeling. The arc above the door, is divided into three arches showing scenes from the apocalypse. Below the arches, on the lintel, basking in the warmth of the yellow stone, are two mermaids. One has a languorously curled tail, the other a straight, single fin. I loved them instantly, their calm, basking strength, and their strong hands. They seemed to be drying their hair, with a pleated length of fabric. I had seen various mermaid pairs; these were particularly good. As I was attempting to photograph them, the young guide came out into the sun. I asked him to tell me about the wonderful mermaids.

'Ah well,' he said, 'they are temptation. They symbolise to the pilgrim the temptation he must be ready for and at all costs avoid. Temptation is always there at his heels.'

And temptation is always a woman. With those scaly tails, the genitals are well protected, so it can't be fear of straight seduction. Maybe it is the temptation of the deep, that man fears. The deep collective ocean, abundant with the kind of wisdom that will always elude death by naming, and the confines of scholarship. How could their calm and strength signify temptation. I loved them even more.

'Where please,' I asked the guide, 'where is the iconography of the male tempter to the female pilgrim, in fact where is the female pilgrim?' I couldn't help being aware of this huge, inherited burden for woman. The exclusion of their true nature from the accepted centres of holiness. I thought of Anna at Bussy saying so emphatically 'I am not a desert father. I want to find my way as a woman, the vital aspects within the spiritual life for a woman, are qualitatively different from those of a man.' I stayed a little longer, loving these good temptresses. Thoughts of temptresses take one easily to Mary Magdalene and Vézelay. Suddenly I could see that nave, a river of crystal clear water, and these mermaids, bathing and basking in the sanctuary of that great church, bringing back to the centre the sacred sense of woman, that a tormented, and male-dominated Church has so fearfully abandoned and excluded.

Once inside this small stone oratory, any feelings of frustration or fury had to subside. It is a very special place indeed. Everything is curves. The low curved ceiling, that flows from columns, that march themselves, in a curve, with the round feel of the outer walls. There are two steps up to the first oratory; small windows set in deep stone walls. Rich fragments of glowing light move round the stones. There is a small wooden statue of Saint Michael. Candles were lit and intense prayers were going on.

There are some frescoes and tiny *trésors* but the most special feeling is in the breath of the space itself. You want simply to be still and in some measure absorb it. At the back there is a smooth, very worn curve of stone like a window seat, where for hundreds of years so many pilgrims must have sat after their high climb. I sat there. I was considerably intrigued by three people who stood before the statue of Saint Michael and together recited, with considerable energy, various prayers and litanies aloud. There was a well-dressed woman of middle age, beside her, a thin, dark, rather frail, spent man and one step ahead of them, there was the man who had the papers in his hand, and who led the prayers. I was fascinated by him. He wore a long, extremely creased, Burberry-type mac with good brown shoes, with the laces tied very unevenly. He wore glasses. His hands were fine, the skin rather translucent. His reddish-grey hair was fairly long, it stood out at odd angles over the collar of his coat, as if it was alive with his obvious energy. He spoke with that breathless speed, in common to many highly intelligent people, who, you feel positively trip up over the abundance of their thoughts. They prayed aloud together for over forty minutes. As they prepared to leave I spoke with the frail, spent man, about prayers and pilgrims generally. They were from Montpellier, they were ardent believers. He told me of a miraculous spring in a private house in Montpellier. 'But really you should speak with my friend,' he said. 'He is a brilliant research scientist, a very famous man. He is staying with us on holiday.' With some trepidation, I approached the scientist outside the chapel; just below the basking mermaids. He was so preoccupied, so intense, I felt in a way as if I was interrupting a fragile instrument, that must play continually in order to live. He darted a fierce glance at me, and then went on to speak very fast indeed.

'A pilgrim is someone who takes risks; is prepared to suffer. To visit places that have inspired man from the earliest times is to receive a little of the energy that has accumulated there ... and possibly to add to it. My work is concerned with the heart of energy, lasers etc.' He kept darting these penetrating glances at me. He was pretty formidable and I could hear the terrible, blundering hopelessness of my grasp of his language. 'Would you say God was energy?' I asked. 'But of course ... of course ... but much more besides ... He is Love.' He said that with great force adding, 'The energy of Love is something else.'

On my way back into Le Puy, there was the sleepy, midday feel of pause; street emptiness; no flow of sound, just the odd step or bark, or car engine, with here and there a restaurant murmur out into the sun.

I paid my final visit to the cathedral by the main entrance, climbing the wide street, where once lacemakers worked all day, sitting outside on the steps of the houses. The facade of the cathedral is a powerful mass of curves and columns, a multi-coloured play of stone in the uprights and fans of the arches. All these great buildings seem to me, to make sounds. Le Puy is a resonating, bass chord, like a Russian choir. More steps, more climb, with more frescoes and carved doors. No one was about. The long, smooth, black 'Fever Stone' is there, making the final step in front of the doors. I lay on it for quite some time, it was hard and cool, excellent for the back after climbing all those steps. If there were any favours around one might as well be open to them.

The bus for La Chaise-Dieu left early in the morning. We climbed and climbed. The land became noticeably poorer, the farms and dwellings more delapidated. The forests, all dark pines, were dense on every skyline. In the end we were the highest part, looking down on endless, forested curves. There were massive timber works every so often. There was the smell of resin and wood smoke. Now and again great lengths of timber were being irrigated, presumably to stop them from drying out too fast. A great sense of height, and that still dark peculiar to pine forests, and soon, a completely empty bus.

I knew that La Chaise-Dieu was very high, a small village in a forested, remote region. I had imagined some sort of 'Heidi' experience. Peace. Solitude. Wise grandfather figures tending stock and carting timber and, of course, the renowned monastic church.

The bus drew up opposite a small, stone chapel with an open doorway. The words Notre Dame de Bonne Rencontre, Protectress of Travellers were written up on the outside. Inside there were flickering candles. I crossed the road full of happy anticiation. The abbey church has two distinguished square towers at the front and a single square tower at the back. The building feels vast, and unexpected in this remote spot. I was immediately there at the side of the abbey church and immediately I felt uneasy. There were so many crows wheeling about the towers, not one pigeon or sparrow. I tried to banish these involuntary and very negative responses. But the feeling persisted. The stones of the church were more refined and even than in some of the earlier Romanesque churches I had visited. The abbey church at La Chaise-Dieu was built during the later part of the fourteenth century. The proportions are very fine; the stone is a calm, uniform, pale colour. I went down into the main street and stood looking back up the smooth, elegant steps that led to the great doors. In the centre of the steps there is a poor, headless bishop. It looks as if a mighty, single swipe took his head with one blow.

In the street, tourist wares had been wheeled out on the pavement. There were racks of cowbells, and hides and fleeces, decorated wooden clogs and pipes, glistening with varnish. There was not a soul in sight, certainly not a tourist of any kind. There was just a churlish wind, and murky clouds gathering. The flight of steps up to the cloisters beside the church and a glimpse of the cloister beyond, was breathtaking, full of austere, Gothic splendour, but there was no warmth in them, no kind of enticement. It was an odd reaction to acknowledge. But I was determined to be honest.

The sky was growing darker by the second. Dumping the baggage had to be the priority. I had anticipated a fairly long pause, here at La Chaise-Dieu, maybe five or six nights. I began seriously to doubt that idea. Just a little way down the street, the Hotel Commerce was advertising rooms. I went inside. It was a dark room with a bar at the far end. Oil cloths on the various small tables were covered with yellowing sheets of plastic. It didn't seem to be a place for food. There were several, small glasses on the empty tables, with the dregs of red wine in them. There was a pile of thick, cold ash in the fireplace. Madame came in from a side door. She was very thin and a little strange. She obviously suffered from some condition that made her movements sudden and faulty. She spoke with difficulty, you were made aware of bright red gums, and shining eyes. She smiled. It was rather an unnerving smile, that seemed inspired more by her condition than her emotions. I was ashamed to think that her odd manner and the general staleness put me off. I tried to compensate for my reaction by asking eagerly if she had a room. There was a room. I followed her jerky, difficult progress up two flights of stairs. There was a definite vivacity in her darting eyes, although I couldn't help thinking that it was probably due to wine more than anything else. The room was clean and cheerful, with a good view down, over tiled red roofs, to the hills and forests. There was a thin cat in a gutter, but no birds; no sound of sparrows anywhere.

Determined to banish weird thoughts and imagined characteristics, I went downstairs to the bar. There were three men in the bar. They wore dark caps, their shoulders were stooped, the joints on their fingers were swollen and puffy; they stared, gripping small glasses full of dark red wine. Rolled cigarettes hung limp on their lips unlit. I said the usual greetings. They stared without making any response. Madame was standing behind the bar, she smiled and then came out into the room and filled every small glass to the brim, without being asked to do so. Then I had to notice that each of them had some facial problem; something at odds and medically disadvantaged with the lips, or eyes or teeth. It was an unexpected average of what looked like, congenital difficulties. Later I was told that the water, which was quite undrinkable, was thought to have been responsible for these kind of defects. It was difficult not to feel slightly daunted by the general atmosphere.

I decided to get the general bearings of the village before returning to the abbey church. Everywhere there was the smell of wood smoke and slightly sour cooking; hot dung heaps in the back of barns. There were encouraging cow splats on the road. I was longing to see some animals, not simply to hear them. I could hear hens scratting behind high barred doors. An Alsatian dog howled from an upstairs window; below his head, trousers were pegged out on a taut washing line. Beyond broken walls, there was the regular moan of cattle. On the wide verges huge lengths of timber lay in great mounds, gnarled and silver-smooth from wind and sun.

In the central square below the church there was a cheerful, modern bar, full of people, but outside it, a machine was digging up the road, and the bar closed at midday.

I made for the church, running up the steps past the battered bishop. I was determined to grasp and enjoy these Gothic wonders. But a manic, fungus chill seemed to seize me by the throat as soon as I was inside the building. A running, green liquid damp was making its way up the pillars, exuding a rich, live quality. I tried desperately to concentrate on the important organ, the wonderful rood loft, all the fine proportions, but I felt totally unhinged by this chilling, suffocating damp. In a little wooden booth, with a special high floor, a foot or so off the stone, there was a custodian lady. Her little wooden booth was obviously to protect her from the damp. She told me sternly that she was about to close the church. I felt nothing but gratitude.

I fled back down the steps into the square to see the cheerful bar close. Then I noticed an unexpectedly enthusiastic lady wearing a wonderful russet suit, it might have been Donegal tweed. Over her suit she wore a sheepskin waistcoat; thick, bright green stockings under the skirt, and a woollen hat perched rather haphazardly over strands of flying hair. She was Mademoiselle Claire. She was over seventy. She liked to be referred to as Mademoiselle because widows got so touchy, if she, a celibate, was referred to as Madame. I asked her where one might eat. Immediately she gave me a list of places where on no account to eat. Mademoiselle Claire was 'in timber', the last of a long line. She suggested that we might lunch together. 'It will be very simple country food,' she said. 'On no account must we consider the F50 menu. It must be the F80 menu.'

Mademoiselle Claire talked with great enthusiasm of heresy, history, education, and the state of France. 'Did I know that Mitterand, on his mother's side was related to your Queen?' I did not. She referred to the bitter cold in the church and the wonderful summer concerts. Archbishop Lefèvbre celebrated mass in the church after his excommunication. Mademoiselle Claire had ordered a bottle of Anjou, but she spoke with such enthusiam, on so many subjects, she quite neglected to pour the wine. Nervously, I asked if I might have a second glass. Horrified at her forgetfulness, she seized the bottle, which then fell across the cheese board, the contents spraying the rest of the table, and various parts of ourselves. In all the subsequent commotion our glasses remained empty. Eventually we parted, with Mademoiselle Claire expressing how delighted she was to welcome me to the mountains.

I returned to the abbey church somewhat fortified. A small party with a guide were just ahead of me, they were suitably muffled up with gloves and scarves.

The choir is utterly spectacular. You enter it from a side aisle. It is like a small church within the other, loftier space. The wood of the choir stalls is warm in colour, it is a feast of amazing carving. There is considerable humour and irreverence in the grimacing faces, animals and chimeras. Tremendous originality coupled with extraordinarily fine craftmanship. In the centre of the choir there is the white, recumbent figure of Clement VI of Avignon, who is buried here. You could understand why Archbishop Lefèvbre might have been drawn to La Chaise-Dieu. Above the glowing wood of the stalls, are the tapestries. They are given three red stars by the Guide Michelin. They are Flemish, and have recently been restored. They are wonderfully detailed and intensely human depictions of nearly all the important narrative moments of the Life and Death and Resurrection of Christ. There are also many details from the old testament. There is a Dürer/Cranach feel in the hair and limbs, although the figures are generally more voluptuous. All the stories are placed in backgrounds of considerable wealth and abundance. Mary Magdalene is a bejewelled, lady of the court. Christ too, is consistently swathed in magnificent robes, with fleurs de lys popping up all over them.

There is definitely a slight pause in the choir, from the shuddering attack of damp. In the side chapels, paintings of saints were rolling down off their supports, with nothing but spores and green death to greet them. Behind the choir, utterly appropriately, there is a fresco of the Danse Macabre. Recently scrubbed of green growth, the drawing and the earth colours are perfectly preserved. Death elegantly greets one and all.

I can't describe the sense of relief I had on leaving the church. The cloisters were brighter. Sitting there in the sun I thought of the history. That same pattern over again. Simple, sincere beginnings, increase of people and prosperity, subsequent power, then turmoil and devastation.

In the eleventh century, Robert de Turlande, a canon of Saint Julian, sought an austere place. But in the well-known way fervour gradually became increase and power. There was building and development and the patronage of Popes. As the guide book says, 'Brilliance, wealth, and religion worked wonderfully together.' Then, of course, comes capture, sacking and general turbulence and finally the Revolution. The tremendous restoration here only began in 1945. 'Tourism, culture, and religious mystique are regaining lost ground. Hope has been reborn,' says the guide book. An interesting understanding of hope.

There was more to see. There was a *Salle d'Echo*. I still felt in the grip of some palpable awfulness, which even the watery sun couldn't dispel. In the old buildings, just beyond the abbey church, there is a hospice for the elderly. Apparently there are three echo rooms, but only one is open to the public. I followed the signs, and found myself in a large, fairly low-ceilinged room. A decorated boss in the centre, gathers up the various, curved segments of roof. The walls were not high. The notice said ... Go into the corner and with your back to the room, whisper into the wall. I began to do this, saying *bonjour* to myself and certainly the whisper came back to me very clearly, as if you were speaking on a telephone. Then suddenly someone tapped me on the shoulder. It was Juliet. 'No. No.' she said, 'You can't play alone, you must play it with me.' And Juliet ran across eagerly into the opposite corner. Juliet was full of life and warmth. She had a blue felt hat pulled down on her head, which gave her a school-girl look, bright rosy cheeks and a marvellous smile. Her skin was brown and soft, although it was very wrinkled. She wore a wrap-over blue apron and blue slippers. We played together with great success, speaking at length via the wall, without any sound heard in the centre of the room.

Juliet lived in the hospice now, having spent a lifetime on a small holding, high in the mountains. 'Juliet as in Romeo and Juliet?' I said. She was delighted and clasped my hands. 'Exactly. Exactly.' she said laughing. At that moment a stiff, very thin man walked across the room on two sticks. Juliet smiled and touched his arm. He didn't seem to see her or take any notice. 'Romeo?' I asked when he had gone. 'Yes. Yes. Romeo,' she said, thrilled that I understood. 'It is sad,' she went on, 'because here the men and women must live separately.' She sighed. 'But it had to be ... it had to be.' Then she came very close to me ... 'But I have free-dom. Freedom. I can sit and walk about how I choose. I can do anything I wish. Oh my dear, every woman should know a little freedom once in her life. Such freedom.' She clapped her hands together with the joy of it all. At that moment a nurse to call her for coffee. She kissed me, patting my cheeks. 'Freedom ... such a gift.'

I went away happy to have the truth of Juliet in my heart. She was such a star. I will never think of freedom again without thinking of Juliet. People like Juliet, just sitting in the sun. Without wealth or brilliance or religious mystique, they probably experience a peace of mind, beyond most people's understanding.

But there was to be no sitting in the sun for anyone that afternoon. Storm clouds had gathered, closing in the sky and pressing down their darkness on to the square church towers and the tops of the pine trees. I ran for cover into the only bar that was open. It was a tiny space filled with red and black formica, with an embossed, carpet wallpaper of huge flowers. There was one sad girl staring at a small black and white television set, where Dougal and the Magic Roundabout were carrying on together. There was a market bus out of La Chaise-Dieu in the morning. With the freedom of

Juliet in my heart, I would catch it and try and find a mountain pause somewhere else.

The market bus was full of people and produce. Still we climbed. At Mayres, a small village, a woman got on who had lived for three generations in the area. She now lived in Paris. She had been staying with her daughter. She was fascinating to talk to because she knew the area so well. She told me of another black Madonna, in a tiny chapel, a Madonna, by whose intercession, drought was relieved and childless couples conceived. I mentioned Juliet and the *Salle d'Echo* – 'Do you know why those rooms were built?' I did not, there was nothing about them in the guide books. Apparently, there had been a large leper hospital at La Chaise-Dieu and the echo rooms were built to enable the lepers to make confession, without the priest having to be close to them. I was riveted. But why no mention of that in the guide books?

The scenery was stunning. The bus driver was an eagle fanatic. He stopped for us to see a milord, close by on the ground, and then he stopped further on so that we could admire the gorge. 'Many many houses are for sale here,' he said, 'and there is a bus every day of the year from Vichy.' I felt he half expected me to leap out of the bus and buy one. There is a great deal of talk, and many jokes about the current English invasion of France.

There was a fair wait at Pont de Dore for a bus or train on to Clermont. I waited with a widow lady who was going on holiday to Austria. The sun was warm. We took it in turn to mind one another's luggage, while we went across to the station loo. Then suddenly a smart white car drove up; a very tanned, elegant couple in dark glasses got out. When I saw them, I immediately felt, that however, round about the route, I was definitely going south. They had a southern 'zing' to them. They assumed we were picnicking and called out *'bon appétit'*. On discovering we were eating nothing, they were horrified, and apologised profusely for the lack of any bar in the small station. The woman drove off again and returned several minutes later with bright green apples and some chocolate biscuits, wrapped in foil. 'I hope you don't feel it's charity,' she said smiling 'but, *c'est l'heure de déjeuner. Bon appétit.*'

During a two hour wait at Clermont I browsed in the university bookshop. I couldn't face dashing off to gather up any more ecclesiastical experiences. Print on paper. What a miracle; all these thoughts and ideas and images, condensed into small, dark marks on a white surface. I found the Editions de Minuit and Samuel Becketts's *Premier Amour*. It was perfect pocket size.

The experience of La Chaise-Dieu had made me uncertain of my route. I planned simply to take a bus south and just stop somewhere on the way. I bought a ticket to Issoire, but on arrival, the impact of the military academy and modern town, didn't seem promising. I felt like a dog sniffing the air. I had to get the right message on the wind. I nearly plumped for Les Jumeaux. It did entice, with its sleepy calm, but there was no station. Then we arrived at a wide street of large plane trees. It was Brioude. From the bus the vibes felt good. I got out full of eager anticipation once again. I knew nothing of Brioude except that something Romanesque was there. It was drizzling fairly consistently as I followed the signs to *centre ville*. A woman hurrying past, offered me some protection under her umbrella. I asked her if she knew anywhere cheap to stay. 'And a meal?' she asked. 'The only place at this time of the year, would be Hotel du Centre.' Grateful for her advice, I took the relevant turnings to find myself beside a battered, and much put together Romanesque church, the basilica of Saint Julien. In the dark porch, in a high niche, there was a statue of a very exhausted, seated Saint James. The distinctive shell was there on the wide brim of his hat, his eyes had a blind stare. His hands had both been crudely chopped off, so it was hard to guess why he was holding out his arms. The most engaging detail were his overgrown toenails. On the wall beside him, I read, that long before the fame of Compostela, there had been a constant flow of pilgrims to Brioude, to the bones of Saint Julian, martyr. The Romanesque basilica had been built on the site of the first oratory, in response to the great crowds of pilgrims.

I was thrilled to find myself, quite unexpectedly in an historic place of pilgrimage. Inside the church I could hear doors being closed and bolted. But the door at Saint James's porch was still open. I went inside for one brief second of amazement and joy at the interior. A fierce old lady, very bent and walking with a stick, a limp crocheted hat coming down like a helmet over her eyes, came towards me. She waved furiously at me to go away. 'It's closed. It's closed,' she said, crashing the doors together. But I had just glimpsed the wonderful, pre-Roman floor, a varied mosaic of smooth, river bed stones. I discovered later that it was as recently as 1963 that this amazing floor was found by accident, when the flag stones were being pulled up to deal with the damp. It is a vast, eastern, decorative expanse using dark and light stones. There are the rhythms of petals and waves, and geometric patterns. I couldn't wait to return. Those mermaids over Saint Michael's porch would feel really welcomed here. There was such a river feel, a sense of the continuous might of water rendering these stone surfaces so smooth.

Hotel du Centre lived up to its name in more ways than one. It was absolutely in the centre. The bell tower of the basilica was close to my bedroom window, at night, when it was floodlit and the bells chimed the hours, you felt wrapped in the sound. There were not many rooms, most of them were occupied by the family. The hotel was a focal point for local life and family celebrations. That first evening, I ate in the dining-room, with the one regular customer. He had a rough, red face and crumpled, blue overalls. He gathered up each mouthful of food with grim attention, as if he could almost hear the taste of the food. In fury he sent back the meat as 'quite disgusting', Madame took it with great calm, no show of any kind of emotion. I felt it was probably a regular response from him, although I myself found the same dish heavy, stringy and resolutely tasteless. After a bottle of red wine he mellowed considerably, pushed back his cap from his head, and went to join the boys in the bar, where very soon he became the life and soul of the evening. But the edge of his laughter, seemed very near some morose and melancholy spot.

On the other evenings we ate opposite one another in the bar, which was full of young men and the depressing talk of unemployment, which apparently was very bad indeed.

I had heard that mass was at 9.30. I arrived next morning at the basilica in good time but there was no sign of life; no priest nor people, nor guidebooks; nothing. By various enquiries in the street I learnt that daily mass was always, unsurprisingly, said in the warm, winter quarters of a tiny chapel in the presbytery. Things were just finishing when I arrived. There were about fifty people. At the back of the chapel I saw the fierce Madame in her crocheted helmet. She attempted a sniff in some kind of recognition of me. I asked the priest for some literature on the basilica and Saint Julian. He knew nothing of Saint Julian, but he had a guide book. Later I found a paper shop in the town which did sell guidebooks.

I returned to the basilica. Outside, it reminded me of one of those hand-knitted blankets made up of small squares, the kind you find in Oxfam shops, where the variety of wools and colours and tension is so mixed. Some squares are bobbled and shrunk, some loose and sagging, some almost too bright. There is this kind of variety in the stones and decorative patterns of the basilica. The tower has a high, pointed roof, with the distinctive, brightly coloured tiles of Burgundy. The church itself is a 'bungey' mass of yellow, purple and green stones. The clustering chapels of the ambulatory crowd in on one another; they made me think of beehive huts on the west coast of Ireland.

Brioude has many very old buildings and interesting architectural details. The narrow streets and squares seem to move round and then out from the church itself. The basilica is the unmistakable centre.

From the guide book I learnt that Saint Julian, with his friend Ferroel, were both Roman soldiers, garrisoned at Vienne. As a Christian Julian was forced to flee, however he was captured and, at once, decapitated. A body was later found with the head of another. It was presumed to be the body of Ferroel, with the head of Julian. The death of Julian and Ferroel was in about 304. The body of Julian was entombed, and very soon prayers for his intercession were answered. A Spanish widow, whose husband was captured, prayed to the young martyr for his safe return. Eventually her husband was returned to her, and increased pressure was brought to bear on the Church, by the local Christians, for some recognition of Julian. The praying and the pilgrimages began to flourish. The pilgrimage of Saint Julian was the most important one in France long before Compostela. Many saints and popes came to his shrine in Brioude.

There are some striking frescoes in the church and vivid Romanesque capitals; man and beast on the edge of power and mystery. There is also a most unusual and powerful crucifix. It is thought to be fourteenth century. It is Christ Lépreux or Christ de la Bajasse. It was brought to the basilica in 1958 from the hospital in Brioude. Christ as a leper, is covered with sores and wounds from the disease. It is unlike so many depictions of the crucifixion, when Christ's pain seems to be contained within himself; this Christ leans down from the Cross with a great expression of love and tenderness, his mouth is open as if he is speaking with someone, he seems to be gathering up the pain of those who suffer to Himself. The crucifix came from the Léproserie of Bajasse, that was south of Brioude.

I could have stayed for any length of time in the church, but that kind of cold does nudge you on, and also, I wanted to find out more of Saint Julian's life and that early pilgrimage. I had discovered that in every place there is a local expert, usual a passionate and personal historian, fired by love as much as anything else. In Brioude I found out, via the lacemaking classes, (there were small boys as well as girls) that the Pommiers were the experts. Madame Rose Pommier, I was told, was the person I must meet.

In this whole region, river is the life force and salmon is king. Very recently on the outskirts of Brioude, the house of the salmon has been built, to honour and extol the extraordinary and dramatic life of this majestic fish. Rose Pommier works there, but she was delighted to arrange a meeting with me in the basilica. We met in the afternoon. She was a very thin, striking person, with deep-set, dark eyes and a bewitching intensity on her subject. She told me that there was a fountain three miles or so out of Brioude, where legend believes Julian was decapitated by his pursuers; immediately his head fell on the ground, a miraculous spring started up from that spot. The fountain, had for hundreds of years been the major source of pilgrimage. I must definitely go out there. Rose also told me of the Chapter of Brioude, once a force as strong as Cluny, but earlier. It was made up of canons, who were simply local individuals from powerful, landed families, not men of religion. Originally they were formed to guard the bones of the saint, but they became ultimately, after many centuries, simply a source of great political power and wealth. Madame Pommier took me later to the public library which is housed in an ancient building, that belonged to the canons. On the ceiling there, on the thick wooden beams, and in between them, there are raised cut-outs in wood, of various coats of arms; an extraordinary run of centaurs, chimeras, griffins, deer and dogs; some duel, some race, all are coloured. For any heraldic enthusiast it is well worth a visit.

While we were standing together at the back of the basilica, there was suddenly a tremendous gust of wings. Sparrows and pigeons were continually flying around, but this gust of bird was mighty and different. We looked up, and there, high above the narthex was the unmistakable, compelling face of a barn owl. Again and again it flew and paused, frantically crashing its white body with terrible hopelessness against the dusty windows. Every so often it would fly the whole length of the church, only to soar up again into another barrier of light. I cannot describe how unbearable it was to follow the flight of that bird, knowing that we were quite incapable to give it its freedom. There were holes and spaces, if only it would see them. Each time it failed, the pause and the stillness became longer, and the fearful despair of the bird felt greater.

We left for the library. We couldn't bear to be there. Later, the whole experience haunted me. The gaze of that particular bird is so involving. I suddenly thought, what if God witnesses in every man a divine spark, which flies within us blindly, like that bird, crashing in terror, punched and pounded from wall to wall, blinded by obstacles and dust, and yet, God knows, that there is a way for natural freedom and ascending flight. What an extraordinary pain that witness would be.

Thursday was market day, as it has always been for as long as anyone can remember. The market stalls are grouped round the church like children at a fireside. In the cool of the main porch, a local, young farmer displayed delicious cheese. There were lilies, cherries, live fowl, bread, apples and eggs. There were hard, tired, waiting faces; treated children running riot, and the men crowded into the bars.

That afternoon, armed with cherries and bread and cheese, I walked out into the country, drawn by the smells of cattle in the buildings at the edge of the town, and the sound of goat bells beyond them, in rich meadows full of flowers. I thought I might find the fountain by the end of the afternoon. It was hot, almost summer heat. I love the way the rise of the heat, comes together with the mounting, midday stillness, when even dogs and birds seem gathered into the pause. No sound; no cars or farm machinery. Then gradually, that still time, begins like a cat, to unwind itself. It undoes, stretching out into the shape of renewed activity; the ordinary coming and going, heaving and carting, cutting and mowing, all over again.

Eventually I came to the main road. Ugly industrial buildings, modern housing and large garages. There was a woman waiting to cross the road. I asked her about the fountain. I was very near, she said. She told me to look out for this large, plain house, and then to walk down into the overgrown grounds. Apparently the house was let out into holiday flats. I found it easily. There was no one about, no sign of life except some clothes on a line. I followed a beaten track in the long grass, it led directly to a stone canopy, built over the spring; a dark pool of clear water, which trickled out into a small stream. Two flat stones bridged the stream. I walked over the stones, and sat on the grass, with my feet in the water. I drank from my hands, the water was delicious and cool; a bit Badoit. My only companions were frogs and newts and butterflies, with a blue dragonfly now and again. I thought of those hundreds of pilgrim feet that must have been here before mine. I thought of the noise and bustle, the songs and prayers, the priests and blessings. Now there was nothing. The woman on the road told me that there used to be a lady who regularly cut the grass and brought flowers, but recently she had died. I wondered about that definite track in the grass; maybe people still came. Then suddenly there was a shriek, two boys on bikes came hurtling towards me. 'Look out, look out, there's a pilgrim,' they yelled, just managing to miss me. Obviously they had made the track, racing downhill, and over the flat stones, and then up the other side. But at least they had said 'pilgrim', which showed some recognition of Saint Julian.

Taking a place slowly is a great privilege. I could wander in and out of the basilica at all times of the day; drawing, mooching, just being there. But Sunday took me by surprise. The weather was awful, a continuous downpour. Everything seemed to be closed, except for the most expensive hotels, well away from the town centre. Every surface was soaked, there seemed to be nowhere to shelter. Back at Hotel du Centre the bar was closed, but a riot of youth, filled the room beside mine. Madame's son and friends I think; nothing but the throb of loud music and the smell of cigarettes.

I kept telling myself that this was a time of challenge. How pathetic it would be to let such small things get to one. I was planning to leave the next morning. I decided to make my last visit to the basilica. The notice said it closed at 6.30, it was then 5.45. I went in and began to draw, when suddenly, the now familiar figure of the fierce old lady, with her crocheted helmet, came beetling towards me.

'Out. Out. Out,' she yelled, irritated beyond belief that I was there again. 'But it says closed at 6.30,' I murmured, 'That's not the point,' she said hysterically, banging those lovely river stones with her stick. 'I'm over eighty ... over eighty. I don't get paid.' Later, I saw her making her way in the pouring rain. Probably her duties, and her fury with them, kept her alive.

The previous evening I had discovered a small pizza restaurant. It was very quiet and inexpensive. To my surprise it opened at 7.30. I went down there armed with books and pencils. My single table faced the glass door out on to the wet street. It was no longer raining, just gurgling and dripping from the gutters.

In some way, the image of that captured barn owl had gone into a deep, questioning space in my mind, that came curiously near to fear and panic. Suddenly meaning, and the pursuit of meaning, became a black, stale dark. This cold, wet, empty, silent Sunday, felt like a truthful cul-de-sac into which I had purposely led myself, leaving Mark and the children, and all the warmth and vitality that went with them ... and for what? My journey had felt like an impulse for search and discovery, now it seemed like a bitter burial. A return to dead space.

I had ordered a salad. I began to read and was enjoying what I read. Suddenly I heard footsteps in the street outside, and a whistle. I looked up. I knew they were Mark's footsteps, and the whistle was his. He always does it when he comes home. The children imitate it, they try to catch me out, but they never succeed. I looked up and there in the doorway I saw Mark, so distinctly. The white jacket, the blue shirt, the worn, but polished shoes. He was smiling so much. He was saying ... 'How are you getting on ...? I want to know.' I suddenly realised I was crying, and the girl was holding out to me the salad I had ordered. It was so vivid; such a presence. But it dispelled the dark. I felt calm and certain again. It was almost as if we had spent the evening alone together.

8
Nîmes. Le Lion de Juda

'To live within bike-shot of Nîmes and with the Saintes Maries as
my summer resort, seems heaven to me, mistral and all.'
LAWRENCE DURRELL

ONCE AGAIN, getting up and going on; a wonderful sense of
freedom. It was a bright, clear morning when I set out from
Brioude towards the station. A glimpse of cows in their stalls
munching lucerne, behind me the ragged height of the basilica. This
time I was really going south. It was thrilling to have the word
Nîmes on my ticket. Bulls, lemons, heat and antiquity. As always
the great pleasure and calm of getting on to a French train. People
reading, knitting and sleeping; the odd remains of picnics, but
òverall, such a civilised, respecting silence.

The tops of the trees were bushy slopes, no longer pines, there
were masses of buttercups, purple orchids, white narcissus; wild iris
in the long grass; bright gorse everywhere. We were in deep valleys;
thrift, forget-me-not, star of Bethlehem, were beside the racing
streams; occasional red roofs against the brilliant green of fresh
leaves. Great, ham-juts of rock, the water clear, not deep, just
constant movement over smooth, river bed stones.

I thought what a perfect dialogue it was; two energies, one
dormant, one released; a counterpoint in perfect accord. The comp-
lement of extremes. Harmony, within intense variety seems to be
the natural order. I remembered the Franciscan priest, John Pick-
ering, at Taizé, saying that he felt it wasn't simply due to heresy
etc., that the Church had so many divisions, but more on account
of the local inclination of different people in different climates, from
different origins, who naturally felt the need to express themselves

within their rites and liturgies, according to their own feel of language and culture.

Richard Burton in his marvellous hoard of thought and language, *The Anatomy of Melancholy*, quotes the orator Symmachus. 'To procure a general toleration, he (Symmachus) used this argument: Because God is immense and infinite, and His nature cannot perfectly be known, it is convenient he should be as diversely worshipped as every man shall perceive or understand.'

La Bastide, a dull, grey place but later the first poppies. At Alès a mother and her daughter joined me. The daughter was teaching English in Marseilles, she hoped to write. We spoke of Ben Jelhoun and his recent novel – *La Nuit Sacrée*. I told them my daughter Sophie had recently been in Alès. I suppose they asked me about my travels. I don't remember, but to my surprise, when we arrived at Nîmes, and I began gathering up my staff and baggage, I felt a tap on my shoulder. A woman of about my own age said, 'I have been listening to your conversation. I live in Nîmes. I have a car. I'm going to take you somewhere.' Delighted and greatly intrigued, I followed her.

We walked a little way from the station to her car. It was a smart blue saloon, I think it was a Peugeot. I remarked what a splendid vehicle it was. 'It is my son's,' she said, 'he died in February, a pot-holing accident.' We got into the car and she told me something of her circumstances. Her name was Libertad. She was Spanish by birth. Her father had been an anarchist. He was forced to flee to France just before she was born. She had lived all her life in Provence. She had four other children, no husband and a very demanding job in the Social Services. Referring to her son she said, 'Against so many people's problems, it is small, but he was such a friend. I miss him very much.'

We came to a high wall in a quiet street. Libertad stopped the car. She told me that the Christian faith meant a great deal to her. It was such a fleeting encounter. But I felt instantly drawn to her, she was intelligent, sensitive and strong. I promised that I would light a candle for her when I got to Compostela. I felt so empty-handed. It was all I had to offer, that promise of a definite remembering.

I found myself outside a high wooden door. A brass plate said something about the archdiocese. There were no other clues. Libertad had told me nothing. I rang the bell. A young man answered the door. He wore brown leather sandals, brown trousers and a white shirt. A simple wooden cross hung very positively round his neck. I began a feeble preamble about looking for accommodation in connection with my journey. He seemed to pause, 'Are you on your way to Compostela?' 'Yes ... in the end,' After further hesitation he asked me to come inside. 'We are just about to have mass, would you like to join us?' 'Certainly.' I was just dumping the baggage, when a bell rang and through the open door I saw this wide cloister, and beyond it a garden with palm trees and flowers. Between the pillars there was a mass of pink geraniums in stone sinks. Then there was the sound of skirts and feet, and several sisters, dressed in long, white habits hurried past. The astounding thing was their youth, and a definite quality of particular confidence. I was very intrigued. There was a large icon of the Madonna outside the chapel. In front of it, on the floor, there was a round, copper vessel filled with sand; in it there were several lighted candles. The door handle to the chapel was a smooth, wooden fish. I knew something different and unusual was going on in these Nîmes cloisters.

The impact of the chapel was extraordinary. Its shape, and basic architectural feel was very Catholic. There was a large space cleared of pews before the altar, and there, on Turkish rugs, this small, extremely youthful community were bowed in prayer, as one might see in a mosque. The altar was a mass of red flowers and lighted candles, unusually abundant for a weekday, evening mass. Below the altar, at either side of the steps there were two icons; one of Christ and one of the Madonna and Child. The icons leant on high lecterns, that were hung with red damask; surrounding them was a mass of white flowers. Some of the community wore long, brown skirts and white shirts. I presumed it was the professed, who wore the full habit. The same rule seemed to apply to the men. Those not in the full habit wore brown trousers and a white shirt. It felt as if many different strands of worship were being pulled together; Eastern, Orthodox and Catholic. I noticed high on the wooden panelling Saint Seraphim (he who stood on the stone for three years) and beside him the Curé d'Ars; that seemed an unusual combination. Suddenly there was a whoosh of skirt and a very tall Sister came forward into the centre of the bowed community. She bowed, she stood. They all stood. She was unmistakably the major authority. She was dark, very, very tall, extremely beautiful and commanding.

The singing during the mass was frequently in four parts,

occasionally there were marvellous strong chords as in the alleluias. The whole feeling was lyrical, and extremely celebratory. I had been thinking vaguely of bulls, lavender, garlic, and the words of Lawrence Durrell. It was as if I had suddenly been plucked up off the street and put down, without warning, in the centre of something unusually intense, of which I had no previous experience. I tried to get my bearings. Just before the words of consecration, a young girl of about twelve or thirteen came into the chapel. She sauntered up and knelt down beside one of the bowed, professed nuns. With a very cursory acknowledgement of what was going on, she started to whisper '*Maman, Maman*' quite clearly. After asking some question, which received a negative answer, she persisted, with a stream of Why? Why? Why not? It was a clear, mother-daughter relationship. I was utterly mystified. The kiss of peace was a very, flowing, loving, kind of dance; one to the other, up and down the Turkish carpets. Tremendous eye contact. I found myself saying lamely '*Merci*' which wasn't the right response at all.

After the mass, there was an obvious discussion about the problem of what to do with this unexpected pilgrim. Eventually Sister Bénédicte, fully professed and probably in her twenties, came forward to me and asked if I would like to stay. Yes please. I felt quite tired after four hours on the train, and I was full of questions.

Sister Bénédicte heaved my rucksack up on to her back and smiling, carried on down the cloister, indicating for me to follow her. The body language here was noticeably normal, easy and free; no processing, no downcast eyes. Everyone seemed full of confidence, there was a kind of unstated exhuberance. We passed a notice which said, 'Silence is Prayer.' I followed Sister Bénédicte up a flight of stone steps, through some double doors into a wide corridor. Everything was bright and spotless; plenty of blue and white. There was the feeling of celebrating enclosure, rather than creeping in under its grey silence. Saint Agnès was occupied. We went into Saint Tibault. It was a pretty, simple room; a bed, a basin, a wooden table, pale green shutters and a Laura Ashley-type wallpaper; small blue flowers on an ochre ground.

Sister Bénédicte sat down on the bed, she was very open, but at the same time very contained. I began asking questions. Yes, some of the Community were married. There were monks and nuns and couples, the vows were the same for all. (I don't know if that meant celibacy all round, or not.) No vow of stability, they went from community to community to assist each other. For instance each community must have a resident musician. They were a contemplative order. Le Lion de Juda et de l'Agneau Immolé. The order was founded in France in 1973 by Brother Ephraim and his wife Jo. There are houses in Jerusalem, Rome, Casablanca, Zaire, Germany, and many other houses in France. It was a charismatic foundation, but completely within, and strongly part of the Catholic Church. This fine building in Nîmes belonged to the archdiocese. The Community were here at the invitation of the archbishop. Brother Ephraim felt reconciliation with Israel to be important. The Church must recognise its Judaic roots. Many of the chants and music were written by Brother Ephraim, by the inspiration of the Holy Spirit.

Some of the Community go out and work in the parish, according to its needs. But silence and liturgical prayer are the centre of our life. Christ will come again. Prayer is our vocation, a fervent prayer. We must reawaken the Church. We want a Church with saints. We live simply, but simplicity and poverty can be beautiful.

Eventually Sister Bénédicte left me. She said there would be supper for me in the dining room. Compline would be later. I would get a call for mass at 6.45 in the morning.

Certainly everything was very beautiful. There was no feeling of a cut-off cloister; more a kind of magical sanctuary. A living demonstration of practical, passionate prayer. I felt peculiarly inadequate to absorb any of it. The Nîmes I had been anticipating seemed not to exist. Outside the window of my room, there was a flourishing fig tree. There were lizards on the stone walls and many birds. Across the street there were mostly modern houses, but there was this high fragment of old wall, just left standing, unattached, almost without purpose. It was made up of many types and textures of stone; chipped flint, and old brick. It seemed to proclaim the significance of random, chaotic fragments, becoming a single, beautiful unit. That wall, was in itself, a Parable of Reconciliation. This Community was utterly different to Taizé, but what both places had in common, so it seemed to me, was a sense of rebirth. Liturgical reinvention, but all from within the orbit of that tattered robe. Wisdom, I suppose is indestructible; from it, regenerative reflection must be endless.

The dining-room was very large indeed and very empty. There

was one place laid. A brown pitcher of water, a basket of bread, a clean napkin, a bowl of salad, a bowl of cherries and a large, unopened litre bottle of red wine and a vase of fresh flowers. I felt extremely nervous. A hatch window opened and a smiling Sister wished me, '*Bon appetit*,' she added that her very special ratatouille de Nîmes would not be long. At that moment Giselle, who had been at mass, came in and sat beside me. She had many Irish friends, and she spoke good English. She lived in Nîmes but frequently visited the Community. I was interested to hear that Giselle also felt nervous. Should we open the wine? Of course, that's why they put it there. I could hear the firm voice of my spouse. We opened the wine, and drank and gossiped until compline.

Giselle told me that the very tall Sister was indeed the authority, known as the *Bergère*. The *Bergère* was voted for by the Community for a period of four years. Giselle was extremely nervous of Sister Geneviève, she couldn't say exactly why, it was just that she was such an all-perceiving presence. 'Wait for vespers,' Giselle said, 'you will get goose pimples. Sister Geneviève will speak then by the power of the Holy Spirit.' Goose pimples were a constant feature of Giselle's ardent life of pilgrimage, to various Holy Places. She was cheerful and kind and said we must get together, but would I stay? I said I hadn't a clue. They may allow you to eat with the Community. Giselles's eyes sparkled. Members of their own families stay, and people on retreat. It will all depend on Sister Geneviève.

I was invited to join the Community. My odd arrival via Libertad, was deemed to be 'of the Holy Spirit'.

As at the Russian Orthodox monastery at Bussy, the sheer quality of everything was beautiful and compelling; music, food and flowers. Breakfast was informal; there was no silence. The various children of the couples were about to set off for school. Everyone dipped bread into bowls of hot chocolate or coffee and then scooped up delicious home-made jam and butter. The priest was a resident member of the Community. He was rather a wry character, very much at one with the rest: He was treated without any hint of dignity or deference on account of his priesthood. Washing up, clearing and laying tables, was done equally, by one and all. Once again, as at Bussy, there were wonderful full-length, gathered aprons. The presence of Sister Geneviève was very much around. There was considerable respect for her. She missed nothing, but she remained aloof, as if strung by some chord to another place; she never seemed to touch down. Lunch was much more formal; sung grace, silence and readings. But the silence became the sound of birds, loud and cheeky in the cloister garden.

Vespers was, as Giselle predicted, fairly goose pimply.

Consistently the atmosphere in the chapel was intense, frequently the blessed sacrament was exposed. The chapel was seldom empty. All the liturgy combined periods of silent, bowed meditation, with sudden movement; standing with outstretched arms, and singing with tremendous, polyphonic praise: antiphons, psalms, and responses. It made me think of frogs and lizards; that sudden pounce and movement, followed by almost uncanny stillness.

Towards the middle of vespers, Sister Geneviève takes the bible from the lectern, and with her eyes closed, and the bible pressed against her forehead, she slowly circles the altar while the singing continues. Eventually she is standing in the centre, below the altar, facing the congregation. She lowers the bible, holding it against herself, and with her eyes open she speaks. She had a very educated voice, it was soft and clear, but the timbre was fairly high. She spoke for between thirty and forty minutes in a manner that it is hard not to describe as trance. The gist of the message was always fervent, and fairly repetitive. Seek Christ. Ask Christ. Come to Christ. Christ is waiting. Christ will come. We must ask and praise.

There was definitely the feeling of a 'raising agent' around, thus, I suppose the goose pimples. But in some way the liturgical structure, and the very professional singing, kept things contained; within some sort of refining control. Certainly, those communities, where a regular, shared prayer is fundamental to the structure of the day, are utterly different from communities without that dimension. I felt engaged by it all in one way, but very reticent in another. Increasingly, I felt open to the various tides, but unable to respond to them with any feeling of certainty.

There is something seductive about days of silence, interrupted by bells and Offices and simple, delicious food. I realised that from the point of view of Sister Geneviève, I could stay as long as I liked.

Giselle insisted on an afternoon sight-seeing in Nîmes, but there just happened to be a freak heat wave. It completely stunned me. We reeled towards the Arena. All I could think of was stillness, and shade. Preparations were in full swing for the Nîmes Feria, a tasteless binge by local accounts, certainly the posters were a gory, graphic run of blood, so unlike Feria posters in Spain.

I had forgotten how intimate the Arena feels, and how lozenge-shaped it is. Giselle was sure there was a chapel, somewhere in the dark under those staggering arches and huge stones. We picked our way over cables and ladders, eventually finding a stack of broken tables and a filthy, velvet curtain. Behind the curtain, in musty darkness, there was a small, severely chipped Madonna. We presumed this to be the chapel.

The street dust, and the thick, still, suffocating heat seemed like a club at your head. Up the steps to the Maison Carrée. Inside nothing; just rolled canvas on the floor, a few students smoking, and the famous, perforated, bronze head. Giselle went off in search of tourist information. I sat down gratefully on the cool steps, among piles of powdered, dry bird shit. On either side of the entrance, were two vast terra cotta urns. A large PISS was written on one, and FUCK on the other. I closed my eyes, and dreamt of returning to those cool cloisters.

Fervour and certainty, interior discipline, one hundred percent commitment to an ideal, these are powerful forces. If you are an outsider, it is easy to feel like some sloth, meandering from place to place, grazing, as it were, the Long Acre, without seeking any admittance to the proclaimed places of purpose.

Suddenly I felt the need to be off and on my way. I left rather hastily. There was no charge. A contribution if you like, but no one handles money; leave the cheque blank, no payee.

In the bustle of Nîmes station I found myself waiting beside Paulette. Without any prompting, she reeled off the saga of her daughter's madness. She wept frequently. She had had to have her daughter committed to an asylum. She was out now, eating a little, but her marriage was over. Her children shunned her, but she did have this job in a chocolate factory. Paulette still collected her washing and her coldness. Was there any hope? Could she believe that Ginette would ever be better? I felt back in the real world, listening to Paulette's vigorous monologue; the whole bric-a-brac of vivid life, such a torrent of experiences, including robbery, faith, her husband's cooking, and the dire descriptions of Ginette's depression and life of considerable squalor.

But Paulette laughed almost as much as she cried. Her face and hands reflected a hard life. We agreed that, of course, there was hope. There was always another day, another season, fresh planting and a further harvest. When the train came we found we could travel for a little while together. At Montpellier I left the train with some of Paulette's cake, three kisses, and much smiling and waving. Once again all I had to offer was a candle for Ginette at Compostela.

Montpellier is really south. I was to make my way from friends in Perols to les Saintes-Maries-de-la-Mer in the Carmargue. I think that my longing to witness the great Gipsy Pilgrimage at the end of May had been central to the whole idea of setting out. The very word Carmargue; a haunting, flat sound; images of salt water, wind, and those indigenous creatures, whose characteristics depend on the unique diet of the delta. Black bull, white horse, flamingoes and gipsies. What a blast of mythic image, just in those few words. Travelling people; once in wagons, now in large cars pulling caravans; from Portugal, Spain, France, Yugoslavia, Italy, Hungary and sometimes Ireland, they gather in this small fishing village for the great festival of their patron saint, Sainte Sara, and the two Marys. Mary Jacob and Mary Salome mother of James the apostle. Santiago of Compostela. Santiago means Saint James.

From Montpellier I knew I could get a bus to Pérols. I had thought Montpellier would be grand, laid back, and beautiful. It was all these things, but on such a scale. So effortlessly chic; fountains, squares, boulevards and gardens, on and on and on. Colourful street artists, entertaining a café society that seemed barely to notice them. The ease and style was for everyone, even mongrel dogs. In a complete daze I wandered about, tantalised and thrilled by every turning. It was the effortlessness of it all. Walking pedigree poodles, or sitting at cane tables, or eating expensive and exotic ice-creams, there was the feeling that it could not possibly be otherwise. I was riveted.

I had walked with all the baggage for about two hours, before I remembered that I must find somewhere to stay the night. All beds here would probably be prohibitively expensive. I was once more in the Rue de la Loge, which opens out into a large market. I suddenly felt my back would disintergrate, and yet I supposed I would have to go a fair distance to find anywhere. Resisting the temptation to thread my way in and out of the market stalls, I turned into a very narrow, street, the Rue de la Petite Loge. Almost immediately I noticed this girl, with flaming gold hair, kneeling at a step, tying up a bag of rubbish. I asked her if she could advise me in which direction to walk to find a cheap lodging. 'Well, come up and share lunch with us first,' she said.

She was Fabienne. She was as dynamic and inspired as her hair. 'We're practising some music first, if you don't mind.' I followed Fabienne up five flights of a dark, circular, turret stairway. She had a tiny apartment of two rooms. It was suddenly quiet, unless you put your head out of the window. Fabienne, who plays the cello as well as hang-gliding and being an architectural engineer, had recently met some musicians; Denise, who was English and her Polish husband. They were trained at Dartington and Cambridge but were finding it hard to get teaching work, because of very un-E.E.C. bureaucratic difficulties. They were planning to busk with Fabienne, this was the practice. While they repeated the Loeillet Sonata, I returned down the dark turret steps, to the market, to get cherries, pâté and cheese to add to the supplies.

I spent three nights on Fabienne's floor. From the tiny apartment there were two keys, one for the share of two footprints, and the other for the douche, which was several stone corridors further on. There was piping-hot water and a romantic view of the stars. Fabienne asked if I would join her and some friends to queue that night for tickets at the Opera House for Verdi's *Sicilian Vespers*.

The Opera House is like some vast, overgrown Pollocks Theatre; faded grandeur, full of romantic resilience; sweeps of stone and marble: balustrades and chandeliers, gilt and plush velvet. The music was thrilling. the audience wildly enthusiastic. And still after midnight, the fountains played, and the laid-back people thronged the boulevards.

From Fabienne's apartment night never seemed to be silence, simply the stars in the sky. From 5.00 in the morning the market was being prepared; by 2.30 in the afternoon it was all dismantled; then, amazing cleaning machines, like small tractors with huge brooms, sluiced and swept the marble surface. By 3 p.m. the place was a mass of tables and chairs, aperitifs and coffee, cigarettes and languid conversations; pauses and glances, with intermittent exchanges of gossip, argument and philosophy, ending with that small, shoulder shrug and a signal to the waiter. I could have watched for hours this subtle, peacock parade, going on everywhere, but I knew I must go and find the bones of Saint Roch. His statue usually portrayed a rather camp, flamboyant figure, lifting his skirts to show a wounded thigh. There was always a large, hound dog leaning mournfully up against him with some morsel in his mouth. I longed to know the story.

Finally I found the church of Saint Roch, who is the patron saint of Montpellier. It was a dirty, dismal place. There was a magnificent white marble statue of the saint and the usual plaques acknowledging favours. There was a litany to Saint Roch, which merited various Indulgences if prayed properly, but nowhere could I find anything about the saint himself.

Then a man came into the church from the sacristy. He was bearded; he wore black jeans and a black vest. He had the pigmentation and general demeanour of one who had become a *coup de rouge*. I asked him if there was any pamphlet or information on Saint Roch. He paused, staring me fiercely in the eye. 'Could I wait awhile?' I waited for nearly twenty minutes. During that time a very well-dressed, elderly man came and sat down at the back of the church. His hands were fine, the skin, oyster pale; through his long, thin fingers, he passed beautifully carved, wooden, rosary beads. His flowing, white hair, the cut of his pale suit, the silver-topped cane that rested against his knee; he might have been a descendant of Saint Roch if wealth and elegance were anything to go by. The bearded man returned with a handful of pamphlets published in 1956. 'How much?' Anything you like, but give it to me, we can trust no one here.' I gave him ten francs. He pocketed it and then said that the miraculous bones of the saint were here in the sacristy. I must go there. Go out past the square to a battered door, which says 'bell not working', knock loudly, you must go there.

I discovered that Saint Roch, rather like Saint Francis, was the son of wealthy parents. His mother, unable to conceive, constantly prayed for a child. In 1350 a child was born to her, here in Montpellier. On the death of his parents, when he was nineteen, Roch distributed his considerable wealth to the poor and set out for Rome. On the way he discovered a village, decimated by the plague. He stayed to tend the sick, eventually becoming sick himself. He retreated to the forest, where a hound, out hunting with his master, discovered him. The hound stole daily from his master's table to take sustenance to the saint. Eventually, the master, intrigued by the dog's regular new habit, followed him and found Roch in the forest. Immediately Roch was brought back to the house, nursed and cared for. On his recovery a hospital was set up at his request. His life was dedicated to caring and tending the sick.

Very soon I found the battered door, with the bell not working. I knocked loudly. A well-dressed, young man came to the door. I asked about the relics. He invited me inside. It was rather dark, then there was this stairway down to a light, open area, rather like a studio or workshop. Suddenly a man and woman came furiously up the steps. My arrival seemed to divert them from a row they were having with each other. The man had long, wild, grey hair, a black shirt, and white braces that held up very baggy trousers, the woman had dark greasy, black hair that clung to her scalp, like algae, she had few teeth, and a rather ill-fitting, brown overall. I asked about the bones and relics of Saint Roch. For some reason that only served to increase their fury. They often said exactly the same word in unison, paused, and then repeated a string of abuse, alternating one with the other, as if the whole thing was scripted. 'Of course the relics are here. Of course. Of course we are the sacristans. Of course. But get out, get out. Fuck off.' I was fascinated by their timing; the general air of performance. I only moved when I was about to be hit by flailing arms. The young man, who had opened the door, was watching with considerable amusement. 'I'm a student. I only live here. They are the sacristans. They're always like this, a bit different, don't worry.'

It was interesting that the bones of such an elegant saint, should be so guarded in such an elegant city. I left, passing designer clothes, a turkish bath, antiques, and many offers of manicure and hairdressing; more squares and more fountains, the screeching sacristans began to feel almost imagined.

Bones, belief, the sculpted images of narrative biblical myth, contemporary cloisters, contemporary fervor and intensity, sometimes they seem like an extravagant, persistent, rather incoherent dream. Then you have to pause, and think into natural sounds, natural forms, natural energies. Maybe sand, dirt, lizard, star, mound, tree, bird or stone, are as much 'my neighbour' as anything else.

Pauses without any particular purpose are real gifts. I stayed several days in Pérols. I minded a house for friends. There were two large shepherd dogs. Rami, named after a famous Carmargue bull, and Doña, a young bitch. There were whoopoes in the garden, they were continually dive-bombed by magpies. The Carmargue was close. That strange, haunting, flat expanse, of salt-moving earth. Its moods and winds, flora and fauna are so particular, like the people, birds and animals. The *gardiens*, cowboys and the *mandiers*, bull farmers, and the many gipsies who live there, coming and going between Narbonne, Montpellier, Nice and Marseilles.

No one knows why the gipsies made the little fishing village of the two Marys their place of pilgrimage. The first accounts of the gipsies entering Provence are in 1427. Perhaps there is something colourful and isolated about the Carmargue which corresponds with their own colourful, strong, but essentially isolated, nomadic life; an isolation forced on them by a history of threat and persecution.

The gipsies are considered definitely to be Eastern in origin, possibly from North India. They allege that they come from 'Little Egypt'. Over hundreds of years they have travelled westwards throughout Europe, but they have never been absorbed by any nation. The similarity to their first ancestors still remains. Their great traditions of music, dancing, horse dealing; craft skills in metal, iron and wood work, remain undiminished despite appalling persecution, suffering and harrassment.

In 1478 Alexander of Moldavia granted them 'freedom of air and soil, freedom to wander about, and free fire and iron for their smithy.' And in Hungary, in 1423, Sigismund, Emperor of Rome, King of Hungary and Bohemia delivered a letter of 'immunity and safe conduct for these travellers'. 'We grant them their supplication, we have vouchsafed unto them our abundant favour, whenever therefore this Voivode Ladislaus and his people Tsigani come to any part of our realm, in any town or village or place, we commit them by these presents to your loyalty. We command you to protect in every way the same Voivode Ladislaus and the Tsigani without hindrance. You should show kindness to them and you should protect them from every trouble and persecution.'

But such good sentiments towards the gipsies never lasted for long. An early edition of the Encyclopaedia Brittanica refers to 'the fury and prejudice by those whose good faith they had abused, whose purses they had lightened and whose barns they had emptied!' and

'A natural terror for their inborn tendency to roam, meant they were instinctively treated as outlaws and felons.'

Consistently their history is terrible. In 1636 at Haddington they were ordered: 'the men to be hanged, the women drowned, and such women as had children to be scourged, and their cheeks burned.'

In 1692 four Estremadura gipsies, caught by the Inquisition in Spain, were charged with cannibalism, and made to own that they had eaten a friar and a pilgrim.

This horrific history of persecution continues to the present times. 500,000 gipsies were exterminated by Hitler. One cannot help, but to draw the conclusion that what Jews and gipsies have in common is a marked divergence from the cultural banner of Christendom, as Christendom saw itself. We are now, so I am frequently being told, 'in a post Christian era'. There are many signs that a new recognition of compassion and tolerance is emerging, as an idea anyway, nevertheless, outsiders seem to remain outsiders. Loss of control and command, as a political idea, seems continually to be read as a negative, but relinquishing control, to allow for creative growth, is an essential part of parenting; and the wild, free-spirited child is often the most interesting.

9

Les Saintes-Maries-de-la-Mer and Saint-Gilles

'Viva les Saintes Maries!
Viva Sainte Sara!'

ARRANGEMENTS HAD been made for me, through friends, to rent a *cabane* in les Saintes Maries for four nights. I was eager to be off, but also a little nervous; people reacted so hysterically to the thought of me being alone, as if it was paramount to walking into a den of thieves. I simply did not believe this would be the case.

The day we were to drive over to les Saintes, it was raining, very muggy, and overcast. The friends I was with had several boats on the Petit Rhône, one needed some attention, it had to be collected from further up the river and sailed down, to be moored by the crane, and then have its engine removed.

The Petit Rhône is wide and very calm. No sign of man, only the sound of birds, the bite of mosquitoes, and the gentle lap of water. High trees bend down with great, full skirts of leaf into the water. There are no rushes, the water runs clear, right up to the branches of the trees; acacia, lime, elder, elm, plane, Russian vine and thick, tall clumps of bamboo. During the whole day, only one boat passed us and only three human habitations were visible. It is hard to believe that the river is navigable from the Mediterranean to Paris, via Lyon. After the rain, there were powerful, strange reflections in

144

the water, as the clouds parted and a watery light filtered through. All through the day we snacked on bread and ham, Pernod and Pastis. At midday we moored under the trees, where there were several loose ropes and a few wooden steps had been dug into the bank. Heavy 'marmite' metal pots hung from the trees, in case you ever felt like cooking over a fire. A friend, who, lived deep into the trees beyond the river, joined us for lunch on the boat. He brought with him two bottles of Côtes du Rhône. We had veal, haricots verts, salad and cheese. The friend apologised for the continual sound of the 'bangers', bird-scaring guns, that went off intermittently to scare the flamingoes from ruining the rice crops. But apparently flamingoes, just like East Anglian pigeons, soon learn that they have nothing to fear. After lunch we made our way back, down river, towards the crane. There were rich pinks in the sky and violet-purple shadows on the water; and always this intense stillness, the feeling often found in a Japanese painting, of a single, small boat, on a large expanse of calm water.

The mooring at the crane was tricky, but perfectly managed. More Pernod while we waited for the engineers. Suddenly I noticed a coif of grey hair and a rather unexpectedly made-up face staring down into the boat. It was Denise, checking up on what was going on. Her husband, Henri, was harbour master at les Saintes. Denise had been at the harbour that morning. She was full of talk of the gipsies' arrival into the village. 'They're coming in all the time,' she said, 'every space is packed with caravans, all the bars and hotels are boarded up.' Denise was invited down into the boat for Pernod, or Pastis. She was horrified to hear that I was going to be in les Saintes alone. As she warmed to her subject it was hard not to feel a twinge of anxiety.

'I'll tell you, listen, listen ... this morning ... it was 9.15 ... 9.15, when I saw this one coming down the street, I knew he was looking out for something ... you have to pay attention then, I noticed this tourist girl, in a mini skirt, not one of them, she was following a little distance behind. Then he went down on to the beach, pulled over this boat, upturned it and there, quick as a flash they were into it and on the job. Skirt up and away, and no precautions, ... No precautions! I waited for ejaculation, ten minutes. I didn't bother after that.' Denise was a vivid raconteur, she continued with more tales of violence from the previous year.

*

When finally we got to les Saintes it was nearly 11 p.m. My *cabane* was in the yard of the stables of the sheriff's house. From here, Carmargue horses are available for trekking. We found the *gardien*, he said that his message was that I could have the house if I liked, it might be more comfortable than the *cabane*. Certainly the house was large, I could have brought half the family. It was the other half of the stables, all on the ground floor. Above, there was an apartment that belonged to the mother of the owner, a highly respected *Carmarguais*. I was assured that under his roof no harm could come to me. The horses had a twenty-four-hour guard.

Before my friends left, we had a pizza together at a little restaurant close by, run by two young Turks. It became home to me for the length of my visit. Piping-hot coffee from dawn and a variety of food until any time up to midnight. The sheriff's house was on the road to Cacharel. Standing there in the yard at midnight, everything was very quiet. All I could see was a rather American sprawl of garages, and white buildings. Beyond the horses' compound there were rows and rows and rows of white caravan roofs. A fat gipsy walked past swigging wine from the bottle, a small, spidery thin child, tagged along behind him.

The sky was strange and threatening. I could hear the horses in the stables. Swallows still darted from roof to telegraph wire. I went in to the large, brown apartment, with its heavy wooden furniture and old, framed photographs of bulls and gipsies, and three fine engravings of Arlesian women in all their finery. I had a choice of three double beds. It was quite a daunting space.

I had no clock of any kind. I was used to being woken by bells and knocks or bustling market and street sounds. Here in the Carmargue, I was woken by the clanging, clippity clop sound of the horses' hooves. The stable floor was close to my bed. The noise of the horses rang out every morning as if they were sounds in my head. Promptly at eight o'clock, the horses were led out from the dark of their stable to stand in the yard. Under a wattle awning, they waited for the tourists, who, mounted, can explore this hypnotic, flat, shifting delta of salt lakes and meres, without disturbing the creatures and plants for whom it is such a rare habitat.

In les Saintes, you feel very much the presence of the delta behind you; you feel remote, in a heartland, that is surrounded by water. The black bull and white horse, with their unique characteristics, seem in some way, as they roam these flatlands, to be the real guardians of it. They are used by man, raised, checked, teased by man, but never possessed; never truly tamed; always respected and loved.

I made my way down the street towards the church, to pay my respects to Sainte Sara, who next day would be feted and processed from the church to the sea. I passed many gipsy families returning to their caravans, weighed down with armfuls of bread and plastic bags crammed with food. They were full of friendliness and the usual greetings. The children were busy buying postcards and sweets, when permitted. The inhabitants of les Saintes seemed less in evidence. Certainly several shops and bars and supermarkets were open. By the sea, in every available space, caravans were packed close together; clothes hung out on temporary washing lines and over walls, any random object; shining metal pots were piled round smouldering fires. There was a tremendous family atmosphere; this was obviously the day for chores and preparation.

The church is simple – a Romanesque church. There is a boat feel about its shape. There are no windows, the only feel of decoration is in the fortifications. The sense is of arches and strength. It was built in the twelfth century and then fortified in fourteenth century. The end is rounded; here the high chapel, like a castle turret, rises above the main body of the building, dove-tailing into a simple bell tower. It is constructed in small, glowing, yellow brick, darkened here and there. It stands very much on its own, harboured, as it were in a wide sweep of pedestrian area, all laid out in yellow stones. Backing off from it are the gift shops, masses of them selling things Provençal and also the particular pieties of the region. Replicas of Sainte Sara and the two Marys and the trident emblem of the Carmargue. A cross, with a heart growing out from an anchor. The Cross is Faith, the Heart, Love, the Anchor, Hope; hope for the peace of a final resting place. Behind the shops, there were a great many bars all preparing to do good business.

I had seen no tourists of any kind. They did arrive later. The locals kept reminding you; beware of your bag; beware of thieving. It was extremely difficult to get into a bank, you had to leave your camera and everything else outside. The main doors at the back of the church were kept closed, except for the processions. The way in, was a very narrow doorway at the side. You step down into this dark, high, belly of space; immediately your eyes are drawn to the arched ceiling and above it, beyond the sanctuary, the little window of the high chapel, where the remains of the two holy women are kept in twin caskets, decorated with the story of their legend.

There is no clutter of statues, no gilded cherubs or baroque organs; no stained glass; it is dark, and simple. There is a niche in one wall, where the two holy women, bareheaded, with tired but peaceful, although pleading expressions, stand in their little blue boat. They will also be processed down to the sea, the day after Sainte Sara. As a man said in one of the bars ... 'Black today, white tomorrow.'

Sainte Sara remains in the crypt, except for her one processional outing. The wide steps down to the crypt are just below the altar. There, in the dark, Sainte Sara is surrounded by lighted candles. On arrival in the village the gipsies immediately visit her, lighting candles to express the offering of their needs and intentions, but most particularly their love, for their own patron saint.

I was just absorbing the dark and peace of it all, when a woman plucked at my arm and whispered ... 'Watch your purse, she'll be after your money.' Then I noticed in the dark, a grey-haired gipsy woman coming towards me. She was old and worn, but strong. Across her stomach, tied very tight, was the flat black apron pocket so many of the women wear. As deep as a tea-towel, it is divided into two pockets at the centre, it would be very hard for any slippery hand to get into it unnoticed. She was just about to speak to me. I said I was sorry, I had no money. Then she put her warm, brown hand on my arm. 'Oh no, not that, not that,' she said. What she wanted was help in understanding the prices of all the different-sized candles. I explained, feeling so ashamed to have misunderstood her. She was from Pau. There were twenty-four in her family. They were on their way to Rome. Her gold teeth glistened in the dark. 'So few places are really beautiful now,' she said. 'It is beautiful here, but not like it was. Fatima is beautiful, but Lourdes, no longer.' I tried to get her to explain 'beautiful'. 'When it is from here,' she said, pointing to her heart. 'When it is from here.'

By now she had gathered up about fifteen of the largest candles into her arms. She then offered me her black purse, which was stuffed with rolls of notes, and asked me to find the correct money for the candles and put it into the box. I did so. She thanked me warmly and went slowly down the aisle towards the crypt, her sheaf of white candles sticking out like bright stems from her rounded arms.

All day, there was a constant stream of people to the crypt. On the opposite side of the church from the two Marys, there is a glass-fronted cabinet, inside there are many small, votive paintings, colourful and very original expressions of gratitude for favours received. What a joy after so many banks of white marble tablets and fat brass hearts.

There is a very large daddy, hauling a limp child from a well. There was one depicting the collapse of a brick wall in Arles, with all lives spared; bricks and babies and shrieking women, but no bodies. There were many bedroom scenes, with usually the sea in the distance. There was a wonderful carriage drama, with a runaway horse. They made me think of the votive paintings at Honfleur, where the Madonna was guiding small vessels through dramatic storms. Then the sound of music outside made me leave the church.

Out in the streets, various musicians were playing guitars, but the more lively virtuosi seemed to remain in the bars. It was not warm. The sky was low; an oppressive, sultry grey. The kind of sky you watch continually.

There was one outstanding musician. He was very fair-skinned. He played on some kind of zither; two brown bear cubs were on chains attached to his ankles. He had a wonderfully deep, very resonant voice. He instantly drew a considerable crowd. Cameras clicked continuously. His songs were Moldavian. He said he was from France, but he had a more Eastern European feel to him. After he had sung two or three songs, he would ask very politely, if the professional photographers (of which there were many) would offer, please, ten francs towards the upkeep of the bears and their parents, who ate so many kilos of raw meat per day. Instantly children, and many delighted, unprofessional photographers, threw their ten franc pieces into the tambourine at his feet. The professional photographers, slung with Leicas and Hasselblads, often with assistants in tow, were extraordinarily patronising. They ostentatiously gave nothing and continued to photograph, with supercilious disregard of what had been said. The singing continued, but the atmosphere became very charged. The singer's gentle bearing and calm, the poignancy of his songs, his complete control, only highlighted the rude greed of these, smooth, designer-clothed, utterly offensive human beings. Somehow their attitude, so keenly and publicly displayed, highlighted a feeling that was definitely there in les Saintes. A feeling that is part of the tormented, banished, persecuted history of the travelling people.

Even the guide book on the Carmargue by Alain Albaric, 1985 begins the section entitled Gipsies with, 'To our eyes (who are we?) the Gipsies appear outlandish in their attire, odd in their behaviour and impenetrable in their language. No other people has awakened such curiosity, fear or malevolence, as they have, since they first made their appearance in Europe.'

The tenor running through the section only exacerbates and perpetuates these dark feelings, born out of endlessly inherited prejudice. To me they were mothers, fathers, grandparents, lovers, babies, toddlers, young people, with areas and feelings in common with all other mothers, fathers, etc., albeit with differences, but those differences cannot exclude the other areas we have in common. There are television presenters, who appear, 'outlandish to me, odd in their behaviour, and impenetrable in their language'!

At two o'clock I made my way back towards the stables. I wanted to be without a camera. I passed colourful spreads of food, and fires; everywhere, random chords sprung and animated the air, plucked from guitars, or struck from fiddle strings. While the men ate, two middle-aged women danced round the fire, waving tea towels above their heads. The smell of frying was mixed with the smell of horse dung. Children ran everywhere, thrown up in the air, caught and teased by tall men with leather boots, large, wide-brimmed hats, flowing hair.

But there were great differences; there were prosperous families, full of panache, confidence and authority and, by contrast, there were thin, taut faces; stiff, bent, unbelievably tired-looking women and worried, shuffling, uncertain men.

Then suddenly there was a clap of thunder, the dark heavy sky seemed about to meet the grey streets with such a weight of rain. I ran. Everyone ran. Heads down, as fast as possible, for any cover. Soapy, grey puddles accumulated so fast. The horses stood tucked up and knowing under their wattle awning. Thankfully I turned the key in the door that led to the large, brown spaces of the sheriff's house. It was 2.30 in the early afternoon, but it was only the beginning.

A monsoon storm continued, unabated for three-and-a-half hours. Great boulders of thunder; brilliant, white banners of lightning, that flooded the sky like a rush of silk. In some way, the dark, trundling rolls of thunder and the white fullness of the lightning seemed to echo the two beasts of the Carmargue; black bull; white horse. I thought of all those meals and fires; the drying clothes; all those excited children penned into cramped caravan spaces, with the tired women and those large, full men. The horses were let loose into a small, sandy corral. The lights failed. All those raucous, celebratory sounds of life that Denise and Henri imagined, were unthinkable now. Relentlessly, the force of the rain battered down onto gravel and tin, tiles and cars, like a throw of spanners. The wind became so strong, I had to close the shutters, otherwise the windows wouldn't hold fast.

It was weird sitting in the dark, listening to the storm, when I had been anticipating golden sands, blue Mediterranean sea. I remember reading Vincent's letters to Theo from les Saintes Maries: he went on about the brilliant blue of sea. There would be nothing now, but saucepan grey. The lights went on again. I longed for coffee, an apple, Evian water, anything. The one comfort were my three calm, female companions in their heavy, dark wooden frames. Young and old, nevertheless, all three shared this sense, they seemed proud and comfortable to be themselves.

This whole region seems in some way to be animated by a female sense. Maybe it is those winds. The gentle virgin wind. The widow's wind, that is the strongest. Maybe it is Sainte Sara and her two elderly female companions. Mary Mother of Jacob and Mary Salome, mother of James.

In the brown dark, I lay on the bed and thought of those women. The ceaseless attack of the raging storm outside made me easily imagine them in their fragile little boat. Legend says, that without a sail, they managed to bob up towards the sands of this delta, remote now as it must have been then.

Both the death of Christ, and the discovery of the empty tomb, were primarily witnessed, so scripture tells us, by the holy women. Mary the mother of Jesus, Mary Magdalene, Mary the mother of James and Mary Jacob. It is thought that the holy women and the apostles remained together in Jerusalem, but that as the Christian community gained strength, their safety was threatened. Legend tells us that they were summarily put to sea by the Jews, in fragile boats, and that Lazarus, Martha, Mary Magdalene and the two Marys, Mary Jacob and Mary Salome, eventually found their way to the shores of Provence. From this moment we have the presence of Sara. But legends vary, some say Sara was the Egyptian servant of the two Marys; others fiercely deny this, saying Sara was a pagan princess living in Provence; she certainly wasn't pushing a broom! There is a capital at Vézelay of Mary Magdalene and a pagan princess, presumably Sara.

The legend says that Sara saw the struggling vessel and ran to the shore and with her long red sash she threw a line to the women and brought them to safety. Lazarus, Martha and Mary Magdalene made their way on to Tarascon and St Maximin, but the two Marys remained by the sea, in the small fishing village which now bears their name, where they were protected, loved and cared for by Sara. Presumably they converted Sara to Christianity.

So from ancient times this trinity of women have been at the heart of the Carmargue, and now in 1990 they are at the heart of this intense, flamboyant pilgrimage.

By 6.30 the storm had lessened, there was no rain, just wind and wet and debris. I made my way back towards the church. Everywhere was a sea of water; the feeling of people, and places alike, was dull, cold, battered and grey. The sea was a gun-metal dark, with great cords of white crashing into the desolate shore.

In the church, far back from the crypt, you could smell the candles and feel their warmth. The metal handrail by the steps into the crypt was almost too hot to hold. In the crypt, a furnace greeted you; a high forest of candles, drooping and bending from heat. On and on the people came past Sainte Sara, lighting more candles; more and more and more. She was completely engulfed in a brilliant white cloak, over layers of blue. Like so many of the black Madonnas, only her head was visible, but she was life-size. Around her neck were gifts, and pinned on her cloak there were tokens and flowers. There was a very quiet, reverent feeling in the crypt, the procession moved slowly, small children looked wide-eyed, as their fathers, often with tears in their eyes, held them up close to the dark face, the bright eyes, the elegant nose.

Just ahead of me, a very large man, wearing a blue denim suit, high boots, flowing, long hair and a deep, leather belt, embraced her. He pressed his huge hands deep into the folds of her robes. Desperately he clung on, leaning his rough, rather unshaven cheek against her smooth, black one. The procession behind him instinctively paused. He found it hard to release her. Then he moved on, but instantly stepped back to her again. With some kind of eager longing he leant his forehead against hers. No one reacted. No one moved. Travelling people respect emotion; whether it is anger or sorrow, it is understood as being a necessary and natural part of human experience. A tall woman with a long, grey plait, placed a large ivory cross over Sainte Sara's head. It hung there, glistening and new in the candlelight. A while later, some lads, purposefully processing towards Sara in the opposite direction of everyone else, fingered the cross, and then looked meaningfully at one another. They began to whisper and take hold of it. Instantly a group of girls came up and furiously pulled them off. One got tugged ignominiously by the ear. They went like lambs, looking full of shame and remorse.

It was eight o'clock when the doors of the church finally closed. It was begining to rain again. There was little sign of life. The elements seemed to have taken complete control of the proceedings.

At the mass the next morning, it was evident how hard the Church tries to both love, welcome and serve the gipsy community, and also to underline the Christianity of the occasion. It was really about witness to Christ's Resurrection, they told the congregation again and again. But it was really about Woman. The wisdom of woman; the wounds and trials of women; the hidden, but accessible strength of woman. The silence of woman, who 'keep pondering all things in their hearts.'

There is a special Bishop of France who is designated to serve the diocese of the travelling people. There were many priests and nuns, whose life-work and commitment was to the travellers. After the mass, the bishop referred to photographers. He begged and pleaded; please, no photographs during the lowering of the relics and the procession. His remarks were greeted with loud cheers from the congregation. 'Let us make this pact,' the bishop went on 'only photograph those whom you have yourselves entertained for a meal.' Hysterical cheers, loud clapping and much arm waving.

I had been warned that in order to get a seat in the church for the lowering of the relics, you must be there by three o'clock. Three o'clock was barely in time. The church was packed but for an hour more the people flooded in. The gipsies, colourfully dressed: flounces, frills, polka dots and flowers. There were many very young expectant mothers, who wore deep, satin sashes below the bulge, accentuating with pride the impending occasion. Black velvet suits, long, flowing moustaches and hair, leather boots and belts and wide-brimmed hats; on and on they streamed into the church, most of the women bearing either candles or babies or both. The tourists were very noticeable, they were slung with cameras and wore loud beach clothes. Many of them having bagged good seats, left loudly in the middle of the service, complaining of the unbearable stuffiness. But from the open doors at the back of the church the crowds pressed in; on and on.

At last the moment was near, all eyes were directed to the window of the high chapel. There, under the dark curve of the roof, the figures of men and boys could clearly be seen fixing the ropes. The small, peaked tin trunks, bolted together, were ready to make their descent. Very slowly the relics were lowered, the ropes had bouquets of flowers tied to them. At each short, careful drop, the congregation called out. *Viva les Saintes Maries … Viva Sainte Sara.* All arms were outstretched towards the relics, many held up lighted candles. Increasingly there was pleading, fervour and longing in their voices. It was as if the people pulled the relics towards themselves, by their repeated cries. *Viva les Saintes Maries … Viva Sainte Sara.* The cut and power in the final 'AH' of 'Sar..AH', was extraordinary. The syllable flew, like some sharp blade into the air, as if to sever the cords and release these hidden benefactoresses to the people. I remember reading Jung, 'in crowds, of particular ceremony, the intellect becomes suspended, we participate without judgement.' Certainly there was great intensity, and to me, the tears that streamed down so many, fine, worn faces seemed completely true and appropriate. The jerk of the cords, the summoning cries, made me think of the moment of giving birth. It felt as if something similar to birth was being witnessed.

As the relics came close the crowds pressed forward; children were held high. There are great blessings for those who first touch the caskets. Once the relics were safely down, resting on an ornate table, there seemed to be a sense of relief; now the celebrations could begin. Sainte Sara in her ice-blue, satin cloak and shimmering crown, waited below the altar, facing down the aisle. Outside, the bearers, and the outriders were in attendance. Sara was carried out from the darkness into the grey stormy light, and slowly the gipsies followed her. Incredible faces passed by, combining age and frailty with such strength; all expressed a deep carthartic emotion.

Soon the procession outside was a happy, singing, ragged mass. I

remembered Corpus Christi processions as a child, when the faithful
followed a scatter of rose-petals. Here the faithful picked their way
through the steaming piles of fresh horse droppings, left from the
four mounted men, who led the procession, flanking Sainte Sara until
they are into the sea itself. On and on we followed the tilting,
crowned figure, until at last, the edge of the water was reached. By
now it was raining. The shoreline was a mass of black umbrellas.
But nothing could deter the sense of release and celebration. The
fiddlers, racing their bows across the strings, were crutch deep in
the stormy water, with the horses and Sainte Sara. Streams of gipsy
women waded out to sea, their wide skirts spreading like floating
flowers, but clinging cold and fast to them when they raced back
again up on to the dark sand. There were crowds and crowds and
crowds, all quite careless of the rain and wind.

That night, out on the road to Cacharel in the Mas du Clarousset,
there is traditionally a marvellous feast. Long tables of between sixty
to a hundred people are weighed down with wine and food and
rose-petals; *tellines* soused in garlic, *anchoïade* sauce over colourful
crudités, huge, grey-green sea snails, with long spikes like some
medieval shield, the feast is the prelude to a night of music and
dancing. The Gipsy Kings, a very fine collection of men, all
immensely individual and distinctive, come to the feast, they are
courted and attended by a variety of local gipsy musicians. The
world famous Manitas de Plata was there, his long white hair and
very pink complexion made him stand out among his more swarthy
companions.

I felt a little paralysed and out of place with the grandees at the
long tables, but I was with friends. It was a strange switch from the
storm, and the relics and procession, to the talk at these tables. I
found that although the local people celebrated the occasion and
loved the fervour of it, few, if any, had actually witnessed the
ceremonies. I was told, 'their emotions aren't real, they're staged;
it's theatrical.' When I spoke of the misery of the storm for all those
families ... I was told, 'Oh but they're used to it.' I found fascination
for them by many, but real human warmth for them from few; some
locals and the management of the Mas were an absolute exception.

The music and dancing was not performance so much as given
and received experience. The young bloods circled round the stars,

strumming and chorusing, as if to rev up the maestros ... to come on, begin, begin. Manitas de Plata demanded considerable attention in order to begin; tables must be moved; spaces altered; still it was not right. But the young men stayed round him, begging him, preening him, teasing him, with their chords and *olé's* and direct, challenging looks. At last, the hips quivered, the arms were raised, the tapping and clapping took him away. At last the voice and the dance.

Manuel, a local gipsy and respected singer from Montpellier, became increasingly saddened as the night wore on and no one asked him to sing. A woman who started to dance, who was not a gipsy, was quietly and firmly restrained by them.

It was nearly six in the morning when we left. A violet, grey-blue sky, frantic bird song, strange blood shadows in the meres and lakes. My friends stayed with me in the sheriff's house for the brief remainder of the dawn.

For the two Marys, the skies had cleared. At last the sea was blue. The same processional route, but this time no umbrellas and many more lobster limbs and staring faces from the restaurant tables.

By the afternoon the two Marys were back in the main aisle of the church, standing in their little blue boat, bedecked with robes and flowers. It was the last chance for the two caskets to be touched and kissed, and for loved objects, handkerchiefs and shawls to be pressed against them. A very thin, young mother came and stood between the two Marys, holding her infant child of eleven days old, close up against the statues. She stared as if in a trance, as if she were taking up some force for her child. The grandmother, in a black shawl and black apron, took her photograph with a Pentax and camera-mounted flash.

Very soon the relics would be taken up once more into their high resting place. There were the same chants. *Viva les Saintes Maries ... Viva Sainte Sara.* But the sound was quieter; a little sorrowful. As the bouquets of flowers reached the high chapel, they were taken off the ropes and thrown down. It was as if these ceremonials made, in some way, womb and tomb as one. It was as if a transitory shaft of joy and celebration only, was allowed; a glimpse of light in order to gain enough strength to return to the travailing dark.

Very soon caravans were on the move. Huge, long cars, seemed to bound and leap round the street corners as if they were animals. Out in the small arena, under a brilliant blue sky, the bulls were teased, and tempted to anger, by young, men dressed from head to foot in white. On foot, a great many of them at the same time, almost a cricket team, they try to cut the cockades off the bulls horns; one bull every ten minutes.

I went back to the sheriff's house to pay Madame Mailhan and pack my things ready for an early start north in the morning. I could hear the caravans leaving; dogs barking; people calling.

My first thoughts of gipsies and their roaming life had been inspired by the poem read to us in front of a nursery fire, of she, 'who left her goose feather bed, with the sheet turned down so bravely O.' She, who went with the Raggle, Taggle Gipsies. Even as a small child you knew why she went. It was to leave the neat, clean, prosaic world. It was to find some way towards the mystery out there, of night, and stars; wild, uncertain feelings that can never be finally named and bounded. Her departure was an act of faith, as all true love must be. An act of trust towards a transforming force.

Next day at the bus stop, there were only tourists. The locals were out in their gardens, walking their dogs, and talking on street corners. The pace of everything was hot and lazy again. I felt eager to be off. Too much diversity, intensity and mystery is exhausting, not to mention all-night feasting. But certainly all the dark talk and hysteria of people warning me of thieves and vagabonds, was ridiculous. Only once had anyone accosted me. A thin woman had rushed up to me outside the church and pinned a medal on me, then asking for money; her scraggy children running round in a staring, applauding chorus. I stopped walking, took my notebook out of my pocket and told her ... you can have a pencil, a notebook and my love; all of that, but nothing else. I have nothing else to give you. She listened, then cackled with laughter, putting her hand to her mouth; then still giggling, she undid the medal.

Months later, the faces of many of the older woman are still vivid and particular to me. Such dignified pain and strength and purpose. It is as if they live in the wound of their history.

*

When the bus arrived I found that the Tourist Office had mis-informed me. It was a round trip, stopping on the way out, but not stopping or taking passengers on the return run. I did then, what I had found more successful than speech on similar occasions. I stayed standing beside the driver looking disconsolate. After a suitable pause, he said ... 'Oh all right, get in.' So we circled the empty squares of les Saintes Maries and then made our way north, to Saint-Gilles.

The Carmargue is unique and mysterious. People say that after many years spent there it still retains its secrets. For a few days it is perplexing. It is somehow bittersweet. It beckons and dismisses. Its route seems to be from earth to sky rather than overland. As we hurtled along, images of the last few days kept springing to my mind.

In the small, cheerful arena, under the one and only blue sky, the lolling, grey-brown, swollen tongue of the bull, desperately feeling for some damp respite in the bright yellow sand. On my last evening I had had supper with the two young Turks, who ran the small restaurant beside the sheriff's house. After much talk of ambitions, politics, the shifting sands of Europe, the personality of Mrs That-cher, one of them had said, 'Of course in U.K., you haven't got a democracy yet, have you?'

Flat land and this wide, high sky. The brilliant green of the rice; birds flying low. The skyline was hardly ever broken, just occasionally there were small groups of umbrella pines.

Saint-Gilles would put me back on one of the great routes to Compostela. To Santiago. To Saint James. What an odd impulse journeying is. The external map you feel impelled to draw, with concrete, bodily movements, from place to place; maybe it is an attempt to transcend a little, the illusion of centrality, that tends to grow about your own time, and place and personality. A journey may feel as if it sweeps towards the skyline, but the sound it makes is always within yourself. The seat of transformation is within.

We crossed the river, and the bus drew up in a broad, shady street. I felt as if I was back in mainland France, from some unattached outpost. The cafés were crowded, the pavements full of people. I made my way up the hill to the old quarter and the abbey church which is famous as a place of pilgrimage; famous for its titular saint,

Saint Giles. It is also renowned for the murder, on the abbey steps, of the Papal Legate in 1208, whose death (some say he got as far as the banks of the river) gave the green light for the Crusade against the Albigensians.

In front of the abbey church, it was very quiet, no bar, a handful of small shops, an ice cream kiosk. Battered, restored and altered, what remains of the church is warm and simple, what is remarkable and quite breathtaking are the stone carvings. Three doors, three tympanum arches, columns and curves and between them spectacular full-length figures of saints and apostles. Saint Michael, shows a willowy, rather androgynous calm, as he spears a fat, pleading dragon; there are friezes; ferocious beasts and narrative biblical scenes. The figures are intensely vigorous and human, with a flow of hair and robes, looser, less Byzantine than some of their contemporaries. There has been horrible damage and fearful mutilation, but what remains is powerfully compelling.

A small funeral procession was making its way towards the steps of the abbey. A priest came out of the church with a little black table, where he set up his paraphernalia of welcome. A hearse quickly nipped in front of the mourners; it was full of wreaths and flowers. The driver, dressed in blue jeans, jumped out and grabbed an old broom from under the piles of flowers. He started to sweep the steps. The thick dust blew back into the faces of the mourners, but the concentration of their grief protected them from noticing it.

The best time to look at the carvings was obviously going to be in the evening, when the sun would be lower; it would have moved round far enough to really seize the stone, with a rich contrast of light and shade.

When I got back to the main street, the crowds were considerable. They were waiting for the running of the bulls. Four slight bulls were raced up the street, one at a time. and then down again, by a clatter of horses' hoofs from behind them. On the way back, a few men would intercept them, with waves and cries. The poor bulls (they seemed very Ferdinand to me) can only run in a direct line. Forced to pause, they stagger to a semi-stop, before racing off in another direction. At this moment all the likely lads run in and jump up to tug at the horns, until the poor bull sees a gap, shakes them off, and manages to go on again. It was all very light-hearted and

relaxed, but the little town was crowded. It was the first time I
experienced some difficulty in finding a room. A tiny attic in La
Biche Gourmande, gave me, in the end, that cold key in my pocket.
It was a small, family hotel. Sunday was Mothering Sunday. They
had many large family bookings, so there was a great buzz of preparation going on.

La Biche is the hallmark of Saint-Gilles. This gentle deer is at the
centre of the legend; another attentive beast to a holy man.

Giles came from Greece, like Francis and Roch he was of good
family. Feeling drawn to the life of a hermit, he came over to France
and lived in the forest below the city. He was befriended by a deer
who let him have her milk, and who became his companion. On one
occasion King Flavious Wamba was out hunting and the deer ran
for protection to his friend. Thus Wamba was led to Giles, who he
found had been wounded by one of his huntsman's arrows. Wamba
was impressed by Giles's sanctity and scientific knowledge. He
nursed him back to health and then gave him lands and money to
build a hospital. Giles died in 721. A pilgrimage to his remains soon
developed. Many cures and favours were granted. Saint Giles is
particularly associated with the relief of mental disorders and cancer.

The abbey was Benedictine and in 1066 was affiliated to Cluny.
The carvings on the facade are twelfth century, they were executed
during a period of considerable prosperity; the pilgrimage was at its
height, trade flourished.

On the Sunday morning there was a large, busy market under the
trees; masses of white arum lilies that, somehow, belong in my mind
to Mexico and Diego. There were a great many Arabs; the old town,
up by the abbey church was apparently their *quartier*. On Saturday
evening I had burst in on a confirmation mass, in the abbey church.
I recognised the Bishop of Nîmes, he had been at les Saintes Maries.
Everything was very relaxed, a small boy danced a positive and
particular jig in one of the side aisles, nobody stopped him. Another
small boy sat on the high base of one of the columns, during mass,
eating a huge piece of delicious, honey cake, when the bishop came
forward after mass to greet the congregation, he got a sticky kiss and
the last morsel of the cake. I also saw the pretty daughter from
La Biche Gourmande. She was on her own. Her parents and her
grandparents, who had ceased practising as Catholics long ago,

were fascinated by their fourteen-year-old daughter's return to the Church. She was due to make her first communion in a fortnight. 'But it's so different now,' her father said, 'she is welcomed to a Church of Love and Hope. We left a Church obsessed by guilt and sin.'

The evening light was dramatic on the carvings; the hands and feet of the figures, were so physical and practical. There is tremendous intensity in the individual expressions. Mary Magdalene, as she wipes the feet of Jesus, with a great rope of hair; the kiss of Judas. There is an abundance of foliage and tracery, beasts and centaurs; the supple, growling, loping ferocity of the lions, the ripped flesh: centaurs, monkeys, sheep, deer, all subservient to the lions' howling, demented hunger.

The bones of Saint Giles are in the large crypt below the church. There was a stairway down from the main church to the crypt. The idea was that the pilgrim should experience a route down to the tomb and dark, and then go up again into the light; this would reflect the rhythm of renaissance and resurrection. The crypt is massive, many arches, decorated with pleated stone, various statues and sarcophagi. It was very cold in there, but such a benign cold, no sense of that manic, gripping damp as at La Chaise-Dieu. Outside, in front of the abbey church, there were always hundreds of pigeons; every kind of speckled, motley bird, batting and cooing from chimney pots, to the dusty niches in the carved stone.

Once again, it was a great joy to be able to return again and again. In the full, peak heat and glaring, blurred light of the midday sun, an American scholar was there with a professional photographer, who knew he should really wait for the evening shadows. The scholar, whose brains I attempted to pick, said rather wistfully, 'I hope you will mention scholars; we are oblique pilgrims.' They were going on to Arles. They were managing to pack in three major sites a day. I felt lazy and happy, knowing I was free to wait for the evening shadows.

By late evening the crypt was closed; everywhere was deserted. With the sun low in the sky, the figures, with these indented shadows, were vibrant and animated; the flow of fur and fleece and foliage was as keen and alive as the expressions in the eyes, and the rhythm of robes, the weight and presence of limbs. I sat on the steps drawing

Saint Michael. Pigeons came and went. An old woman dressed from head to foot in black, with a shawl over her shoulders, and thick, grey hair, piled into a tousled bun, crossed the street with a large, black umbrella. Although the sky seemed clear, I felt that her sense towards these things, would probably be accurate.

Then a man and his dog came slowly up the hill towards the abbey. His head was strong; a square mass. The hair was dark, the eyes deep-set, the whole impact, thick and rugged and dark, otherwise he seemed worn, his skin pitted and weathered. His clothes hung from him as if they had no serious purpose. It was as if they just happened to be there, loose and creased and old. The jersey was a bright, royal blue. Frayed and torn, it seemed an unexpectedly vivacious colour, as if it might have just blown on to him in passing, rather than being a garment of considered choice. Beside him, walked the ugliest and most confident dog; a mongrel; a terrier cross, that had a small, black head, and a fat, barrel body, marked with a mixture of dirty grey and black spots; slabs of marks, that seemed like gross stains, without identity, white slipping to a mess of grey; grey, sluggishly unable to be black.

The dog came and sat down in the shade just below the steps of the church, a narrow, red collar round the small neck, seemed to declare to all the world, the obvious quality of his life. The man went and bought an ice cream and came and sat down on another flight of steps in the shade, just yards beyond me. We nodded to one another. Then there was a violent cascade of wings from every height, hundreds of pigeons flew about the man and his dog. They flew behind him, above him, below him, between pecking feverishly at the rough, broken plaster on the wall opposite, just behind the man. The wall belonged to a fairly derelict building. There was a battered door, but no window on that side. The front, on the other side of the street, was one of the small gift shops. The man finished his ice-cream. Then, from the lolling, baggy pockets of his jacket, he took handfuls of corn, which he scattered to the birds. Immediately many more descended, cascading about the place; they alighted on his hands and head, shoulders and arms. He continued to scatter the bright grain. It encircled the mongrel dog, who sat like some proud monument, as the birds pecked and scuffed and cooed all round him. Some time later the man went across to the battered door, and went into the building. A few moments later, he came back with a plastic bowl full of water. He then filled the large pot-holes in the black tarmac with water, making two or three journeys into the house to do so. The birds batted and fluttered and drank from the clear water, brushing the dog's nose in their eagerness; he never moved. There was a sense of ritual and permanence about it all. These two, this man and his dog, were undoubtedly the real guardians of the abbey church.

'Do you feed them every day?' I asked. 'Every day,' he replied, 'Are you drawing the carvings?' 'Yes.' His voice was husky, the regional accent was very strong. I asked him why the birds pecked so persistently on the broken cement finish of the house, exposing the lathe and plaster to all weathers. 'They need the saltpetre,' he said.

Some while later he came across to me. 'Have you found the rabbit?' No. 'A thin rabbit, come and look.' I followed him, and stood exactly where he indicated in front of the abbey facade. But I could see no rabbit. 'Take it slowly. Look quietly. Look quietly.' I still found no rabbit. Then he showed me, and there, brilliantly clear, racing up the side of oak leaf tracery, a thin rabbit. It is there in the main pillar on the left as you face the church.

For an hour or more, he told me the history of Saint Giles, the murders, and intrigues, the womanising monks with their underground tunnel system as far as Aigues Mortes. He talked of Cathars and heresies, Albigensians, and the greed of man; the repeated patterns of history. 'Now, the Arabs are here. The French fear the Arabs. They are here, because they live in houses no Frenchman would live in; they do jobs no Frenchman would do; they raise families on wages no Frenchman would manage. It is the way of the world.'

He walked with me down various side streets, showing me fragments of carvings, particular windows and details. Above a door lintel, he showed me the stone head of a woman, he told me how the eyes appeared to follow you, up and down the street. 'In the moonlight,' he said, 'she lives; those eyes are everywhere.' People in the street greeted him with respect. A rather crazed, young woman, very thin and strange, raced out of a house. In an over-excited, disjointed manner, she told of some film on television with Marilyn Monroe; she was almost incoherent; explosive in her speech; demented in her gestures. He calmed her, he stroked her hair, patted her hands and told her gently to go home.

For twenty-five years he had lived alone in the battered house. He seemed like some wise thread, that runs through history; the seer at the gate, who is often passed by, because his outward appearance is not a proclamation of any kind. He perceives so much, because he remains outside scholarship and social position, and apart from the judgemental forces of political and commercial progress. He never told me his name, but like Juliet at La Chaise-Dieu his memory will remain with me always. He and Juliet needed no artifice on which to project and make the marks of their experience. They were poets of presence.

I arrived later than usual at La Biche Gourmande, to be surprised by a very warm and public embrace from Monsieur, while his wife, mother in law and the chef, looked on smiling. 'Because it is Mothering Sunday, and we know you are a mother, and you have no one here to embrace you.'

The shape of a journey, north or south, west or east, is extraordinarily defined and unique as it takes place. There is something headlong, free and expansive about south; west seems more serious, but still it has an open, liberating quality. North needs a deeper breath, a more serious stride.

I certainly felt a jolt of sadness as the train took me north from Nîmes towards Toulouse via Narbonne; that last southern scoop before the landscape alters. It was a long fast train, an important train from Cannes to Bordeaux, but for over an hour it waited at Narbonne, with cryptic announcements on the loudspeaker referring to delay, but giving no detailed information. The passengers seemed intrigued, but not frustrated. Eventually the train moved off at a fairly grudging, impractical pace until it came, once more, to a full stop, this time for over three hours! There was still calm and humour from the passengers, and it was possible to get out and investigate.

It was a *manifestation*. To me that sounded like a vision or apparition. But it was neither, it was a demonstration by the citizens of Lézignan, against a proposal by the S.N.C.F to cut local services and put on more high speed trains. The Lézignan women out on the track, were firm and vociferous, but full of smiles. The Mayors looked uneasy, in the their broad, striped sashes. The police were there in force, a group of quiet, charming, completely detached young men. The passengers seemed prepared if necessary to sleep the night. The consensus of opinion was that the village would lose out in the end, so they should be allowed their protest; their point of view should be recognised. Only bewildered non-nationals, about to lose boat connections at Bordeaux, showed any real signs of distress.

I was bound for Rocamadour, a complex route with a variety of changes. The four-hour delay meant a night at Toulouse, which had once been an important stop for pilgrims to Compostela. I left the train full of enthusiasm.

Toulouse is a vast and important industrial city. The home of the aircraft industry and a large centre of medicine and medical research. But the once central basilica of Saint Sernin's, has been almost throttled, by the thrusting, vigorous streets that surround it.

My visit was frustratingly brief. So brief, it left me feeling bewildered and uneasy. The basilica is built in a warm brown-pink stone, not the clear pink of Tournus, a heavier, more earth-bound colour. It has a high, telescope, Pisa-like spire, the sharp, final point rising needle-keen out of a mass of roofs and curves and domes. It is a very fine, coherent example of Romanesque architecture, but it so overwhelmed by the city, it cannot breathe or expand into any space. The treasures are rich and numerous, caskets of sacred bones, marvellous, carved wooden figures; there is so much. I began to feel a despairing, aching sense, there was just too much for the time available. In the end I sat for almost all the time I had, on the floor in the ambulatory, before the marble relief of Christ in Majesty, which has been moved from its original place and is now set in a curved wall with other reliefs. This Buddha-like Christ, has a large, comfortable belly, and a right hand raised in blessing. The long hair, flowing well back off His strange, full face, accentuates the unusual, protruding, oval blanks of icon eyes. It manifests a combined male-female strength, and an interior energy, which is very compelling.

One of the reasons for my brief visit, was that a requiem mass was being said when I arrived. The nave is very high, a breathtaking space of eleven bays, the arched ribs of the roof correspond wonderfully to the high arches between the pillars in the side aisles. The space is huge, calm and uncluttered. During the mass I remained at the back of the church. The mourners were a small handful of frail, bent, elderly people, they seemed intensely distressed. No sound came from this huge nave to greet the young priest's declarations, he had to make all the responses himself. He was the voice of both celebrant, choir and congregation. From the priest's address, I learnt that the deceased was a market stall-holder, who had worked with the Resistance. He was also an accomplished sportsman, well into his seventies; a master of Boules. Eventually this little knot of mourners made their way behind the coffin, and out from the vast basilica of Saint Sernin.

Sernin, who brought Christianity to Toulouse, was put to death by pagans in Toulouse in 250, by being attached to the body of a ferocious, white bull.

10

Rocamadour

'More things are learnt in the woods than from books; trees and rocks will teach you things not to be heard elsewhere – you will see for yourselves that honey may be gathered from stones and oil from the hardest rock.'

SAINT BERNARD OF CLAIRVAUX

ROCAMADOUR. ROCAMADOUR. The name sang in my head, as I made the long journey up now, up and up and up through such dry, burnt land; mud-brown, hippo-flank rivers, staring, brittle stalks.

Rocamadour. It is a beguiling, beckoning word. Like ripples in a lake, the sound goes round and round, opening outwards, then closing in again. Although I planned to go further west in the end to reach Compostela, the Carmargue – les Saintes Maries – was the most southerly part of my journey. Having turned from there I felt I was making some shape towards return.

There were many moments when fatigue was just a physical thing, aches and bruises, mosquito bites, the back, a grizzly red charge, gripping the base of the spine; and often from the cancer scar itself, violent shooting pains; only to be expected the radiologist had said after the burn up and that long infection. But physical pain however acute and persistent is always somehow a remove from self. You can observe it, move it, alter it, or you can abide within it, thrashing about, tense, angry and apparently powerless, but there is always choice; there is always an outside feel, with regard to pain and bodily fatigue.

There seems to be another fatigue. A clouded, uneasy, dry, but sharp fatigue; a fatigue of spirit. Here you may be overwhelmed. Suddenly the field of choice blurs; it goes under, although with enormous effort it can always be retrieved; almost always. Staring

out of the train window at the parched, brittle landscape, I felt
something similar within myself. So many believers. All that beautiful, vivid, proclaimed faith. The rich confusion and struggling
witness of these sacred places. This Christ, this tympanum, man/
God in glory could seem terrifying and utterly ruthless. Sometimes
I have felt that the gaze of God from the face of his Son is a radiation
blast almost to ashes in an instant. Then there is the awful realisation
of this derelict, no man's land between belief and disbelief.

There are degrees of certainty, which, you know in your heart,
can never be abandoned. Their irrational presence within you is part
of their power. Moving back is not possible. Moving forward is also
out of the question because, there is nothing there. Just as the poet
can only attend, listen and wait for the inspiration or idea; only when
it presents itself, can it be grabbed, so, in a similiar way, faith, or
belief seem to move, inhabit and persuade, according to ungovern-
able laws of chance. Waiting and attendance can be a dark,
baffling experience.

A variety of beds and faces, the demands of a foreign tongue; they
are continual challenges. They can be a spur, full of challenge and
excitement, but to proceed with them, is, to some extent, to throw
a rope across a ditch. Every part of you must be concerned to spring
the ditch, make the next bank, take the next road. To look back, or
down, is perilously close to losing ground, losing purpose and
even identity.

I had set out feeling beckoned by the places, by the route itself,
by the legends of saints and pilgrims, the builders, and carvers, the
general roaming pulse of people everywhere. Then, sometimes, I
found myself in this, dry, forsaken, barren spot, where it is peculiarly
soundless and without resonance. Anger is a kind of temptation
then. It might animate things. It might be some kind of sound. But
I couldn't say, Oh stuff belief, it's just a cultural nursery for the
unthinking idealist. I couldn't say that, although I could stare into
that idea. I had to go back to the roots of those certainties, which
seem incessantly to proclaim belief, and the sacred quality of life.
The magnetic mystery of a loving unity, with no created thing
outside its consolation. An unthinkable reality. The vast orbit of
Divine Regard. Some organic, transforming force; some energy
without, that knows, and is part of, some energy within.

Up and up, still, dry, scrubby land; fine, soft-red, biscuit bricks, odd-shaped meadows. G.K. Chesterton said of Christianity, 'It is not a question of being tried and found wanting, but of being found difficult and not tried.'

It was a day of glaring, full heat, such as I could not believe would ever happen when I was in Normandy. Figeac and a change of train. A wait in the sun, a handful of local people, a very bright station building, with a considerable garden of ornamental trees, roses and lavender.

Say Rocamadour. Think Transformation. Think without division. Think Love.

At last after rumbling on for ages, with waits and changes, dry heat and dirty windows, at last we were right up on the spine of the hills; uneven, jigsaw puzzle fields, thick hedges, long grass and wild flowers; goats and bees and dark, deciduous woods. The ground was green again in places, where it must have been spring fed.

Rocamadour. A deserted station, no passenger but myself. Opposite the station a small *auberge*, no other habitation, just the sense of height stretching out under the sun. There was a parked van. A young woman with long, fair hair was reading a book. I lumbered across, dragging the baggage about me. Simultaneously we said 'Taxi'. She moved some bread and fruit from the seat beside her. I got in. 'Which level?'

I had been once before to Rocamadour. I knew that the dwellings mounted haphazardly up the cliff face. A mass of tourist shops, hotels and houses were on the lowest level; the shrine, the other chapels and shops, were higher up on another level; and above them, on the summit of the cliff, there is the castle. Sanctuaries or ramparts, was the official choice. I had been told that there was some sort of hostel, convent, on the top level, by the church. We drove there, past a peculiarly deserted, sandy space, a large, closed café, and the guichet for the *ascenseur*, which operates up and down between the various levels during the day.

In the middle ages, the penitential climb of 216 steps on your knees, was the only way to the shrine. The sense of stillness and great height was amazing. Across the deep valley of the Alzou, you could see the opposite cliff, curving unevenly round, lower than the sheer, perpendicular rock face, on which I stood.

> Houses on the stream
> Churches on the houses

Rocks on the churches
The castle on the rock.

I walked across yet another monastery garden. I rang the bell. I could hear its echoing clang, within the building. A man answered the door. He would go and get one of the Sisters.

A Sister came. She looked stern, probably all manner of important, pressing things were uppermost in her mind. She stepped out into the garden closing the door firmly behind her. She was young, not more than thirty-five. She was distinctly unfriendly. She did not believe I was any kind of pilgrim. She was utterly fed up with people such as me. 'Don't worry. Don't explain' I pleaded. 'Just tell me you have no room. It doesn't matter' Another older Sister came to the door. She seemed a bit uneasy. She tried to say that there was a bed for one night, but no longer. The two Sisters argued together. 'One night, but only one night. Do you understand?. You probably don't understand. It's very difficult for us. We have schoolchildren, large party bookings. Only one night, is that clear?'

By now I was inside the building. But this surprising, fierce unfriendliness didn't really dispose me to want to stay. They showed me a small, cool, comfortable room. The older Sister tried to placate the younger Sister. 'She's tired,' she said of me, trying to persuade me to drop the baggage. But the younger Sister persisted with her glowering looks and obvious irritation, not only with me, but now, with the elder Sister also. 'She can't understand what we say. Only the one night, she probably doesn't understand that.'

Eventually I cut into their conversation, 'One thing is perfectly clear to me and it does not need to be expressed in any language. Your looks and manner have made your 'unwelcome' abundantly evident.' There was a pause. The younger Sister walked away. The older one said she had been to Yorkshire and that England was a very beautiful country. She was anxious about the keys. She was anxious about everything. I said that as I had not eaten all day, I would go and find something and arrange a bed for tomorrow. The Sister seemed to think I would leave, never to return, and that the door would remain unlocked all night. I felt the temperature rising again. Eventually I was on my own, a cool key in my pocket and the baggage dumped on a hard, narrow bed.

I was feeling rather 'sodish' by now. Sod Sisters. Sod pilgrimage. Sod the lot. Most of all sod my stupid, delapidated self, for carting baggage day after day, when I had been advised not to walk or stand! Such negative thoughts, utterly pathetic, did give me the energy to bound down the steep path – The Way of the Cross – to reach the level of the sanctuaries. There were no tourists. Everything was empty and quiet. The Sisters in their ramparts, felt far away.

There is one hotel opposite the steps up to the sanctuaries. It is the only hotel on this level, behind it there is a road out into the country, no shops, no dwellings, nothing. The dining-room of the Hotel is a curved, shaded terrace, overlooking the valley, it faces away from the town; far below you can just see a small scatter of roofs, and the Moulin de Roquefraiche down by the river; the rest is a wild, open landscape; the winding ribbon of cliffs beyond, on the other side from Rocamadour; there are trees, and scrubby green meadows below, and birds everywhere; buzzards, crows, kestrels and eagles; pigeons, sparrows, and the bell-clear call of the cuckoo.

The Madame at the Hotel Sainte Marie was very welcoming. Out of season the price was surprisingly competitive with the rampart Sisters. I had dinner on the terrace of the hotel. There were few people, just a murmur of intimate conversation now and again, and the sun going slowly down. I waited for the first star to flicker into the sky. It was a cool, blue-green sky, but full of light. On my way back to the ramparts, I peeped through the keyhole in the sanctuary door. Candles flickered in the rich, empty dark.

When I reached the convent, it was in darkness. By the time I switched out the light in my room, the moon, a sharp, crescent slice, directly opposite the bed, seemed to signify that sheer pulse at the heart of mystery. The parched, No man's land, was probably a necessary place, within Divine Regard, like all the rest. There is no place beyond Divine Regard. That gaze is summons, birth and destiny. It is the regenerative speed of Almighty stillness.

The next morning the smell of clear, warm, vibrant air from the open window, was like a spark, to fire the day. I felt wonderfully rested and eager to be off. I made my way down various passages, following the smell of coffee and the clang of cutlery.

In a large dining-room, a very laid-back party was having *le petit déjeuner*. An architect, a painter and a priest. They were apparently setting up, in the museum of the sanctuary below, a large, wall map showing the routes to Compostela, painted by the architect, and a colourful, jolly, hanging, designed by the artist Gilberte Basso, and executed in appliqué by ladies from Goblin. They were part of a catechetical organisation, creating and distributing visual aids to inspire the young and faithful. They too had been told to leave as soon as possible, but they seemed extremely relaxed and in no hurry to move. The elder Sister came into the room, when she saw me she gasped ... 'We thought you'd left last night. How clever you were to find the dining-room.' 'Come on Sister, she's a big girl now,' came the cry from the table.

After breakfast we all made our descent from the rampart Sisters. The map and hanging were admired and re-adjusted. I asked the priest about the Community at Nîmes, Lion de Juda, did he know them? 'Yes. Yes. All very beautiful, but we are not angels. They are not earthed; not of this world.' I looked at the well-fed, happy children on the hanging; bright colours, skateboards, air balloons, boats and aeroplanes, leaping ponies, colourful haversacks. It was a waving toytown pilgrimage, all cosily tucked into a *coquille* shell. Not very earthed. Not particularly pilgrim. Only recognisable as 'of this world' if your world is a humming, bourgeois paradise, bright with holidays and leisure.

It was wonderful to have the baggage in a room in the Hotel Sainte Marie. That cold key in my pocket, was the star of my journey. The hotel was immediately below a great overhanging rock, with melancholy dark streaks running down over the lighter, ochre stone. That rock seems to possess and protect this strange town, that climbs 150 metres up the cliff. The hotel was immediately opposite the wide stone steps, that lead through, under an archway, to the levels of the chapels, gift shop and museum, and the final, shorter flight of steps up to the sanctuary itself. But the hotel is very much on its own. The calm terrace is well away from the tourist buzz, and there is the little road out at the back, behind the hotel, which goes down into the valley. Two or three times a day I walked out on that road, and always last thing at night, and I never met a soul, car or dog, nothing.

It is perfectly possible to visit the sanctuary without being part of the buzz below; skins, hides, bells, medals and earrings; baskets and lavender, wine and cheese; large, snarling nylon creatures, and small, cuddly ones; *croque monsieurs*, ice-cream and candy floss, and even a small train, tooting its way through the lower streets. Rocamadour calls itself a city, but it has the feel of an eccentric village.

There is something so particular about this valley; an ancient, wild intensity. You feel drawn to listen to its silence. Something profound and mysterious is going on, something lyrical and majestic. The high, curving cliffs, the native woodland, overrun by wild honeysuckle and briar roses; so many flowers, and the constant, gliding flight of large birds. The vivacious applause of insects and small birds: bright winged finches, and a mass of ochre and white butterflies, and others with blue, white and green markings. The butterflies must be a feature of the terrain. In the high chapel of Saint Michael, there is an early fresco with ochre butterflies.

More and more I was certain that the crucial ingredient to all sacred places, is the host ground. This host place, that by some mysterious quality of energy; some factor of presence, draws man to shelter, reflect, pray and make sacrifice; whatever happens to be the expression of the time.

The caves and overhanging rocks in this valley were prehistoric places of human habitation. Dolmens, tumuli, all the usual evidence, suggest that Rocamadour was a sacred place long before Christianity. Possibly there was a cult of fecundity, there remain local traditions to indicate this. They may have preceded the Marian shrine.

Of course legends abound, faint facts, fusing with imaginative conjecture, are gradually made into a concrete narrative, with lists of illustrious names to add colour to the underlying mysteries.

It was early in the twelfth century that the first mention of worship of the Virgin is made. The present small statue dates from this time. There was a considerable scrap in 1076, between two different abbeys, about who should administer the chapel. The Pope had to arbitrate to resolve the dispute. It was peak time for flourishing pilgrimages. The great routes to Compostela and the stops at Saint-Gilles, Le Puy, and Vézelay, could be encouraged to encompass Rocamadour. There is an eastern proverb that says: No bones and no miracles . . . no pilgrimage. The pilgrimage to the black Madonna already existed. Monks and hermits had lived in the surrounding area for some time, but the real boost for Rocamadour, came with the discovery of the body of Amadour in 1172, at the entrance to the oratory.

This complete and preserved body was sufficient evidence to claim sanctity. The body of Amadour was left beside the shrine until it was finally destroyed by the usual pillage and turbulence. But the holy body brought about a great increase of attention for the shrine. A book of miracles was scrupulously kept, although the Virgin was always credited with the favours, over Saint Amadour. Once again, as with Sainte Sara, there are servant myths. Was Amadour the servant of the Mother of God? Possibly he was Zacheus, or the husband of Veronica, who wiped the face of Jesus? The new testament characters, seem all too easily to have bobbed up on to the French coast.

Saints and kings made the pilgrimage to Rocamadour. Henry II of England, Saint Bernard, Saint Dominic, Saint Antony of Padua, Saint Englebert, Archbishop of Cologne. Simon de Montfort wintered at Rocamadour during the beginning of the Albigensian Crusade in 1211, although he is certainly not claimed to have been a pilgrim! In the fifteenth century the English occupied Rocamadour, this was really the end of the pilgrimages until a major procession in 1562. The extensive restoration is all nineteenth century.

Today the constant stream of visitors are both tourists, and organised, church pilgrimages. A group of children were being prepared for confirmation while I was there, the pilgrimage was part of it. A loving, old priest had brought them.

'We are so happy, so happy to be here,' he kept saying to the quiet, tidy group of children. 'However tempted, however difficult, however dark ... there is always a light in your heart. Love that light. Increase that flame, it is Love. The love of God for you.' I could understand what the father at La Biche Gourmande meant about his daughter, being welcomed to a loving Church.

It was certainly very different from preparation for confirmation as I remember it. I mostly remember the fun of a choosing a name. I chose Thomas as in Thomas More. During the ceremony we waited in a long queue, crawling gradually towards the bishop on his throne. To my horror, when I got to the mitre and the holy, jewelled hand. He said Thomasina ... Horrified, and determined not to be confirmed as a mouse, I remonstrated, to the huge embarrassment of the standing clergy. However, the bishop did begin again, this time with Thomas, pure and simple.

The sanctuary itself, is small and very dark, candles burn there night and day. From the black, cave ceiling, covered with dust and cobwebs, hang model boats and the famous bell that sounds, when anyone in danger at sea, invokes the Madonna of Rocamadour. There was also a painter's palette. I asked the rather enigmatic and dour resident priest, about its origins.

'Oh,' he said, shrugging his shoulders, 'some painter gave a work to the shrine, and just left his palette up there.' 'And where,' I asked, 'is the painting?' 'It soon got disposed of,' was the curt reply. I couldn't help feeling, that perhaps, the jolly hanging, set up that morning, might soon be disposed of. I asked the priest what proportion of visitors were pilgrims as opposed to tourists. 'How on earth do I know,' was his fair reply. 'Poulenc, the composer, came as a tourist and experienced a great religious conversion.' The museum has the original manuscript of the Litany to the Black Virgin, which Poulenc wrote after his visit.

It is hard to find the small chapel ever still. There is always a steady flow of people, and the constant click of handbags, and the roll of coins into the candle box. Far away, in a small canopied shelf above the altar, is the tiny, stiff, black figure of the Madonna. Her recent crown, and the crown of her Son, don't take from her strange austerity. She is very thin, her breasts are fallen, the wizened, little, old man figure of her Son, rests on her knee. He is not held by her. She seems, from photographs, to be kept together by pieces of metal. Her face is full, the eyes closed. She is knowing, attentive, intense and contemplative. Without the photographs, she is just a tiny figure, but there does seem to be this numinous charge about her, and the chapel itself. She seems to peg down the place, keeping some strength gathered there.

I suppose worship and prayer are really forms of refined attention. Maybe the object, so acutely attended to – figure, or icon – maybe the object acts as a kind of long stop, to the intense directives beamed towards it, thus building up a reservoir, from which it is possible to release back some of the quality generated.

But the ground itself, beyond the sanctuaries, was for me the experience of sanctuary. Out there beyond the streets and steps and buildings, out there, the quiet was so charged. The bird and insect life was vital, and celebratory. The light was pale during the heat of the day, simply a fullness over everything; moss, sticks, lichen, flowers, dry wood, sharp stones. You couldn't look in any direction without finding a dense, thrilling, small world of form and texture and life. It seemed secret, because I suppose it felt so unseen and wild.

Again and again I walked out towards this soft, high, just undulating horizon, where the cliffs gradually move closer together at the end of the valley, to part again, and spread out into the next shape of open ground. A wooded, growing, dense quiet, regenerating itself, without any interference from man. On the road out, there was a track up to the right, by a large, single stone cross. It curved its way up and up. There were fallen stone walls, behind some of them there were deep wells, occasionally there was a broken wooden door, propped up by growth and ivy. As it climbed, the path widened; it became a matted carpet of pink convolvulous, orchids, onions in flower, lad's love, thyme and camomile. At the top you were equal to the height of the cliffs across the valley. One evening, when I had gone further than usual, I came into what might once have been a small meadow. I saw a tiled roof through some trees. I walked towards it. I supposed it would be a deserted dwelling, but as I got closer I saw there were geraniums in pots, and just down from them, a small, neatly planted vegetable garden. There was a stack of firewood, and yet there seemed to be no road up to the house, no entry except the steep track I had used. Another thing that struck me, was that the house had few windows; and those there were, were very small indeed.

The next day I came again, this time I decided to do a circular trespass. Round on the far side, there was an open door, into a small oratory. There was a Cross on the stone wall and a prayer stool, nothing else. At the hotel everyone denied that there could possibly be an inhabited house up the track. But Madame made some enquiries. She told me later that a hermit lived in the house; a woman.

Each day and each evening, and then again in the moonlight, I walked out there. I could never bear to think it would be the last time. Sitting up on the dry ground, the birds and butterflies so close, there seemed to be such sound in the silence. The horizontal, narrow runs in the rock on the cliff opposite, reminded me of the robe at Vézelay; those close, Byzantine sloops, and swirls and scoops. It was as if the strength in this silent, but mysteriously full sound, could only be understood as some kind of pain.

I had often worried about how I should cope with language, to describe architecture, because I have such inadequate knowledge of the subject. But sitting on those warm stones, one afternoon in the sun, staring, watching, almost being taken up into this unique stillness, I realised with sadness, that this was the experience I would be unable to express.

You know in your heart that you must not say, I will come back here, or bend down, to take up flowers and stones. You have simply to greet the charge and be there; with everything as it is. You just are, perplexed, bidden; intensely moved.

Each night, the moon was a flood of light, with a thousand stars, picking out the sharp, white, path stones, as if there was some language in them. Nothing seemed to be haphazard.

There is a very clear echo in the valley. During the day, while I was writing out on the terrace, I heard voices calling R O C A MAD OOOUURRRRR. On the last midnight, after the bells had sounded, I walked out to the end of the valley. I called aloud, one by one the names of the children. Mick, Ralph, Martha, Magnus, Sophie, Jacob and Joseph. The sounds flew round the valley, several seconds of clear, uncanny call. The best two, the sound going on and on, were Jacob and Joseph ... It felt as if those names sped into the midnight rocks, and would remain there, in some way, to guide the named.

Rocamadour remains for me, above all else, this spirit of place; something complete and tangible by the sheer force of its intangibility. Within that simple, listening experience, there seemed to be all I sought and all I would ever find. A continuous, live cantata of silence; the hinge and sum and fulcrum of the rest.

The next journey was so complicated by frequent stops and changes, that the young man at Rocamadour station insisted on sellotaping his written directions into the back of my notebook.

> Rocamadour to Brive direction Bordeaux
> Brive to Niversac direction Agen
> Niversac to Les Eyzies.

II

Dhagpo Kagyu Ling

'For him who perceives in truth and in wisdom, how things are
produced and perish in the world for him, there is neither being
nor non-being.'

SAMYUTTA NIKÂYA

IN HIGH SUMMER Les Eyzies is packed. It is cave country. It is in
the heart of the Dordogne, and its rich prehistoric past. Here
on a high, forested rib of land, La Côte de Jor, above the river
Vézère, between the villages of Le Moustier and St Léon, in 1970,
His Holiness the 16th Karmapa decided to build his European seat.

A vast gift of land from an American made this possible. There
are various dwellings scattered about at some distance from each
other, private houses, restored farm buildings, cottages and some
recently built additions. Not all the dwellings belong to the same
line, but all are the property of Tibetan Buddhists. The site for the
temple has been decided on. The French authorities have recognised
and given much support to this Tibetan Foundation, but one local
American lady, who would see the top of the temple from her
bedroom window, is at present holding up the proceedings. Maybe
the auspicious moment is not yet. But teaching, meditation, study,
and healing, flourish here. Lamas come and go, some permanent,
some visiting. There are monks and nuns and lay people of many
different nationalities, who live and work and study, permanently or
semi-permanently in a great variety of accommodation. There are
various courses open to vistors throughout the year. The tall prayer
flags, on their high masts, billowing, or damp and fallen, are the
surest indication of a Buddhist Community in residence.

It was to Dhagpo Kagyu Ling that I was making my way. 'Ah,
Dagpo,' the taxi driver said, knowingly. Monastic retreats, far from

the madding crowds, must give considerable business to the local taxis, as many visitors and pilgrims come without cars.

From the train window in Brive station I had seen the unmistakable, red and yellow robe of a Buddhist monk. He was being seen on to a train for Paris. Two young people were carefully explaining his picnic to him. He was receiving their intructions with a great deal of laughter. Lamas seem to laugh easily, they are full of smiles, between their calm, seriousness. That monk on the station platform, was a welcome signal that I was going in the right direction.

At Dhagpo, against the rich, lush green of the surrounding meadows and forests, the Tibetan habit is spectacular. Red, called here *bordeaux*, signifies compassion, the yellow, primordial wisdom. It was a French monk who greeted me. The next day was the begining of a short course in meditation.

After Taizé, Nîmes and Bussy, the general tempo seemed so much less. Perhaps it was because the proportion of large empty landscape to resident people was so high. There were, maybe, twenty-five residents at Dhagpo and perhaps twenty more on the course, and the prayer flag territories went on for as far as the eye could see. It was much wetter and more wooded than at Rocamadour. The trees were higher, there was a forest quiet and the kind of full, saturated greens of some Chagall fields, with every so often a colourful monk in them, instead of a black horse.

The 'Welcome' seemed complicated. Perhaps that was because you chose your cost, according to your income. Many people found this difficult, if they felt that their incomes varied considerably. There was a choice of vegetarian food or otherwise. There was no particular emphasis on meat, one way or another. Everyone seemed to be themselves, there was no overall style, no overt indication on the person of the philosophy and transformation towards enlightenment, being sought. Monks and nuns wore the habit, everyone else dressed in the most normal, relaxed, everyday way. Most people had a mali – a string of wooded beads similar to a rosary – used during the recitation of a mantra.

There were families who lived there with children. They lived in their own separate houses. The children went to local schools and enjoyed the freedom of the wild surroundings. There was no attempt to involve them in the Pujas and Practices. But the philosophy of compassion to all sentient beings was always in the air. A small note, written on a paper napkin, was pinned one morning to the kitchen door:

Butterfly eggs, on no account damage, close door carefully.

The little cluster of eggs remained. Everyone was very careful, but as someone remarked, there's not much for them to eat on a wooden door.

I had initially ticked dormitory, but Pascale persuaded me to go for a single room. It was Pascale, who kindly initiated me into the general run of things. She was French, about twenty-five, I think. She was living *ensemble* with an Italian, called Davies. I kept thinking I must have got his name wrong. Davies. Yes. Yes. My Father was a tennis professional, Davies. Davies Cup. Pascale and Davies lived in the next village, they came daily to Dhagpo. They had both been studying Buddhism, for some time; Pascale for longer. In the following January, Pascale would start a three-year retreat. Three years, not in silence, but intense practice and study, and no contact with outside world, although letters might be written and received. Malika, a young Swiss woman, who slept in the forest in her own tent, was also to go on the retreat. Not surprisingly, Davies looked sad and brave about the whole thing. He was a large man, when anxious, he seemed as vulnerable as his size. The lamas only accept you for retreat if they feel you have achieved stability. Everyone does a job. Pascale was to cook for the group.

One of the nuns living permanently at Dhagpo was a widow with grown-up children. She had built her own cottage in the forest. There was another young nun, who seemed in the depths of acute depression. But she obviously wanted to remain and she was given every assistance to do so. No one would ever refer to another, in any critical or judgemental way. There is something very striking about highly intelligent people, able to discuss any subject, but without judgement of any kind. There was a noticeable difference when the uninitiated arrived for the course. Suddenly we were all caught up in light-hearted judging and assessing of people, things, books, films, weather, food, politics. We had a long way to go!

At one level, as my journey continued, I felt calmer, deeper; more still, more complete in some way; more naturally at ease with myself. But every so often the burden of the book, and the language, could seem bewildering. I would be thrown into a state of panic. Would I have enough information? Would I get it right? Perhaps when I thought I understood, maybe, I was getting it wrong. Perhaps the book would be a string of gaffes and loose suppositions. Maybe my elegant, civilised publisher would feel his act of faith in me, 'Just go. Just go,' had been wildly misplaced.

The first impact of Dhagpo on me, was obviously the difference here from all the other religious houses I had stayed in. The images; large coloured photographs of lamas, smiling and serious. The complex, highly coloured posters, (methods and colours, as in icon painting, follow certain rules). Creatures, clouds, jewels and flowers, and the flowing, particular presence of the Bodhisattvas.

The language; a whole new vocabulary of reference. Refuge, Ignorance. Karma. Enlightenment. Transformation. Right action. Right attitude. Sentient Beings. Transience. Gross or subtle. To refrain from. To act skilfully. Then, at the centre of all the teaching, the Triple Gem of Buddha: Dharma – the teachings. Sangha – the Community, Puja, referring to the different chants and intercessions to various Enlightened Beings: Tara. Mahakala. Tchenreizi (spelt differently every time I asked). Then the various teachers and teachings: Manjusri. Sakyamuni Nyingina. Padmasambhava. Milarepa.

The line here at Dhagpo was Karmapa. The monastic community of Karme. Dharma. Chakra. Then there were the various vehicles; Hinayana, Vajrayana, and above all Dharmakaya, the Buddha nature, that pervades all sentient beings. It is present in all, but must be realised. It sounded very similar to 'the kingdom of heaven within you'. Then there was Samsara, that sounds like a round sigh. It refers to the state of transmigration, the continual movement, on and on: rebirth; the cycles of existence. There was so much. In every word you could feel these rich, profound traditions of thought and teaching inspired by compassion. Inspired by Gautama, the family name of Siddhartha, son of the ruler of the Sakya tribe in Nepal. He probably lived 563–483 B.C.

He left his palace and wife, and son Rahula, to seek some answer to the problem of suffering. On his enlightenment he became known as the Buddha. He assembled together communities of monks and nuns, to teach the Four Noble Truths, and the following of the Eightfold path; teachings towards Enlightenment. His wife, Yaso-dhara became one of the first nuns, and Rahula entered the Sangha and became an eminent Arahat. From a state of Enlightenment, all sentient beings will be loved and served. Enlightenment, and the realisation of Buddha nature, is sought out of compassion for all sentient beings, and not, as so many people seem to think, for some kind of private and personal Zen buzz.

All the residents work hard in a variety of ways, much of the work is physical. The days begin early. All the meals were very generous helpings of good, nutritious food. The vegetarian dishes were par-ticularly inspired. The new buildings were a little way down, away from the original farmhouse complex, where the lamas live, and where the shrine room is. The new buildings are strong and simple, wide-covered verandahs connect the blocks of bedrooms to the dining-room and kitchen. Everything is made to the highest possible standards, the bathrooms, are specially designed for disabled people. There is a cloister feel to the rooms, that look out on to the forest nearby. The colours were blue and brown, extremely calm and beautiful.

'In the beginning,' Pascale said, 'the lamas feel that the quality and peace of the environment, greatly assists meditation.'

All the time, you feel that there is this strong desire, above all else, to preserve the teachings that were so severely threatened by the Chinese invasion of Tibet. The foundation seeks to maintain the great oral tradition of the teachings, making them available in the best possible surroundings, to as many people as possible, I heard no reference with sadness or longing for Tibet or the East. Everything is Karma. The teachings are a live force. It is intended now, that they should be made available to the West. Men, who have lived for thirty years or more in the Tibetan mountains, seem marvellously at peace and ease, in the Dordogne landscape.

We sat out on the wide verandah eating supper. Pascale with her answers, me, with my questions. Scores of ants calmly traced live patterns across the scrubbed wooden table, in and out and sometimes over our plates of steaming food. With reference to the ants, Pascale said, 'We just try to do our best. But we don't get worked up about it.'

All round the buildings was the run of the forest, and from its dark, green depths came the continuous mantra of the cicadas; a vivid, urgent sound. Pascale had shown me the prayer flags. They are covered with the mantra to Tara. They are printed from wood blocks in Dharmsala in India. The close writing is interspersed with line drawings: lion, horse, tiger and peacocks. The flags make this constant, tugging, batting, trumpet-sound into the air, as they blow the mercy and compassion of Tara across the world. In Tibetan Buddhism, Tara is venerated as the goddess of mercy, the female counterpart of Bodhisattva Avalokiteshvara. Originally she was an Indian goddess. She is always depicted with one hand pointing to the earth, to indicate her ceaseless compassion for the suffering there. Not far from the flags, immediately behind the shrine room, was a long verandah, where, carved in teak, prayer wheels on greasy poles were waiting to be swung. On each wheel is carved the great mantra. Om Mane Padme Hum. The jewel in the lotus. The jewel is Buddhist doctrine, and the lotus, Buddhist scripture. This mantra, unlike many others may be used by all, even the uninitiated, it does not need to be given to you by a lama.

The prayer wheels were themselves stuffed with written mantras. At odd times throughout the day people would circle the building from the right, turning each wheel as they went. Pascale explained to me that virtue may be accumulated by circling any sacred object from the right, that could include a lama.

Eventually in the cool dusk, the gong was sounded and those who wished, made their way to the shrine room. I went with them, but I felt hedged in by some kind of anxiety; maybe it was just being fairly tired, there had been a great deal of speaking and translating. The piles of shoes and sandals outside the shrine room door, indicated the number of people within. I had never witnessed a Puja before, only meditating assemblies once or twice in London; a day at a time, with teaching. I was on the threshold of yet another great, human tradition, full of images, teachings, symbols, and history. The world seemed to be awash with facts, data, legends and marvellous artefacts. The life of every individual also, seems awash with a personal history of such intensity; trials, tribulations, anxieties, failures, ambition and isolation. There must always remain, so it seems, a gap between the experience of feelings and their expression, and understanding. Words will never carry the whole burden; there must be other means.

I kicked off my shoes and added them to the pile. There was something rather liberating just about that. There is always so much to let go of. All the new words, went round and round in my head, and the names of all the people. I was constantly having to ask a name more than once and then I immediately confused it with the wrong person. All these words were like flies buzzing round, and in and out of my brain, reducing it to a colander; a tattered vessel full of holes. Eastern thought, Western thought. Turbulent past history, turbulent present history. Chants and prayers and silence. Gestures of blessing, penitence and sacrifice; gestures of witness; gestures of offering and greeting. Beneath it all, what was going on? What was the force behind this great, sighing, grinding, lump of Samsara; this beast, this creature, twisting and turning, from cause to effect, on and on. A tidal flow of movement and change, effecting both quark and kingdom, monetary illusions and mollecular structures.

As the initiated entered the shrine room, they held their hands together, pointing them to their forehead, then lips and heart. Between each gesture, they knelt on the floor prostrating themselves, that is letting their forehead touch the ground. They did this three times. I was reminded of Bussy, the kissing of the icon and the touching of the ground, also, three times. The externals often seem different at first, but there is much that is the same, a great deal unites all external worship, and prayer.

The impact in the shrine room was of red (*bordeaux*) and bright gold; cushions, mats, walls, people; purple and gold. It was a simple room, not particularly large. There were only windows on the verandah side. The whole of the end wall, was 'shrine impact'. In the centre on a wooden throne, there was a thin Buddha, draped and surrounded by flowers. Behind the Buddha, there was a large coloured photograph of His Holiness the Karmapa, the last head of the line. He wore a magnificent high hat, and robe. On either side of the throne, there were ornate glass cabinets, housing many more buddhas, and significant and very colourful paraphernalia. On a narrow ledge, like the front of a dresser, there were seven small bowls, offerings and water respectively: rice, incense, candles, flowers, biscuits, shells.

Everyone was quietly gathering up purple mats and cushions from the end of the room, by the door. On either side, next to the wall there were cushioned benches, this was where the monks and nuns and lamas sat. Everyone else settled themselves somewhere on the floor in the centre of the room. There was a huge gong on a stand in front of one of the cushioned benches. A yellow dragon raced round the side of the gong. The initiated also had with them long thin folders, covered with silk or damask, which they rested on a low wooden stool in front of them. This folder housed the various chants used. Soon everyone was still, cross-legged, kneeling or in a half lotus position. They waited for the arrival of the lama, who would lead the Puja.

The only lama I had seen since I arrived was Lama Phurtsela. At mealtimes, he sat in the corner of the dining-room, smiling continuously. He was a moving mound of colour. Every so often, he would break into hums and chants. He might suddenly clap his hands in a greeting, or simply for the sound itself. In a smiling, expansive gesture, he might unwind, and then rewind, the yards of *bordeaux* that hung from his shoulder, over the gold, of primordial wisdom. His face, was so creased by continual smiling, that his eyes were hard to detect in this happily crumpled countenance. From every table you felt his presence in the corner of the room. He spoke only Tibetan, with a smattering of French words, just enough to make his loving gestures and greetings possible. He was a very tall, large man. He walked with a rolling sway. You felt that the bones inside the body, must be as supple and free as the smile. You couldn't imagine any edge to him; within or without. He was a large, smiling flow of red and gold. But there was another Lama Phurtsela, hardly recognisable from the first. When Lama Phurtsela led the chanting, his general softness became galvanised into an incredible power of voice, timing and rhythm. The thundering, deep voice would rise and fall like a boat sailing over rapids. The sound and speed, would be punctuated by small throws of rice grains into the air, a sudden clash of cymbals, a shake of bells. The ceaseless flow of the mali beads through his fingers, like a sifting, race of corn, would suddenly be interrupted, and he would roll the beads into a bundle, and strike them with the side of his other hand, making them into yet another instrument of timing and expression.

Because I love Doctor Samuel Johnson very much, I have often thought of his ungainly shape, which housed, not only the great mind, but so much humanity; such frailty, love and sadness. Somehow I felt he would have loved Lama Phurtsela. The ungainly shape, suddenly struck by a particular focus into nothing but accomplishment and grace.

The evening Puja, the chant to Tchenreizi was like the soft, persistent murmur of bees over a field of flowers; a continual rising and falling. Within the chanting was the recitation of the mantra. The same phrase, on and on and on; everyone in their own way, and at their own pace; the smooth beads dropping fast through their fingers. On and on, very fast, until this strong rope of sound became the only presence in the room. It hung there above the heads of the people, like the glow from a constant fire; the action of smoke, but the presence of flame.

Suddenly it seemed futile to remain outside this experience, gathering facts and data, trying to be attentive to the outer experience of everything. I felt as if I had come into a beautiful house, or garden, or was the guest at some feast, and instead of simply tasting the food, or walking in the garden or wandering through the house, I just badgered my host for the names and genus of the plants, the history and dates of the objects, the exact recipes and contents of the food. In the end I could hear my host say simply. Be here. Taste the food for itself. Just look and be with these objects and their immense variety, be with these plants and shrubs and flowers, their smells, shapes and shadows. Let them be. Give them space and you will know them as they are, and not as they might be labelled for you.

So rice, petals, sounds and silence, all became a presence; a hollow dark, like the trunk of some great tree, that rose higher and higher and yet reached so far down, that nothing might be left below. In this hollow dark, my own spine seemed to echo the tree's shape; a straight sapling, not hollow enough, but ready to echo outwards into the hollow trunk and this tall, reaching darkness.

After the Puja, when everyone had gone, having gathered up their mats and cushions, I suddenly saw, in a different way, the two bright, rampant lions, in white and green that roared round the throne on which the Buddha rested. These lions, like the yellow dragon on the gong, were beasts of value; they were part of the praise; they were protectors of the teachings. How unlike those howling, raging beasts in the stone carvings on the facade of the abbey church at St-Gilles.

The speared, writhing dragon of both Saint Michael and Saint George, is never dead, but simply pinioned; the head always seems to be rising upwards as if pleading for life, forgiveness, and attention. Maybe when we spear our dragons, we divide ourselves. To insist on fight, division and conquest continually proclaims duality. Maybe if dragons and mermaids were welcomed into the centre, and allowed to be expressions of a flourishing, live force of rejoicing, the mysteries might be sustained with less division. Judgemental certainties, as a means to achieve power and political progress might give way to the new order, which is being so ardently sought by so many nations, called 'the peaceful solution'. Perhaps there might be more than one head of state, like Vaclav Havel, who can use the word 'Love' as a natural political expression.

In a letter from prison, Vaclav Havel wrote of 'doing something positive in life, which is the expression of a moral imperative, or simply a love for people.'

The lions and dragons at Dhagpo were there to preserve the teachings from negative forces. In Christianity the poor dragon is synonymous with negative force. His scaly form from the deep caverns underground echoes the scaly tails of the poor, banished temptress women, from the depths of the oceans. Perhaps those mermaids from the lintel at St Michel d'Aiguilhe, might rise up out of banishment, and on the backs of roaring dragons, ride through the narthex, up the nave and into the sanctuary, to be at last within the place of celebration; puffing incense from the dragon nostrils and dropping scales from our eyes. Such a presence might resuscitate vigour and banish blame.

That night, watching the same moon over a fresh forest, I could only think of unity; the single summons. All this diversity of teaching and rituals seemed simply to mirror the incomparable diversity of nature itself. A single regenerative force, seemingly unstoppable, in its endless manifestations of species and breeds, but always operating within the shape of birth, flowering, and a gradual dying back into decay, towards ultimately, death. A return in some form, to the regenerative ground. Diversity of expression, but unity of purpose. A life maintaining purpose. A refining purpose, towards a greater, and maybe unimaginable unity. The sense of something other, something beyond, something supramundane, seems a factor common to all tribes and peoples. Some powerful intent towards transformation seems to be a natural instinct.

'Let nothing live in thy working mind but a naked intent stretching into God,' writes the fourteenth-century author of *The Cloud of Unknowing*.

Night and moon always seem full of 'naked intent.' Staring into night and moon seems to drain thought of definition, and leave only that mysterious certainty, which cannot be claimed or known; simply sought.

Bede Griffiths, the Benedictine monk, who has lived for the last thirty-five years in India, says in his book *The Marriage of East and West*:

> The narrow-mindednesss which has divided the Christian Churches from one another, has also divided the Christian religion from other religions. Today we have to open ourselves to the truth in all religions. Each religion must learn to discern its essential truth and to reject its cultural and historical limitations.

I suppose that must apply equally to individuals, who, after all, go to make up the various religions. Is the essential human truth, an ability to love and be loved? Certainly without love, degeneration and pain make extraordinary progress.

The practice – the Puja – was three times every day. 7 a.m. 2 p.m. 8 p.m.

The next morning I woke just before the gong sounded. There was bright light, tremendous birdsong and a heavy dew. Still half asleep I ran up the hill. As I got closer I could hear that the chanting had already begun. Outside the shrine room a young Vietnamese man was waiting. He, like me, felt too shy to go in. Encouraged by one another, we kicked off our shoes and found to our surprise that Lama Phurtsela, two other nuns and two others were all who were there. Strangely, everything in the shrine room felt intimate and ordinary, not baroque and foreign. Chants to Tara, angels or saints, within all this sacred scope, there seems to be simply, a profound purpose, naturally connected to the rhythms of being and living. Just a 'naked intent' focused towards Compassion, Realisation, and Transformation, achieved by Practice and Diligence.

*

The Vietnamese young man was called Marcel, he and his sister Lyse had come from Marseilles for the course in meditation. They had lived all their lives in France. Their father was a pharmacist. Marcel was hoping to go into the same profession. He was anxiously waiting for exam results. He was a most thoughtful and gentle person. Lyse had spent some time in America, she spoke very good English. She was physically slight, but strong in mind. They said that their parents were Buddhists; they had a shrine in the house, but their mother was equally at ease with Catholicism.

As the course in meditation was not due to start until the afternoon, the three of us walked to Le Moustier and on to the meadow beside the river Vézère as it runs under the heavy, dark bulge of the rock Saint Christophe. The light on the poplars, animated by a continuous breeze, made the frail, small leaves, tip and turn like sharp crystals in the sun. The sky was blue, between fast-moving clouds, the bright light reached into the various greens, giving them extraordinary vitality.

Several summers before, maybe ten years ago, we had swum and picnicked with the children in this exact spot. I could see the children clearly; sketchbooks, cameras, butterfly nets, brown limbs; teasing and joking; each one positive and different; collectively such vigour and life. Six of them between seventeen and ten. I could see the picnic on the ground; always remains in an instant; crumbs and pips and rind. There had been blue butterflies skimming over the clear, cool water. Marcel and Lyse found it hard to believe. They had not been to that part of France before.

Lama Jigmé Rinpoche, superior of the monastic congregation here at Dhagpo, gave the course on meditation. He was in his forties, very quiet and gentle, but there was a contained strength about him. There seems to be something very resolute and compelling about lamas, from my slight experience. Perhaps it is something to do with the emphasis on oral teaching; the power of the line. You feel that simply to be with them, is quite as important as to speak with them.

Lama Jigmé spoke in English, which was very handy for me. I was the only English speaker on the course. A young man, a resident at Dhagpo, translated as we went along, with more flourishes of metaphor than the direct and simple words of Lama Jigmé. But the essence was certainly the same.

The essence was the need for clear mind. To relax, then meditate. He spoke of the posture; a straight spine; the breath, the eyes not closed, but focused down. He spoke of allowing thoughts to rise, but not grasping them. Follow the thought to its source of arising. The place of meditation was important; a place made by you; a place without sounds and distraction. To see mind, to know mind. Recognise the tendency to grasp; develop the sense of 'wellness of being'. Allow thoughts, but let them pass; do not allow thoughts to obscure and intrude.

Understand how mind is related to body, and air, and breathe related to energy. Become aware of emotions and find their source. See their roots in self. If you look and are aware, that increases wisdom aspect.

The essential of continual practice and diligence was stressed again and again. But, and this was stressed most emphatically, meditate for the benefit of others, not from desires for self. Buddhism seems to point to weakness and ignorance by avoidance, not condemnation. By skilled action, ignorance is avoided. Blame and judgement seem to be no part of compassion. And the avoidance of blame and judgement help to maintain the necessary equilibrium for meditation and practice.

Lama Jigmé's voice was quiet and even.

'Breathe in something for others. Breathe out to give love and compassion. Regular practice of meditation is purification and the accumulation of merit.'

After each teaching session there was a time of meditation. In the stillness, a leg might be moved, a knee lifted; I often envied that movement.

The combination of the teachings and the meditations and the hours of practice, made the days deep and full, with very little slack in them. Walking in the forest I came upon a piece of paper in cling film, pinned to a tree, with the message on it. 'Please go no further, retreat area.' There seemed to be no path, nothing, but peering through the trees, I could see in the distance the battered roof of a white caravan.

In the evenings, after the last practice, there were long walks; narrow tracks, through woods, and fields, full of poppies and daisies. You might pass other prayer flags, and the occasional farmhouse. There was considerable discussion of 'life on the path', people comparing notes of the various routes that had led them to

Buddhism; personal problems, dreams, a haphazard contact, something read, or the attraction for the philosophy of compassion for
all creatures, and its non-duality. Common to everyone seemed
to be the idea of growth and transformation being possible and
necessary.

Cathy, who lived not very far away, had been Catholic and then
Rosicrucian. She was now an ardent Buddhist. She seemed content
and happy. She went regularly to mass and received communion.
'The Church is like a very beautiful house, there are wonderful
things in it and wonderful people. I love Christ. He is an emanation
of compassion. I love his Mother. But there are other beautiful and
important things outside the Church. I love them also.'

I walked for several evenings with Cathy. We picked wild mint
and sage and then came back and made a *tisane*, by then it would be
dark, only the moon and the cicadas. When Cathy heard I had had
cancer, she was insistent that I should go to Lama Jigmé to be given
a particular mantra; a mantra for long life aspect.

I did go to Lama Jigmé, I wanted to ask him how Buddhism
regarded Christianity among other things.

Lama Jigmé said, 'Out of compassion Christ took form, and gave
the truth. He was a founder of the truth.' '*The* truth, or *a* truth—?'
I asked. Lama Jigmé paused, then smiled broadly and said most
emphatically, '*The* truth. Then ...' and he bent down and gathered
up the little Tibetan terrier at his feet ... 'then ... there was
interpretation.' He smiled broadly.

Indeed, there was interpretation, and the founding of Christendom, more often than not at the point of a sword.

Lame Jigmé also said that it was perfectly possible to practice
Buddhism without believing in reincarnation. There is, it seems in
Buddhism, this certainty, that by particular, consistent actions and
practices, transformation will gradually occur, and the truth, the
Buddha nature, will be realised. At one level, talk of Purgatory, has
a great deal in common with the laws of Karma. Both seem to refer
to our intrinsic responsibility for all our actions, and the need, in
the end, to transform them. The compassionate help and assistance
of the many and varied Bodhisattvas, and the past great teachers, is
very similar to the whole idea of the guidance, help and attention,
that through intercession to the Saints, the Christian may benefit
from. There is so much in common at the heart of both these great
traditions. Both stress the need for love and practice, continually.

Perhaps that demanding simplicity is too commanding and clear for the sophisticated modern mind.

I knew I would get no peace from Cathy if I didn't mention the cancer. I told Lama Jigmé that it didn't worry me, I didn't think I minded at all the idea of dying. Lame Jigmé became concerned, almost stern.

'Long life is most important. The gift of a human life is so much, so much. One must pray for long life aspect.' He gave me a mantra. A long one, to Tara; for long life aspect.

Cathy was pleased about the mantra, but it wasn't enough. She had just heard that a very wise lama of Tibetan medicine was staying at another of the houses over the hill. I must visit him. We made the walk together. It was a small farmhouse, quite dwarfed by its prayer flags and prayer wheels. I gave my medical history to a young woman, who was screening the old and frail lama from many others who had come from afar to visit him.

The message came back, expressing unequivocally, that I must immediately take a course of Ratna Sempel. It had to come from Dharmsala. It was full of gold, the scrapings of pearls, and various plants that must be gathered at night, on particular, auspicious phases of the moon. I was advised to get it through Chocila. This meant another walk to another Buddhist centre. La Sonnerie. Still Tibetan Buddhism, but another line from Dhagpo.

We were greeted with kindness and calm. Yang Chen would send me a course of Ratna Sempel to London. 'If they send it to you direct from Dharmsala, it is often intercepted, as it is thought to be drugs,' Yang Chen told me.

There were storms and heavy rain the night before I left. Paschal was to drive Marcel, Lyse and me to the station at Les Eyzies. Happily the train time just allowed us to participate in the practice at 2 p.m. To Mahakala. This was the most powerful sound. Tremendous use of the gong and cymbals. Lama Phurtsela was in great voice, gathering up the sound and charging forward faster and faster, with these powerful invocations. It was a chant to protect the teachings and ward off negative forces. An exhilarating pound of energy.

It was hard to leave the peace and strength of Dhagpo. Peace and strength are certainly the products of great diligence. The kind of diligence to daily detail, that Thérèse Martin discovered. The greatest attention to the smallest issue.

I was beginning to feel very tired. It was as if I had gone out into some meadow, and had gathered up flowers; so many flowers, all with different smells, and textures. Undoubtedly there was abundance, great abundance. At first the abundance in itself is delightful, intoxicating, then there just seems to be too much. Perhaps the thing to look for was the source, the hidden strength in the darkness of the meadow ground that gives up nutrients and moisture on which the flourishing meadow depends. A life upwards towards the light, from strength, in a hidden dark. Hidden dark; final light; and between them the continual, changing evolution of life. Without the hidden source, there could be no abundance. Without the regenerative darkness, the light might attend in vain.

I was on my way to Lourdes. A long journey. One change at Toulouse. As the train batted on, all the thoughts, faces, sounds and people, seemed to roll away from me, out of this gathering lap, and back on to their own ground. I wondered why I felt so tired. That kind of flattening, grey tiredness, that is bland and dull and empty.

In the usual way, I found myself beside a sad lady, not a widow this time, someone who had been visiting her mother in Toulouse. Her mother was in hospital, dying of cancer. She described to me the pain of pain; how it could hold you apart, when what you longed to do was come close together. She lived in Pau. She was making the journey into Toulouse every other day. She was longing for it all to be over, but she was dreading the emptiness, the lack of resolve between them, that she felt sure would remain. She was in her late sixties, but her childhood relationship with her mother, seemed as if it was yesterday, without the intervening years of marriage and children. I listened, marvelling at the depth of intensity and capacity that is in every human life.

Compostela was coming closer. It had not been in the original budget, but I was determined to get there. Lourdes, then Compostela. At Pau the smart, sad daughter left the train. She said she never usually spoke about herself, but it had helped. She thanked me. I had only listened. 'One forgets,' she said, 'how natural all these problems are; how commonplace this kind of pain is.'

There were only two of us left in the carriage. Lourdes was the end of the line. Lourdes. Great crowds once again. People think about miracles and holy water, but it is not about that. Apparently it is about penance.

12

Lourdes

'It is better to say I'm suffering, than to say –
This landscape is ugly.'

SIMONE WEIL

I REMEMBER MY grandmother's small bottle of Lourdes water. A very cloudy glass Madonna. The precious liquid never seemed to be used, it just evaporated away. I remember her great length of rosary beads, also from Lourdes, that hung on the wall beside her bed. All her pieties had seemed strange, but endearing, because they were part of her, and her struggle, in her old age, towards some kind of atonement for a rather romantic past. Romantic anyway, as it was handed down to us. Her long affair with a Frenchman, when it ended, or maybe because she could not end it, she tried to take her life, by jumping from a window. She broke her hip, and always walked lop-sided after that. Everything about her was at an angle; the wide-brimmed hat, the head, the mouth, the whole expression; all of it seemed to be a part of some sadness, a search for some forsaken self, that she seemed to find in her Catholicity. A Catholicity of rosaries, candles, blessings, novenas, and the greatest joy of all – her son. Born to her late, after her return to the original marriage bed. Her son became a priest; her most dreamed of, expiatory gift to God.

I left the train thinking vaguely of her, and the deep trench that her faith had been. Something gripping and sad; something dark, full of sorrow and longing.

Lourdes didn't seem like France. It was wet and cold. Heavy grey

194

clouds over dark, green hills, hardly mountains. It felt like Ireland.

I wandered vaguely down the hill, riveted by all the brightly painted hotels. Madeleine, at Lisieux, had told me of a convent opposite the Grotto, but it was after 9 p.m. and the convent was a considerable distance from the station.

The bright hotels, that in Ireland might have read 'Atlantic View' were here, instant reminders that you were in a place of pilgrimage. More pilgrims come to Lourdes than Rome or Jerusalem, over four-and-a-half million a year.

I wandered on past these eager, hotel façades, all with 'vacancies' in the window. Hotel Saint Thérèse, Saint Teresa, Saint Jude, Saint Antony, Saint Anselm, Pious 12th, Holy Nazerath, Angelus etc., etc. There was even Hotel Solitude in the middle of it all.

Although it looked as if it might rain any minute, I didn't feel beckoned by any of the vacancies in the windows. Every so often something said 'Grotto'. I vaguely wondered if I should go there, but it was in the opposite direction to all the hotels.

The streets were completely deserted. Suddenly I heard footsteps behind me. A tiny, cheerful couple were coming very fast down the centre of the road. They recognised me. I had asked them which platform for Lourdes, when we were racing for the train at Toulouse.

They were Roger and Josephine Arpin from the mountains of Saint Maurice. It was their holiday. Usually they went on holiday to relatives, but they had all died. They had been before to Lourdes. They told me to follow them to a very cheap lodging; many were very, very dear. Roger indicated the gleaming hotels all round us. They raced on, laughing and arguing with each other about the right direction to take. Two nuns looked extremely disapproving as we clattered past. At last, shrieks of joy, they had found it. La Familiale. A small hotel above a gift shop. Yes, there were rooms.

In the rain and grey cold, nothing seems more bleak than an empty gift shop, full of Marian pieties. A little girl was doing her homework in the shop. Encouraged by Monsieur, I bought the English guide. A fresh one, brought out after the Papal visit in 1983. Business was certainly not booming. In the little dining-room, Madame, was working away at figures, on her typewriter. There was a party of school girls, that was all. Josephine and I had a *verveine* together. I also had soup and an apple. Roger had gone off to a bar. 'He's a little like this,' Josephine said, indicating with her elbow, frequent drinking, 'but we manage.' She was very amusing and direct, and quite convinced that there was no cheaper bed in the whole of Lourdes.

My room was four floors up, very small indeed, but with a large bed. The mattress was a dumpy mound of lumps and horsehair spikes and old brown feathers; as soft as cold porridge. There was a tiny square window looking out directly on to the Fort. I remembered that before the Marian Cult at Lourdes, this remote area of the Languedoc had had a fierce history; among other things the whole town was put to the sword by Simon de Montfort during the Albigensian Crusades.

I knew that the bed would play havoc with my back, but there was no space to think of putting the mattress on the floor. There was hardly space to stand. One night I thought, and Lourdes is a place for penance after all, not miracles. I had been told this so many times on my journey. The contemporary stress, is on a place of reconciliation, prayer and recognition of the Cross; our part in the Cross.

The next day, my back made it abundantly clear to me that I must find fresh accommodation. I thought I should seek out the Convent of the Assumption first, and then return for the baggage, if I got offered a bed. I visited the *cachot*, that was nearby. The *cachot* was a disused prison lock-up, that a cousin of Bernadette's family made available for the Soubrious when they were destitute. It was empty at the time, because it was felt to be unfit, even for prisoners.

You always have some preconceived ideas of a place, particularly anywhere as well known as Lourdes. People often mention the horrors of the gift shops; all the tasteless kitsch; the whole commercial bandwagon. I was expecting that, and real mountains. There is no drama about the landscape, there is typical, ash-white, spa stone, green hills and the racing river Gave.

The shape of the town and its relationship to the Grotto is laid out in such a way that you can easily visualise the walk, taken by the frail, asthmatic Bernadette from the *cachot* down to the area known as Massabielle, to collect firewood. It was here that the apparitions appeared to Bernadette, in 1858. It is quite some distance down the hill, past the fort, to the river, and then on to what must have been a wild, wooded area. High, under heavy, grey-black, overhanging rocks, is the Grotto, only a little way back from the river. The Gave is a wide, fast-moving, dash and swirl of greenish water.

Just as at Rocamadour, it is perfectly possible to go from station
to Grotto without passing the gift shops, and the general trading
buzz. The vast basilicas, both above and below the ground, the baths
and grotto, the hospitals and Way of the Cross, they are all in the
enclosed domain of the Grotto, separate from the other town. In
fact I felt sorry for the traders, they get continual flack from journal-
ists, but obviously what they sell is what the pilgrims want, and buy,
again and again. It all seems like a very legitimate market force.
Certainly the objects are fairly mind-blowing, but not all the in-
novations seem to catch on. A life-size, moving crib, was continually
empty; the nodding donkey outside, to the strains of Corelli, seemed
no incentive to entry.

That first morning, when I visited the *cachot*, it was fairly quiet,
it was early in the day and not the peak season, there were few
pilgrims. First, you go into a low-ceilinged room, which is full of
photographs and memorabilia, then a Sister sorts people into small
groups, ready to cross the narrow passage into the *cachot*, which is
a single space, four by four-and-a half yards. There is a very shallow,
low, stone sink and beside it the chimney breast, with an open grate.
There are two shuttered windows. The slate window sills are deep
enough to sit on. The atmosphere is grey and still. People simply
come in, and stand and stare in silence. It is hard to imagine that a
family of six ever lived here. They had two beds and a table. The
windows could never be opened to let out the smoke from the fire,
as the flies and smells from the yard outside would have been
intolerable. It must have been terrible to wash clothes, and cooking
pots, and bodies, just in that small sink. I sat for some while on the
window sill beside the sink. Maybe Bernadette and the family had
sat there, or possibly, it had housed pots and pans and plates. How
damp and dark it must have been. Living in such terrible, brutalising
conditions, faith would be forced, either to become dead and bitter,
or heroic. The usually vague, comfortable, middle ground, would
seem impossible. If you believed in God, and His Love, and His
Mother, with her love, you might very well think of little else. It
would be the only imaginative thread, to lead you, to some extent,
away from a living hell.

In that little room, it was impossible not to feel close to the young
girl, with the dark, serious, heavy-lidded eyes, the full mouth and
the round face, framed by a headscarf; the shawl, and the gathered
peasant skirts. Bernadette had severe asthma, she was always unwell

after her recovery from cholera. That walk down to the grotto, for the fire-wood must have been exhausting for her.

Bernadette, the simplicity and dire poverty of her short, dramatic, public life, subsequent to the eighteen apparitions, feels real and close to you in the *cachot*. Finally 'Aquero', That One, which is how Bernadette referred to the Madonna, gave her name, after insistent requests from Bernadette, encouraged by the parish priest.

I am the Immaculate Conception.

From that moment, the parish priest, Father Peyramale, was convinced that the visions were authentic. Consistently Bernadette remained firm and calm against intolerant and aggressive handling. She insisted that there were no miracles as far as she knew. Lourdes was not about miracles. The lady had said to build a chapel above the grotto, and to pray, especially for priests, and to process. The lady had simply indicated to Bernadette where the spring was, and said she could wash her face there. Clean water, would have meant far more to Bernadette, living in the *cachot*, than we can imagine.

There were many other springs and Marian shrines in the area. Lourdes might have remained, simply a chapel by a river, with local pilgrims coming to the place. In 1862 the Bishop of Tarbes authorised the cult. Huge crowds came. The professionals, the Garaison Fathers, moved in. They were expert organisers of visionary moments and subsequent pilgrimage. The *domaine*, the land surrounding the grotto, was bought. The train came.

The Catholic Church, particularly in France, was consistently threatened during these times. In 1870 the Dogma of Papal Infallibility was defined. In 1871, during the Paris Commune, the Archbishop of Paris was murdered. Catholics needed to show strength and solidarity. In 1872 there was a pilgrimage of twenty thousand to Lourdes, predominantly of Royalists. There seems to have been more to the founding of Lourdes than Bernadette, her visions, and the fairly low key demands of Our Lady, for a chapel, prayers and processing.

I made my way up on the outer edge of the town, to the Convent of the Assumption, which is a substantial building, standing alone in its own considerable, high grounds. The back of the convent looks out across to the Grotto, the river, hills and woods, and the vast area of green grass, where pilgrims picnic and pray. All through the day small groups celebrate mass, up and down the banks of this belting pulse of green water.

The convent had been a school, now, like so many of these religious houses, it is a retreat house. It accommodates both large, organised retreats, and small, personal pauses, for those known to the Community.

The Sister in charge registered some surprise, that I had not written in advance. Prudence again, or rather a lack of it. Although I feel inclined to believe in the alternative prudence, of letting things happen. At first the Sister found definitely, no bed; no space whatsoever. Then after another look, good heavens yes, a cancellation. There was a bed after all. The Sister escorted me upstairs and showed me into a room, with its own douche and lavatory. In the room was a small writing table. The bed itself was marvellously hard. It was certainly the highest standard of accommodation, comfort and privacy I had experienced.

There were about fifty Sisters from various Orders from all over the world, staying in the convent for a week's retreat. They were from Canada, South America, the Philippines, and various parts of Africa, also France itself. I would eat with the Sisters in silence. Three meals a day; please attend all meals. There was a rota for washing up, laying of tables, clearing etc. There was not only a key for the room, there was a series of keys available, to open the gates on the private route, under the railway and into the *domaine*, the area of the Grotto, basilicas etc. There were two libraries in the convent and one small salon, with a balcony, looking directly across to the Grotto. The price, including all three meals, was less than La Familiale. Roger and Josephine would be amazed.

I felt very grateful to Madeleine's advice. The convent was extremely bright and cheerful, the Sisters were young and active, full of humour, and very hardworking, between the regular hours of Sung Office in the Chapel.

But there was something about Lourdes itself, which made me feel deeply apprehensive. From the small salon I saw the Grotto just as I had seen it before on so many postcards, all my life. There were the flickering candles and the steady, slow stream of people. I must admit, I felt nothing but dread at the idea of going down there. I don't know why, but there seemed to be this cold, grey dark over it all, despite the vast, white statues; that kind of harsh, screaming white, that is almost as bad as chalk slipping on a blackboard.

Again and again I made my way down, and up, and down again. I was perplexed and miserable at my own chilling dismay and deep unease. All day there were people waiting outside the baths, waiting to be admitted through the blue and white curtains; many more women than men. All day there were bustling crowds at the brass taps, filling plastic water containers, bottles, and glass madonnas, and washing their faces and hands, and drinking. It is very clear water. It has the cold sting of stone in it. I washed my face, and drank from my hands when there was a free tap. All day, groups from all over the world, bearing banners of their town, parish, country, or organisation, gather for mass by the river, or to make the steep Way of the Cross, up the wooded hill above the Grotto. There are long queues for candles, huge candles, that are never able to burn themselves out, until February, when a giant fire, cleans up all the long, left-over lengths of wax.

Every afternoon there is the Procession of the Blessed Sacrament. The sick, who are able to walk, gather under the trees on metal benches, which have *malades* written on them in blue and white enamel. The place, in front of the Basilica of the Rosary is contained by a great swoop of steeply rising, balustrated walkways, that run up to either side of the door to the Basilica of the Immaculate Conception. Every afternoon the balustrades are packed with people watching the progress of the procession.

The procession moves out from the Grotto itself. The *brancardiers*, the officials of Lourdes, keep the crowds in check. The procession always takes the same route, from the Grotto, down the esplanade, and upwards towards the basilica. On past yet another crowned Virgin, into the area directly in front of the church, where the sick are waiting in wheelchairs, and on stretchers, or in the rather wonderful, rickshaw-like vehicles, with their bright blue hoods, a protection against sun or wind or rain. They are pulled, rather than pushed. Every day, before the procession is due to start, you are suddenly aware of a flurry of activity as nurses, nuns and *brancardiers* race their rickshaws to get the sick into position.

Different pilgrimages head the procession each day. The shape and feel of the procession alters with each pilgrimage. There are always the priests leading, and then the canopy and the Blessed Sacrament held high in its star of gold. Once the processing is over, the priests walk slowly among the sick. Again and again the blessed sacrament is raised in blessing over them. This is sometimes the time of miracles. Certainly there have been many miracles and dramatic remissions of chronic disease, sometimes at Lourdes, sometimes months or years after a visit. Authenticating miracles is a fairly grisly business. Miracles are not emphasised now. People say: I'm not here for a miracle; just for hope, peace, and reconciliation. But when you see crumpled little people in pushchairs and lying on the stretchers; distorted limbs, lost, stiff expressions, the concept of cure must be somewhere in the mind of the brave and loving parents and carers. The majority of the sick do seem to be old, and to be women; rows and rows and rows, tucked in by brightly-knitted nursery blankets, a mosaic of coloured squares. From dawn to dusk the *domaine* is a buzz of movement and activity.

In front of the Grotto itself, there is a large area of smooth stone; it is sometimes closed, sometimes open, depending on the time of day. Always a steady stream of people, move slowly round the Grotto, below the dark niche in the rock, where the tall, white statue stands. Bernadette, when shown the statue exclaimed, 'My God, how you deface her.' She was also shown an icon of the Madonna, and was said to have felt 'Aquero' was more like that. But her reactions were virtually disregarded, the blue sash is there, as Bernadette said, and the rosary beads, and the clasped hands, and the eyes lifted to Heaven.

The extraordinary force of simple, accumulated pressure, is brought home to you, by the marble-smooth surface of the grey rock, where every day, for over a hundred years, hands have felt their way, as they go towards the spring, now covered under glass, and out once more into the light.

In the evening there is the Candlelit Procession, it takes the same route, as the Blessed Sacrament Procession. Everyone carries a lighted candle. The hymns, the Credo, the Salve Regina and of course the Lourdes Hymn itself, sound out clearly above the crowd, from a loudspeaker system, but it seems to lessen rather than encourage the voices of the pilgrims. Intermittently there are warnings given against crime. Thieving is a major problem.

The Basilica of the Rosary, and above it, the Basilica of the Immaculate Conception, are nineteenth-century gothic. High, pointed towers rise up against the hills. The buildings are constituted in a grey-white cold stone. Accommodating spaces for vast crowds, never cease to be built. There is a new Sanctuary of Lourdes, inaugurated as recently as 1988. It has a rather sombre South Bank, feel to it. It can accommodate five thousand. It is used for conferences as well as worship. The main Sunday masses are usually con-celebrated underground in the Basilica of St Pious 10th, inaugurated in 1958. This basilica has a capacity for twenty-five thousand. It is rather like being in the rib cage of a whale.

There are other chapels, the Chapel of Reconciliation, a little room, with wooden cubicles on every side. Robed priests wait with their breviaries open. Above the cubicles is written the language within which confession may be heard. Margery Kempe would have been delighted, her non-existent access to foreign tongues made the sacrament of penance in faraway places, like Rome, Jerusalem and Compostela, a considerable trial for her. It often gave rise to more scruples than a sense of forgiveness.

There are Foyers of the Missions, Pavilions of Vocation and many cinemas, with non-stop films on Bernadette and Padre Pio. And of course there are the shops and cafés, with easy ramps for wheelchairs.

For me, the *domaine*, was a grippingly sad, grey, somehow static place. Thousands and thousands of people, all with inward looking eyes, as they stare out. I felt nothing but increasing alienation and dread. I have many friends, who have been greatly helped by visits to Lourdes, both as the sick, and as parents of the sick, and as helpers of the sick. Thinking of their joy and comfort with the experience, only made me more perplexed and anxious, with my own dark, miserable, utterly dejected sense.

Of course, as I processed and wandered generally about, I had to wonder where my feelings were rooted. Why did it seem so to me? Was it muddled belief?

There is a strong mix in Lourdes of papal preoccupation and the dogmatic edge of the Immaculate Conception. For me, the whole Madonna bit can be difficult, because the inconography, almost all the images have been made in the language of a male view of female purity. Maybe for women, their view of purity, might be of strength; real form. Something wise and known; way beyond girl. That kind of female expression is hard to find. I can cope much better with mysterious, little black stubs of Madonnas, as at Le Puy or Roca-madour, they seem like coals of fire grown cold, but they still remain alive with energy and mystery.

The need to define Papal Infallibility as late as 1870, has always seemed to me, to demonstrate a lack of faith in the gifts and power of the Holy Spirit to mankind. The message of Christ is so huge, so clear, perfectly understandable by anyone. Love God. Love your neighbour. Love your enemies. It seems enough to be going on with. Who needs dogma? Continued emphasis on papal authority seems to infer this lack of faith. It seems to put Pope before the Holy Spirit as guardian of the Church.

In his book *The Marriage of East and West Bede*, Griffiths writes: 'The fact that Rome became the centre of Christendom is an accident of history, and the Bishop of Rome only acquired his present position after many centuries. One may hold that this development was providential, but there is no reason to believe that the present structure of the papacy is permanent, or that the Church may not acquire a new structure in the context of future history.'

Even though it may not always seem so, history, like the river Gave moves fast and furiously.

Perhaps it was the nineteenth-century religious art, that so depressed my spirits. Without the disciplines that are imposed on icon painters and Buddhist artists, it is easy for sacred images to become increasingly decadent. Without some sense of abstract awe, images easily deteriorate into extremely sentimental human terms.

I heard many complaints that times had changed. No one made the Way of the Cross on their knees. The *brancardiers* talked to one another as they wheeled the sick, once they would have been saying the rosary. There was less silence. People even spoke in front of the Grotto. People even picnicked by the river. 'Everyone now is egoist,' one local lady said. I'm still not sure what she meant to imply.

It got colder and colder. I found the walk up and down the hill from the convent quite a task. Most of the nuns on retreat buzzed up and down, taking in two processions each day. I felt ridiculously wretched. Perhaps I had just run out of steam. In the convent grounds, against a far wall, beyond rubble and overgrown grass, there were thirty red-brick, disused rabbit hutches. Each one had an arched wooden door, under a curve of bricks. They were beautifully made, stepped in tiers, to follow the sloping shape of the ground. I began to find them and the river, the two most sustaining sights.

Life at the Convent of the Assumption was a comfort. There was something very earthing about those silent, five-course meals. The were always so carefully presented; the napkins rolled carefully and put back afterwards in the numbered cubby holes. There were generous supplies of red wine. Throughout the meals taped music was played. Vivaldi, Beethoven, a minuet, a pavane. The tables were hexagonal. In silence, character comes strongly to the fore. The diffident, the humorous, the disapproving. I became fascinated by the physical resemblances. The feel of the the skin, and the thin, almost vanished lips. The watchful, rather wistful eyes; a kind of attending wisdom. Many were small, rather homely figures, but full of energy. They reminded me of old-fashioned nannies, as in *Brideshead Revisited*. Nannies that might be found knitting in the upper rooms of a large house. Nannies, who know so much of what goes on, but say so little, unless asked. The glance, the pause; a language of nuance and inference, while folding clothes or stirring tea. While ecclesiastical dramas run on in the grand rooms and curia corridors, maybe these simple 'nannies' keep the fire going; mending and stitching, giving comfort and consolation. They are certainly a strong force always to be relied upon.

One evening three Sisters approached me. I was, they realised, a Little Sister of Saint Charles de Foucauld, might they speak with me, they had friends in the Order. I couldn't believe it. A second time. I had to ask what had given them the idea. They became very shy, and then blushing they told me ... 'Well ... the little Sisters wear blue ... and their clothes are often very worn and shabby ...' This must have been my rather long and faded Hobbs skirt, a cast-off from my daughter. It had gained a certain patina of the road, and had become increasingly comforting to me because of that.

There was a diverting small group of people staying in the convent, not nuns, and not on retreat. Tell us about Margaret, they asked eagerly one morning. Well, I have never voted for her, I began. No. No. not that Margaret, they interrupted. Margaret. Margaret, your Princess. They were eager for news. One young woman was keen to put me in touch with Charismatics in Kent. Denise spoke in tongues. She explained to me that whereas Lucifer can understand prayer, he realises that the Our Father, or Hail Mary are addressed to heaven, tongues on the other hand are safe from him. They are a direct, coded route to the Almighty.

As the grey days passed I wondered about the baths. There were always long queues. Some of the nuns were bath addicts, some had never been. All stressed that the point was penance. It was an act of faith.

One morning there was a blustering north wind between heavy showers. The *domaine* was practically deserted. No one was queueing for the baths. I paused by the sign. I was promptly ushered in through the blue and white curtains. There was the sound of piped music. More blue and white curtains and then into the waiting cubicle, which takes six bodies at a time. A pilgrimage from Kildare was bathing, so the helpers were all speaking English. There were one or two strays, not from the pilgrimage. I was assumed to be a stray. 'Dutch or German most probably, she can't understand a thing,' I heard one of them say of me. 'Petticoat and bra on', they yelled, 'everything else off.' Dazed women peeled down their clothes. One elderly woman was busy unwinding bandages from a raw, superating wound. But you could hardly look, speed was the thing. Another curtain, and there was the bath, like a narrow, stone cattle trough, just a step down. Utterly paralysed, and very grateful to be assumed to be Dutch, I stared for a second into the clear water. Then the ladies, one at each side, with horrifying speed, yanked off the bra and petticoat, and threw a large, wet length of mutton cloth, over the body, presumably in the interests of some kind of modesty. 'In now, sit down, sit down, not your head.' I suppose for speed they pushed on the shoulders. I felt as if I had gone through some fairground curtain, into a ghost train, where things flapped at you, and voices called. One of the women grabbed up a small, white statue from the end of the bath. 'Kiss our lady and say your prayer ... now.' The statue was put to my lips. It was all over in seconds. A dunking. Mutton cloth off. Clothes on. No towels.

Seconds later, I was beside that marvellous, loud, pounding river. There was a curiously warm feel on my wet body. Water and stone once again. A place of water and stone. For me, some sort of atrophied sadness; something frozen in time; something beyond any coherence I could tap into.

The last day was glorious, with a really warm sun. I met many English people at the café tables. Pilgrims from Catford, Croydon and Carnarvon. All were thrilled with Lourdes. For most of them, it was a longed-for visit. 'She'll get you back if you ask her, she'll always find a way,' one man said from his wheel chair. They talked of peace of mind and spiritual healing. Rita, one of the helpers, described how suddenly, many years ago she had decided to take a child suffering from Down's syndrome to Lourdes. She had cashed in all the family savings. Her husband had been furious. But from that beginning, they now had a regular business, taking the sick to Lourdes. They had a special ambulance vehicle, with a lift for wheelchairs. Rita said that the benefit for those, isolated by disease and disability was incalcuable. Suddenly on the pilgrimage, in a group, they were wanted and loved. They were the priority. It was often hard for them when they had to return home.

In Rita's party, there was a very charming Yorkshire man – Bill Alexander. He was over eighty. He had been to Lourdes four times. I asked him what Our Lady meant to him? He was eager to reply.

'She's the love of my life, Jini. It's like this. In the war we'd have photographs, wouldn't we, the wife and kids. And we'd look at them, and feel close to them. That's how it is with Mary. I have her there, at home, up on the piano. I took up the piano when my wife died. A bit of Beethoven. A bit of Scott Joplin. I'll turn to her when I'm playing ... What do you think Mother? How is it? It's all right lad ... Carry on, carry on. Lourdes is sad. Of course it's sad, but it's wonderful. I'll tell you this, Jini, if they don't feel it when they come, then there's something wrong with them.'

I was glad Bill felt so certain and so happy. I was glad also, that I had my ticket for Spain, booked to Irun for the next morning. From there, as soon as I could, I would make my way to the far west of Galicia. To Santiago de Compostela.

13
Santiago de Compostela

> 'Give me my scallop-shell of quiet,
> My staff of faith to walk upon
> My scrip of joy, immortal diet,
> My bottle of salvation,
> My gown of glory hope's true gage,
> And thus I'll take my pilgrimage.'
>
> SIR WALTER RALEIGH

LOURDES STATION WAS deserted. Nobody was bound for Irun or Bayonne, so it seemed. By midday I would be in Spain. I felt drained and derelict. It is almost a relief, when the body makes all the demands, then there is little energy left for the mind. It seems to float in some grey pond, where there is no reflection or movement, simply a staring, numb soup of stagnant being.

I remembered reading that Madame Martin, mother of Thérèse, when she was very ill with breast cancer, had been taken to Lourdes, and she had hated it. She said she had never felt worse. It had been awful. She lost her dead sister's rosary, the bottle of Lourdes water leaked, their provisions were uneatable. She tore her clothes, they missed the train, her daughters complained. Once again you are left with variety; the subjective response. One man's meat, is another man's poison, something like that.

I couldn't wait to go and yet I felt sad. I was getting so close to the end of my journey. We had had a plan that Mark might meet me in Compostela, but funds didn't allow for it. Mine hardly allowed for it either. But Saint James is the archetype of the pilgrim traveller, and his city Santiago, his city, high in Galicia, it must in some way be the point of resolve.

I was very sad that my journey had to be hurried. By train through the night, instead of on foot all the way, taking the ancient routes as so many have done and are still doing today. Still, Margery Kempe's seven-day sail from King's Lynn to Compostela must have been very tough and hazardous, although not on foot. Perhaps the interior way is the one that counts in the end. No journey can be more dark and difficult, unexpected and hazardous than that. There is always somewhere this deep, searching sense, that you are, in some respects, unlike anyone else, and in this, there is a very particular purpose.

The train came. Nearly all the carriages were empty sleepers: crumpled, sallow bedding, crumbs, cans, plastic bags and water bottles. The spaces were stuffy and exhausted, the windows were opaque with dirt, streaked with brown stains. And yet this overall emptiness was peculiarly full, as if the bodies that had been there, had left some part of themselves behind. Poor train, it could not possibly be otherwise. It had started at Pisa, from there to Genoa, Marseilles, Toulouse, then Lourdes, and from there over the border to Irun.

Very slowly, with endless shunting and pausing, we made our way. Sometimes there were half hour pauses beside high banks and factories, scabby, industrial spaces. The abstract patterns in the window dirt, were almost more lively than the landscape beyond them. After Bayonne I strained for some sign that it was really Spain. But the gritty banks of buddleia, valerian, and maiden hair fern, the allotments and drizzle, almost made me half expect to see Brookwood Cemetery. Occasionally, the dark, high banks, gave way to concrete living spaces; grim towers of flats, the windows blinded with lengths of washing that had no hope of drying.

At last it said Irun.

Irun. I had imagined nothing in particular. Just a station and the usual waiting places that go with it. But Irun is not a station. It is a vast building site waiting to become one. Girders, cables, cement sacks, broken glass; people lying on cardboard in the cement dust. The loos were made. And there was a small café, the rest was noise and grit, drills and cranes and general chaos. No computer working for cash cards, no timetables, no telephones. It was midday. The only train to Compostela was at 6.30 p.m. travelling through the night, arriving at Orense at 7.05 in the morning, change there, and wait for the 9 a.m. train to Compostela.

Loud rain, railed down on to every surface. I realised I must get to a bank for cash; that would mean carting the baggage, as there was no place to leave it.

I crossed the tracks and came out on to the streets, beside a

derelict, domed church of incredible gloom. I felt grateful for the
pounding rain, it was at least a live force in some way, and it made
you move on. It was certainly more live than the boarded shops,
litter, and dog shit. What could I do with all the hours of waiting?
Any sort of philosphy or calm completely deserted me. I tried to
remember that a far worse fate would be to live in Irun. Poor
Irunians.

I could find few bars or cafés. But there were banks. In the end I
found a small bar with sawdust on the floor, and a dining area. The
patron, shuffling from table to table in his carpet slippers, was
serving bread and soup, a thin, transparent liquid, with jabs of pork
fat staring up out of the steam.

I thought how easily resolve and purpose diminish into the soft
trash, of self absorption; the stupid illusion that one's minimal
hardship has some kind of relevance. How you decide to look at a
situation, will dictate how you feel towards it. You are still in
command if you choose. There is always choice.

Back in the glum station café, several waited. A man attempted to
sweep the green-tiled floor, but there was so much loose cement, he
might have been drawing in the sand, with his long, stubble broom.
An Italian sculptor, expansive on two or three brandies, asked me
where I was going. 'Compostela? Ah ... pilgrimage. Well then, all
this,' he indicated the grey dereliction and chaos, 'all this is fine for
you. Every trial is good. Just part of the struggle, part of the journey.'

That was how it should be. But the grey of Lourdes had tunnelled
me back somehow, into this cul-de-sac of hopelessness.

Then a surprising teacher of immeasurable quality came into the
café. He was a little fair-haired boy of five, called Jonathan. His
father, wore his hair tied back into a pigtail, Mahabharata style.
They looked worn out, Their clothes were crumpled and spent. The
father was struggling with the child's bag, into which a bottle of
milk had been spilt, all over the clothes. Both were calm and gentle,
utterly without complaint. I suggested that if he liked, I would stay
with Jonathan, and he could go to the loo and wash out the bag
properly. This he did. He was French. They lived in Gap. They
were on their way to Setubal in Portugal. They had been travelling
since the previous evening.

With a small bag of peanuts, some sodden biscuits and a
plastic car, Jonathan remained calm and happy, and completely
undemanding for over six hours in that café. His father was a guide,

for off-piste skiing. Out of season he roughed out for a sculptor. He had first seen mountain snow when he was twenty. Instantly he had known that his vocation was snow. He had fallen in love with the mountains. Jonathan's intense pleasure at being with his father made up for everything else. He obviously felt complete just to be with his father. It never occurred to him to ask for anything. His security and peace of mind were there, in the love and trust he had for his father. Watching them together, made me think, that if any individual, really loved and trusted God, then they would experience that calm and stability, at all times and in all places.

At 6.15, they boarded a train that would reach Lisbon at 9 a.m. the next morning. Jonathan was a memorable child. The night train for me, was free to be boarded at 6.30. It was very clean. Everything was pale blue, with light, varnished wood. At last I was really focused towards Compostela. In the bright, cheerful carriage space, that would soon leave Irun, my spirits rose. All those shells; on doors, on lintels, in floors: in tapestry, frescoes, wood, steel, and stone. All those shells leading you like stars towards Santiago. Santiago, this eccentric place of pilgrimage that has grown out of legend, into its own myth, beckoning, believers and unbelievers, scholars and convicts (apparently for some offences in Holland and Belgium, the offender may choose to walk to Compostela, instead of a prison sentence).

A woman from another carriage came in to tell me to join her. On no account travel solo ... No. No. Not solo. It is dangerous, very dangerous. She was hectic and hectoring. At 6.30 on a bright evening, her stories seemed simply exaggeration. I stayed where I was.

At last we were off. The seats were comfortable, but the rolling stock was no relation at all of the smooth run on the S.N.C.F. lines. We hurtled and bucked, rocked and plunged like jumping beans. There were frequent stops, soon the carriages were full. Three times, haversacked English people asked, 'Is this first class?' And they were amazed it was not, which must say something about British Rail.

A young, very serious Swedish couple came into the carriage. They spoke a slow, measured English. They had travelled extensively together, South America, India, Egypt, Turkey, Greece. Proudly they told me of all the rail trips they had taken in Spain. But they had spent very little time out of the stations. All their travel had brought them to the conclusion that there was no place that was a patch on Sweden. Why? Because Sweden has hills and fields and rivers, our land is the best. They were getting out at Palencia at 1 a.m. in the morning. They began to regale me with tales of horror on the night trains. 'They put chloroform on you while you sleep, and then take your purse, You mustn't be alone with the men. You mustn't be alone on the night train.'

There were men everywhere. There seemed only to be men. I decided to heed their warnings. I went to find a carriage with a woman in it. I found a very charming couple alone in a carriage. They would be on the train all night, they were going the full extent of the journey. The Señor was frail, he looked erudite and distinguished. He was full of charm and courtesy. His wife was considerably younger than him. Her ambition was to keep the curtains drawn, to put people off coming into the carriage, so that we could both lie flat out on the seats. Señor would remain sitting upright. I could lie flat beside him, with my knees up. Many, many people would get on at Miranda. The Señora was enthusiastic that my inability to speak Spanish could help in keeping people out. I could just refuse to understand them. I hoped she was right.

The Señora was a very vivacious, engaging person. I was sad that my Spanish, was little more than a sign language. Very soon the Señora got down a picnic basket. There was a bottle of wine, white linen table napkins, ham rolls, cake and tomatoes. They insisted that I should share with them. I felt restored by their company and generosity. Although my back was very painful, I had grown to realise that it would never actually fall apart. It was simply pain, and at the end of the journey, there would be a flat, hard, surface once again, floor or earth, it wouldn't matter. After the wine and rolls and cake, the Señora took down a flask. I thought it was coffee. In fact it was sweetened hot milk, which I regretted very much, but without drains, or open windows, or ground, there was no alternative but to drink it.

Tolosa. Alsasua. Victoria. Miranda. Burgos. Palencia.

The picnic was packed away. The Señor, his black beret off his head, slept upright. Both of them had changed into slippers. The Señora had a small, lacy pillow; smiling, she said goodnight and lay flat out on the seat, a large fur coat and scarf tucked over her. In the moonlight she might have been a child, all you could see were a few dark curls, and the small feet, in soft black slippers. I lay down, as she had directed me. Because the curtains had to be drawn against the corridor to discourage people, I could no longer see the moon. It felt as if you were being trundled in a wooden wheelbarrow over craters and pot holes. I thought of Jonathan and his father. The night felt as if it was a length of experience out of time. The only reality were the bumps and voices, the station lights, a pause, and then the slap, slap, slap of the doors closing. That you had any other life or name, or being, seemed simply illusion. I just thought Dawn. The shift of dark. Strands of light.

Occasionally people looked in, but they always passed on. Then at Leon a square-headed man, with pale cream shoes and white socks, came purposely into the carriage. He said something to the Señor, but he never moved. He indicated the sleeping Señora under her black mound of fur. He went on talking as he put his bags up on to the rack. I had no alternative but to give him space between myself and the Señor. He was eager to speak, but he was greeted with nothing but silence. The corridor outside was packed. There was no shape or texture to the sky, just a great slap of darkness. I longed to find tentative skeins of light, beginning to seep, imperceptibly into the dark. The man jutted his square chin, horribly close to mine. Lean on me, he said. If he was not attempting to touch me, he was staring at me with grim, pickaxe, eyes. Twice I was forced to jump up swearing. I wished the Señora would wake. Each time the man would apologise, but he would stare on, and begin the whole procedure again. I showed explicit distress and left the carriage, but in the corridor it was worse and more of the same. It was most unpleasent. You feel so furious to be trapped, by awful, rampant male hunger; it is so pathetic. My swearing and fury only seemed to encourage him. At last there were streaks of light in the sky; mountains, buildings and telegraph poles were just discernible. To be flooded sick with intense loathing is hugely debilitating. At last, at some station, he peered out and read the sign and it made him move. The bag was down. I stared at the floor, willing those awful pale shoes to get lost, once and for all. He went out into the corridor, saying, that now I too could lie down flat, like the Señora. I thought he was gone, then suddenly he came back, and grabbed at me. This time my Anglo-Saxon expletives worked. The Señora woke. He was gone. The train moved on without him. Loathing and fury leave a terribly bitter and rank taste. The Señora apologised for sleeping. She said her husband was deaf.

'Listen,' she said, sitting up, full of life and sparkle. 'You must say this very loudly, if it happens again *Adondiba Steth. Adondiba Steth.* (my spelling is phonetic) She made me repeat the phrase after her. Luckily I never had any cause to use it.

Then, at last the night was past. Like blind cattle, we had crossed the breadth of Spain. Even if it was not on foot, I felt that there must be some legitimate pilgrim travel in that roughly bundled night.

Seven o'clock. Orense. The Señor and Señora were washed and brushed and had changed out of their slippers. 'Compostela is nothing like Lourdes,' the Señora said, 'Compostela is heart and life, you will love it.'

There was not much heart and life in Orense 7 a.m. The only loo was overflowing; one panel of the door was missing. In the station bar a group of men were drinking brandy, they looked as if they might have been there all night. Several sad, tired women sat at small, black tables. I joined them, and stared at black shoes, white socks and sugar papers. There was one man in a huge Joseph Beuys overcoat, and homburg hat. The fabric was so worn; there was a shine on the elbows and cuffs, like a snail thread over smooth stones. Form and texture are such a consolation. With the animation of light, you are never bereft of extraordinarily rich and complex harmonies, to remind you that anything may be beautiful, and nothing is as it seems.

By 9 a.m. Orense was full of life. The little train to Compostela was simply two carriages. Very slowly it climbed and climbed and climbed. There were rocks and shade, steep ravines and still water. The land was increasingly dry; gaunt, black pine-spikes, demonstrated the continual devastation of the land from fires. By the railway line, there were foxgloves, daisies and butterflies. But the land was very poor; tumbled stone dwellings, fallen walls, bracken running into the little pockets of pasture; sometimes goats; sometimes buzzards. The climb went on. This dry, deserted land felt as if it was a spiral of smoke curling its way up and up, far from the cities and traffic and people below.

Many of the stations were well kept, with flowers, and brightly painted wooden surfaces. At last the land began to level out a little, as if we might be reaching a plateau. There was more cultivation. There were well-made walls, cool corridors of vine, with cows sheltering in them, and the distinctive, carved wooden store houses for the maize, that looked rather Russian, but are particular to Galicia. It was similar to Ireland, without the emerald green. The yard dogs, the odd-shaped fields, the flat, sharp, tooth-stones, making the dividing walls, the single women working: straw hat, broad brown arms, apron and gumboots.

That terrible trundling night seemed like a boulder hurled back down now, and out of mind. This was Galicia. Here legend says Saint James walked and told of Christ, before he was summoned back to Jerusalem, where on arrival he was beheaded by Herod Aggripa. James was the first apostle to be martyred. His death is a fact, the rest is legend. Legend tells how angels and/or disciples managed to sail back to Galicia, so beloved of the apostle, bringing with them his remains. The boat sailed up the tidal estuary, the Iria Flavia, to what is now Padron. Oxen pulled the huge stone sarcophagus, until exhausted, they could go no further. So there, in a small field, where the oxen stopped, the sarcophagus was buried.

It was later, in the ninth century, when a shepherd was tending his flock that he saw one night, a bright star hanging low over a particular spot in a field. He told the local priest, who decided a hole must be dug in the spot indicated by the bright star. This was duly done, and all Christendom was delighted and amazed to find the buried remains of James the Apostle, brother of John the Beloved, and son of Mary Salome. The thought that bones, so closely connected with the life of Christ were available to trusting pilgrims, sent waves of delirious excitment through the believing world. There were pilgrims, prayers and processions. A church was built to house the remains of the saint, Santiago, from the field of the star. Campo de Stella, finally Compostela.

The insignia of the shell, is noted in the guide books, but its origins are not discussed. It is simply the sign of the pilgrimage and the saint. But there are legends that say either an early pilgrim or one of the disciples bringing the remains, was forced to take flight from vagabonds and took to the water, where he nearly drowned, on reaching dry land and safety, he was found to be coverered in scallop shells.

All the legends have been consistently debunked by scholarship. It is myth, but a myth that inspires people, in 1990, throughout the year, to come to Santiago. On foot, on horseback, by boat and plane, they make tracks from Holland, Belgium, Italy, France, Germany,

Great Britain, France and Ireland, in fact from the four corners of the earth. Pilgrims follow the great medieval routes, starting in Arles, Orleans, Vézelay, or Le Puy, or even further from Cologne, Geneva or Frankfurt. Over mountains and plains, on and on, in the footsteps of history, with the shell, like a lode star to guide and encourage them. Vast cathedrals and small, Romanesque chapels, bridges, barns, rivers and plains link the pilgrim, to the past, to those dramatic and dangerous journeys, of risk and disease, penance, indulgence and absolution. For many contemporary pilgrims, inspiration is often cultural and anthropological, rather than consciously spiritual. But for whatever reason, *El Camino*, The Way, is a live expression of contemporary European culture. A unique link with the past. An affirmation of individuality. The search, and expression of purpose within experience.

Santiago de Compostela has a shining new station. Pale stone work and glass, blood-red girders and iron work, incorporating a mass of scallop shells. The rich colour of the ironwork reminded me of the *bordeaux* of the Buddhists, signifying compassion.

It was midday, hot and dusty. Another visible pilgrim got off the train. He was a very tall, rather gaunt figure. He was an historian from Brazil. He was bound for Madrid. He was carrying two heavy suitcases. He just had this one day to spend in Compostela. Together we began the climb up from the station, through busy streets, and parks, past bright shops, past the Place Vigo and then on up into the narrow streets of the old city. Continually there were glimpses of fine architectural detail, carvings, numerous churches, cool courtyards, high, ornately traced balconies full of flowers; the sound of birdsong, and the fast clip of feet rushing past. Together we went at a very slow pace, my book bag had become intolerably heavy. The back felt like a hot crush, without any strength or power. It is a steep climb. Like dogs straining at the leash, we sniffed the air, longing to sense our first glimpse of the cathedral.

Round another corner, past more strong stone buildings and into another large, still sloping square. There was the blast of pipes; melodies and instruments reminiscent of the music of Ireland. A dancing, haunting sound, full of the tapping feet of Kerry and Clare. These rhythms of celtic merriment and melancholy were so far removed from anything ecclesiastic.

We were at the back of the cathedral. Wide stone steps, and below them a fountain, and then the towering height of the building itself.

In those first few seconds, Santiago declared itself to me as a uniquely celebratory place, so far from the rest of the world, so high, so vibrant, so effortlessly on fire with the joy of itself.

I had no other thought but how to dump the baggage, how to be instantly rid of it and be free to feel the stunning charge of this place. Santiago is a university city, tall and very good-looking students fill the streets, as at Oxford or Cambridge. They are in great contrast to the rural people of Galicia, who come in daily for the market, they are very small indeed; dressed in black; milk churns or baskets on their heads; they come round street corners everywhere.

A group of female students came forward to offer me advice. They are all very keen to speak English. They knew of a convent. Two or three times I was eagerly taken and directed, up here, down there, but each time the convent I had been directed to was now an extremely expensive hotel, or a priests' seminary. I suddenly felt as if I would really die, collapse; become just a lump on a stone step. My general state was clearly obvious to many passers-by. Groups of little old ladies and more young people, all kept coming forward full of energy and gestures to point me towards *habitaciones*. They were all so concerned, but all pointed in consistently opposite directions, arguing madly among each other at the same time. Eventually a young girl, recognising the situation, firmly picked up my rucksack and took me by the hand, and marched me up to a small side street, *hospitallo*. We went into a newsagent that also rented rooms, mostly to students from the university. There was a room. It was on the first floor, with a tiny balcony, ideal as the Señora pointed out, for drying clothes. The mother of the young family who ran the shop, took charge of me. She was, as her daughter said 'inclined to nervousness'. She was indeed. She alternated between hectic arias of castigation, and expressions of frantic anxiety to one and all, to long bouts of rather dejected silence. Then, her fine, strong face grew soft and vulnerable. She looked as sad and lost as a child. I called her Madre Musica. We understood one another well.

At last there was a hard surface, and the absolute end of travel. I was really in Compostela. I lay on the hard bed listening to church bells, and voices, greetings thrown across the street like balls to be caught, fielded and returned; car horns, and the constant clatter of feet; the general dynamic fugue of street sounds.

During one of my expeditions in the wrong direction, I had been whisked by one of my young guides, through the giant dark of the cathedral itself, and then out the other side, into the place de España Obradoiro, under the towering, baroque, escarpment of stone over the main entrance. Even in my delapidated state, those trembling towers, peaking like full sound up into the high clear sky, seemed incredibly alive. The pinnacles on either side of the triumphant apostle, were like leaping flames; the strength of it all is effortlessly vibrant. I longed to return there. My room was only a few strides away, past the Church of Saint Martin and then down to the place of the Immaculada, and into the cathedral.

Sometime later, without the baggage, I was at last, simply a pair of eyes in this staggering place of pilgrimage, with the final cold key in my pocket. The cathedral has three main doors. I walked through the church and out on to the steps the other side. I was utterly in awe of it. There is extraordinary energy and presence, like some potent draught. I wanted to take it slowly. I felt I had to suspend all the usual language of responses, and just become used to being there.

I wandered about the city. I walked past dark green, very wide, stable doors, that opened into cool mysterious passages. So much stone. It is some kind of granite flecked with gold. Most of the streets are narrow and cobbled; there seem to be few cars. Everywhere little steps led up or down, into and out of narrow walkways. Always the height, the solid mass of churches and towers could be glimpsed ahead. Throughout the day Galician music is piped out from the various gift shops, so that it is the sound of the street. Silver and jet are the two textures, exquisite jewellery, silver shells, spoons, plates and jugs and always the apostle, and outside every shop large baskets full of scallop shells from the sea.

There was no hurry. I had a week to amble and observe. I went back into the mysterious dark of the cathedral, knowing how easily I could come and go, again and again. The central form of the church is Romanesque, but the work of centuries has added and embellished from the first work, creating continually from that first ground. There are plenty of baroque whirls, abundant racing schemes in shining dark wood and gold, as well as the first, simpler stone.

In most churches you pause, reflecting on a past calm. Themes of other times manage to engage mysteriously with contemporary, local life. Usually there is something that jars, something that seems out of place, while other details, an arch or font or carving, come positively to greet you. Then gradually, piecemeal, your looking and absorbing begins.

That kind of thing isn't possible in this cathedral. A blast of energy, some kind of continual current, seems to bound out from the centre; an organic thrust happens, second by second. The totality of form and vision, image, shape and texture, seem effortlessly to be this live whole, sprung into its own unimaginable force. Life-size angels, trumpeters, candelabra, gold and ebony. There is a puff of cherub cloud over the focal point of Saint James, his gleaming head and halo, and the reliquary of his jewelled cape, glistening there above the altar. The first words that came into my mind and perplexed me were, sacred erotic. It if as if every thread of dynamic force known to us, and to creation, is somehow gathered into a working whole, demonstrating diversity and unity. It is like a plunge of sound glanced off every space and surface. And it happens now, minute by minute, a palpable charge.

Jan Morris in her book *Spain* describes if as 'fizz'. It was quite beyond anything I had ever experienced or imagined. Coming back two or three times a day, it was like coming for a 'fix'.

The appropriate entrance for the true pilgrim, those who have walked the way, the *El Camino*, those who have had their card stamped at the various refugios, is up the high steps from the Obradoiro, and into the small narthex by the Gate of Glory, the work of Mateo in the thirteenth century. Unlike many carved façades; biblical figures'; angels and beasts, and the presiding Christ in glory, on numerous other cathedrals throughout Europe, where consistent mutilation and damage is part of the experience, here at Compostela, you find all is intact. A human hum of perfect heaven. Everything is in harmony: apostles smile and chatter, angels attend. Musicians play above the Christ, who, unlike the tense, sometimes severe Christ of Châtres or Conques or Vézelay, is a benign, peaceful, Buddha-like figure. It is a figure of Love rather than power. Huge hands, both apart, welcome the pilgrim in a gesture of great blessing. On the central pillar, a very fit and calm apostle greets the pilgrims. There is a sense of joy and arrival. I particularly loved the scaly beasts of the deep, below the pillars that support this full celebratory heaven. They yawn and grin and scratch, and suck their talons and claws. Maurice Sendak must have seen them. Here, in Santiago is *Where the Wild Things are*!

*

Many pilgrims were in fact very depressed by a mass of scaffolding in front of the Gate of Glory. It made close inspection of this masterpiece very difficult indeed. It was a pity that there was nothing to explain the reason for the scaffolding. Apparently, for over twenty years it had been the ambition of a priest – Father José Lopez Calo – to have the intruments of heaven copied. The scaffolding was there for this purpose. Many distinguished musicians and instrument makers from all over the world, were staying in Santiago, to measure and photograph the instruments of heaven and then make them. Beards, and pigtails, the fat, the fair and the lean, sped up and down the metal steps of the scaffolding, with rolls of white parchment under their arms. I spoke with several of them. All of them agreed on the unique energy in the cathedral. 'Scholarship of any kind has to be suspended here, for at least three days.' 'It is like an explosion every few seconds, incredible.'

In the streets of Santiago, as well as students, and local Galicians, there are the priests. Up the steps and down the streets, you continually meet them in pairs or alone, sometimes in small groups; black berretas, and long, black cassocks, the direct descendants of Don Camillo or Father Brown. They are there in the bustle of the market place, where every day the women sit astride huge, wicker baskets, to count out into kilos, the small, green peppers of Padron. Sizzling in oil with almost every dish, they are very strong, but sweet also. Meat, fish, fruit and flowers in the shade and in the sun, large crabs in the glistening spittle of their last breath. In the market the women are the workers; carting and carrying, pushing wagons and heaving crates and boxes. The older women, often in black, carry armfuls of bread and lilies.

Throughout the day, in numerous dark churches, there is the anxious, passionate whisper of prayer. In the side chapels before colourful saints, the same small women, their rosary beads in their worn hands, give the impression of praying without ceasing. Every evening the enclosed Benedictine nuns of the Monasterio de San Pelayo, sing the Office. Fifty-two nuns, of every age, their black habits and bright red breviaries, are spectacular, below a magnificent gilded, baroque bank of colourful saints and angels. The back of the convent looks over the Plaza de los Literarios and the Plaza de la Quintana, it is a tapestry of shuttered windows, all with strong, iron grills over them. On each window sill there is a flourish of red geraniums. From here the New World and all its problems seem remote. It is hard to believe that Columbus has already set sail.

There are many maimed and fraught individuals who beg constantly in the cathedral doorways. While I was with the Buddhists at Dhagpo, someone asked Lama Jigmé about the problem of itinerant beggars. How should we respond to the beggar? 'Always give something, however small,' Lama Jigmé said, 'As a mark of respect for their human identity.'

There was a man and a woman and small child outside one doorway of the cathedral. I assumed all three were together. I gave the woman all I had. As I turned away, the man came furiously after me, waving his smooth, pink stubs of arms, and shaking his toothless mouth, with its bright, keen, raging red gums. Still furious he followed me down the steps. From then on I made sure that I was always weighed down with some change. Whenever I saw him, I gave him something. On my last evening I remembered the many candles I had promised to light for various people on my journey, when I got to Compostela. First there was Saïd from Kensington Market in London, then Jimmy and Leni at Taizé, Libertad at Nîmes and Paulette for her mad daughter. The cathedral doesn't encourage candles. You have to buy your own in the town; large ones in their own holders. I noticed that people put many in front of the statue of Saint James as a flourishing slayer of the Moors. I decided on the crypt and the relics themselves for my candles.

As I was coming back up towards the cathedral, my arms full of red candles, I saw my friend, waving his stubs of arms at me. I had no free hand to search for any change in my pocket. But as I got closer, I realised that his waves were in greeting, not in demand. Eagerly he pushed open the two heavy doors. He was all talk and smiles. He was now the giver. I thanked him. It made me understand Lama Jigmé's point exactly.

The days flew by. Again and again I returned to the cathedral. To Mateo. Just behind the Gate of Glory, facing down the long nave, there is a small statue of the master who created this wonderful work in stone. Tradition suggests you knock your forehead against his, hoping to obtain some measure of his gifts.

There was always a steady stream of people climbing up the steps behind the altar, where they may clasp the saint by the neck, kissing and touching his cape of relics. It is as if all the scuffs and scars and scabs of the journey of that tired, worried figure, you have seen again and again, in the worn robe, wide-brimmed hat, staff, and leather bottle, it is as if his wear and tear has been transformed into gems, just as he is transformed. He is no longer an anxious traveller, but a witness to the peace, perfection and resolve of heaven.

Feet of every description peep out from the dark of the confessional boxes on either side of the nave. Margery Kempe must have cherished her absolution from here.

The murmur of masses and liturgy continues throughout the day. On random, important feasts, the vast *bota-fumeiro*, a silver incense-burner five feet high is swung by six priests in an arc in front of the altar, from ropes to the lantern above. The air is filled with white smoke and the excited, cheering applause of the pilgrims.

In the Plaza Obradoiro there is the magnificent Hostal de Los Reyes Catolicos. It was built by Isabel and Ferdinand to house the pilgrims. Now it is considered to be, possibly, the most outstandingly beautiful hotel in Europe. I was told conflicting tales of the hotels' contemporary hospitality to pilgrims. Some said that those who received a Compostela, verifying their genuine pilgrimage, may eat three meals for three days, or one meal for one day, in the hotel's kitchens. I felt I should find out the facts.

The staff were immensely courteous. They said that three meals for three days was given to the pilgrims in the hotel kitchens. I was given a slip to gain entry to the kitchens and seek out some foot-sore pilgrims for lunch the next day.

In spite of all their courtesy, the hotel staff certainly do not like the pilgrims loitering about in their magnificent hall. Down dark passages, past the garages, through a little garden, then up and down more passages, until the evidence of steam and cooking smells lead you clearly in the right kitchen direction. Great hunks of red meat, large gleaming fish, the deft pull and slap and cut of the chefs at work in various different kitchens. Then the huge, hot sluice of the washing-up, tired, aproned women in caps, going about their business with a certain degree of exhausted resignation; quite unlike the flourish and panache of the cooks.

A very heavy wooden platter is loaded by the chefs. That day it was spinach soup, some dark burger, mountains of chips, a large orange, and a generous glass of *vino tino*. It is quite difficult to carry a heavy breadboard, without sides of any kind, and all these objects on it. It looked and felt extremely precarious. Concentrating madly on my wooden platter, rather as you might at an egg and spoon race, I mistook the direction, and found I had pushed the door through into the hotel dining-room. Immediately an appalled mob of major domos rushed to redirect me.

The room where all the hotel staff and all the pilgrims take their meals, looked like some leftover sixties' bar. The red carpet shone with dropped food, ground in. But the space was cool and comfortable. There were many women eating, from the hotel staff. There was no sign of a pilgrim.

Then suddenly three sunburnt men walked in. They were definitely pilgrims. There was a Frenchman – Michel – he was fifty-eight from Le Mans, he had walked 1600 kilometres from Le Puy. Paul, the tallest and most relaxed was a banker from Amsterdam, he was twenty-three. Friso, another Dutchman was the youngest. He was nineteen. He had been walking for three months.

For the next four hours they eagerly regaled their adventures. All three, with quite different motives and intentions agreed on one thing, it was The Way, *El Camino* that mattered. The Way was everything.

For Michel it had been a serious and definitely religious experience. He had made an Ignatian retreat in preparation for the journey. He was an austere man. As he recounted his experiences, his eyes lit up and he became increasingly animated. Two words brought to all three an identical reaction. Aubrac and Figeac. Aubrac for its danger and isolation, a day's walking in dense fog and deep snow, with nothing but God and a compass, as Michel put it. People had died there. Figeac was memorable for the violent and threatening distaste of the parish priest for all pilgrims. Each one, at different times had been hurled abuse by him, and sent off to the police. 'I can't wait,' Michel said, 'to visit that priest in a suit and tie and get out of a clean car, and and then ask him who his neighbour is?'

The real horrors, even worse than rain and tempest and unfriendly priests, were the dogs. Recently a woman had been savaged to death by dogs. Michel had taken a gas gun as protection against dogs, but he had never used it. He had killed two vipers.

Spain was deemed to be far more welcoming than France. In France, Friso said, 'I felt like a clochard, a vagabond, an oddity. Only in Spain did I feel the welcome of a pilgrim.' Friso was very endearing, very frank and open. He had gone to grow up, to find out who he was. 'You have to get away from your family,' he said, 'in the first two weeks I was terrified – no bed, no place – then suddenly I thought, it's nothing, just get up and walk twenty kilometres, that's all it is. One night I sat for seven hours in the pouring rain, no shelter, no tree, no wall, nothing. I couldn't believe it. It was terrible. Then afterwards I thought, it's not so big a thing, not really.'

For every story of rejection and dog or pig horrors, there were wonderful tales of welcome. A bishop's bed with duvet, everything, and no charge. The Benedictine welcome always seemed to come top.

Friso had found a small house on the route, in France, near Lousine, with a large placard on the cottage wall, with the sign of the shell and a notice that read: Compostela 924 k Drinking water. Friso had knocked at the door and found a great welcome. Every night the family lay a spare place at the table in case a pilgrim comes by.

The blessing at Roncevalles was holy, different, definitely special. They were all well and both glad and sad that it was over. But Friso felt uneasy. He wanted to keep walking. He didn't want to return home. He wasn't ready. With his rucksack on his back, he felt free, different. He wanted to go on. Both Paul and Friso were ardent admirers of Sir Ranulph Fiennes. I stressed that my connections were remote, bloodless, less than incidental. But they were still inordinately pleased that we should have the same name.

All of them stressed the power of silence. The need to be alone and find oneself in that silence.

As they talked together of The Way, the obstacles, the people, the different refugios, the signs; crosses and bridges, passes and chapels; with groans, again and again, at the word Figeac, you felt the great importance of physicality in the quest. Moving alone, with silence as the single companion, seems a most profound means to register the natural balance of world without, and world within.

Continually the talk had to be of return. Return must be within the shape of every adventure, and certainly of every pilgrimage.

It occurred to me that to meet a genuine woman pilgrim somewhere near my own age, would be interesting. Vaguely as I wandered about Santiago, I had my ears pricked as it were, to discover such a person. There were various art tours, with erudite guides. There were several, worn, solitary men, but few women. Paul had said that a woman was on her way, travelling with two children, but my flight was booked before she was due.

Then suddenly I saw this smiling, open face, fair hair flying, blue jeans, pink shirt. Without thinking I said in English, 'Are you a real pilgrim?' I usually started with: Do you speak French or English, but luckily Gustava spoke English and she was a real pilgrim. She was German. She was a doctor. She had promised herself this pilgrimage after her fiftieth birthday celebration. She had four sons, they were wonderfully vivid as she described them, and obviously very close to her. Their ages were between fourteen and twenty-six. Her husband lives and works at the centre of the Arts, worldwide. 'Black tie, is our natural uniform.' Although Gustava is a doctor, she felt that she wanted, in some way, to widen her sense of herself, beyond her profession, marriage and motherhood.

She had walked for ten days alone, starting at Astorga. Her first night at Ponferrada, on a damp mattress in the presbytery cellar, had been the hardest. Her son Cornelius had said as she left ... 'I hope you find what you are looking for.'

I asked her what she had found. 'I have sown seeds,' she said, 'Now I must go home, live and work and wait for the harvest. I'll tell you in two years.'

We had delicious meals together, walked out of Santiago to a small Romanesque church and bussed to Padron. Gustava was full of tales; eager with all the adventures, but she was also very happy to be going home. 'Certainly it had been difficult, sometimes grim,' How had she coped. 'I trained myself to remember the faces of the children, they were so clear, as if they were with me.'

Gustava, like the others, stressed that 'The Way', to be one who is 'on The Way', was an extraordinary feeling. She told of the joy of continually seeing the sign, a yellow shell, on blue ground. 'When you come to a crossroads, that shows no sign, nothing, then your heart is so heavy. But then suddenly it is there again, on a stone wall, a barn, the bark of a tree. Your joy then is indescribable. Involuntarily you cry out for joy.'

I asked Gustava why she had gone. 'For my sins,' she replied smiling. Never has anyone seemed so loving, open, caring and sinless. Gustava is a Catholic. She explained to me that although you may be absolved of sin, the sin is itself a separation from God. She had wanted to work through that separation. 'Also I wanted to thank,' she said, 'thank for my life and health and my immediate family and I wanted to pray for two particular people.'

I thought of Cornelius's remark to his mother. One is always looking. Perhaps finding, is simply, looking further. 'Looking' is life. Maybe a pilgrimage puts that 'looking' into keener focus.

Just as at Rocamadour and Vézelay, it was sad to be in Santiago for the last time. It is easy to try too hard to see and feel. To be filled with excitement and longing, and miss the point completely.

I wondered what I had been looking for. Certainly the adventure with cancer had been an impetus. There had been some sense of urgency after that, urgency towards a deeper understanding of oneself; the nature and opportunity of one's being. Obviously quality of life depends on the kind of trigger you choose.

Carl Jung once said, 'To my mind it is more important that an idea exists, than that it is true.'

Santiago certainly exists, the place itself and the myth of the wandering apostle. All those routes, all those shells, all those shrines. Botticelli may have conceived Venus, born out of a scallop shell, but the figure of James, without any foundation in fact, only the roots of legend and myth, was born so many years earlier with his shells intact. A bright star, a shepherd, and the birth of an archetype. James, close to Christ, but still, simply one who is 'on The Way.' Everyman. The Wayfarer. The Pilgrim. When it suited the times and the culture, he was turned into a soldier, devastator of the infidel. Today he has shaken back down again into being, a simple, pilgrim force.

There is such freedom in the myth of James and in the final celebration of the cathedral itself. A healing feast for the psyche. The present Pope has been to Santiago, but the myth led the Pope. The myth retains its freedom. Like some extravagant theatre of texture and imagination, its lack of certainty is its strength.

I met a very laid-back Dutchman who said, 'Santiago is a circus, the Benidorm of the blind mind.'

Maybe only the 'blind mind' dares to acknowledge the extreme circus of the human condition. Our mad mix of images, feelings, hopes and fears. In the cathedral, high above the ambulatory, cherubs wave phallic fronds from between their legs, acorns are at the tip, every so often they burst into flower. Huge, sultry angels lazily guard the canopy of this womb-cave, where altar and saint, glow with a full, wide-awake welcome. A very positive and indi-viduated James is the happy focus of anyone who enters the cathedral, and gathered round him, there is the triumphant expression of all those wild, rich feelings that may lurk as threat and disease, if they remain unclaimed and hidden.

Maybe 'blind mind' and 'scholarship suspended' allow the psyche sufficient freedom to connect to this burst of human and sacred inheritance.

On my way to the airport bus I met Frico. He was very happy. He was not going home. He was going to walk to Finistere. Paul had given him his carved staff. He was on his way, a gleaming scallop shell from Australia stitched to his rucksack.

Bearing garlic, pimentos from Padron, Santiago cake, more books, tapes of Galician music, and a colourful clay image of the saint, I returned home. I felt excited and eager to see all those very beloved family faces; so much zest; so much variety.

But to my surprise as the weeks passed, the most disorientating dark gripped me. Like a demented dog I went from room to room, to park, to library, to every kind of public and private place trying to write this thing. The images, the people and places remained so clear, yet nothing satisfactory would happen.

Then gradually it dawned on me, that some sort of intellectual pride held me back from the only possible conclusion.

It is not enough to seek and care; to pay lip service to all manner of ideals. Real witness is what counts. Why is it so difficult?

It is something to do with leaps in the dark. Recognising that truth is hidden. But transformation towards truth is something else. It is practice and diligence as Lama Jigmé said.

Referring to belief and faith Thomas Merton wrote,
'We do not see first and then act; we act, then see.'

'Sir, we know our will is free, and there's an end on't.'

DR SAMUEL JOHNSON
late one evening to a
badgering BOSWELL